Conceptual Metaphor Theory and Its Application on English Teaching in a Selected Medical University

概念隐喻理论在医学院校英语教学中的应用研究

张 冉 牛军伟 著

图书在版编目(CIP)数据

概念隐喻理论在医学院校英语教学中的应用研究 = Conceptual Metaphor Theory and Its Application on English Teaching in a Selected Medical University：英文／张冉，牛军伟著. — 郑州：郑州大学出版社，2023.7

ISBN 978-7-5645-9702-3

Ⅰ．①概… Ⅱ．①张…②牛… Ⅲ．①隐喻－应用－英语－教学研究－医学院校 Ⅳ．①H319.3

中国国家版本馆 CIP 数据核字(2023)第 080854 号

概念隐喻理论在医学院校英语教学中的应用研究 = Conceptual Metaphor Theory and Its Application on English Teaching in a Selected Medical University：英文

策划编辑	陈文静	封面设计	苏永生
责任编辑	吕笑娟	版式设计	苏永生
责任校对	张 楠　张馨文	责任监制	李瑞卿

出版发行	郑州大学出版社	地　　址	郑州市大学路 40 号(450052)
出 版 人	孙保营	网　　址	http://www.zzup.cn
经　　销	全国新华书店	发行电话	0371-66966070
印　　刷	郑州市今日文教印制有限公司		
开　　本	787 mm×1 092 mm　1／16		
印　　张	15	字　　数	453 千字
版　　次	2023 年 7 月第 1 版	印　　次	2023 年 7 月第 1 次印刷
书　　号	ISBN 978-7-5645-9702-3	定　　价	52.50 元

本书如有印装质量问题，请与本社联系调换。

新乡医学院博士科研资助项目成果

Foreword

Shirley is my PhD student from 2016 to 2021. When she was a PhD candidate, she tried to use metaphor in English instruction which I think is an available approach. I asked her what is the problem she wanted to solve in her instruction and was told it is students' English competence and how to help students shift from General English to Medical English smoothly. Then we began to work on this topic.

This book consists of six chapters. Chapter one introduces the research problem, research questions and significance. Chapter two briefly reviews the history of metaphor study, metaphoric competence, medical metaphor, metaphor enriched college English for General Purposes (EGP) teaching. Chapter three describes the methodology, the research design and the materials as well as an experimental research of metaphor enriched teaching and learning. Chapter four presents the implementation of the Metaphor Enriched English Language Instruction to the first-year medical students. Chapter five presents the result of the analysis of data collected in the study. Chapter six refers to major conclusions and recommendations.

The significance of this book: First, it is an empirical study on metaphor instruction which last for one semester. Two teacher participants applied the metaphor-enriched materials to their class and the effectiveness was proved. This is a great reference for other teachers in this field. Second, she collected all her supplements and edited a supplementary booklet which is beneficial for both teachers and students. Third, she adopted multimodal teaching materials in the study which made the instruction interesting and easy to understand.

George Bernard Shaw once said: "You see things; and you say, 'Why?' But I dream things that never were; and I say, 'Why not?'". This is also my educational philosophy. I am glad to encourage Shirley to do research on her favorite topic and hope that she can keep moving on this path.

May 2023

Preface

In recent years, English Language Teaching (ELT) in China has been criticized for being test-oriented and of producing "deaf and dumb". English learners who are competent in grammar but incompetent in communication. In order to change this situation for better, the "College English Teaching Reform Project" put forward by the Chinese Ministry of Education aims to strengthen the practical English instruction and improve the English language proficiency of college students. However, for college students, in their EGP (English for General Purposes) curriculum stage, the problem of "naturalness" still exists due to the imbalance in language forms and concepts between their native language (Chinese) and target language (English). In their ESP (English for Specific Purposes) curriculum stage, there is disconnectedness due to the changed contents and vocabulary. Therefore, how to improve the English competence of college students and how to migrate smoothly from EGP to ESP is an urgent issue for teachers and researchers.

Conducted in a medical university, this book tried to make metaphors as a bridge to enhance the language competence of students, especially metaphoric competence, as well as their medical knowledge by adding medical contents to General English language instruction. Three teachers and more than one hundred students participated in the Metaphor Enriched English Language Instruction (MEELI) which lasted for six weeks. Three units from the textbook, the nervous system, the cardiovascular system and the immune system were supplemented according to the unit topics. A metaphoric competence test was chosen as the pre-test and the post-test tool to verify whether there was any improvement. The researcher did the classroom observation and filled the checklist for further analysis. Then the feedback of each supplementary unit from teachers and students were collected. Statistical Package for Social Science (SPSS) and qualitative data analysis software NVivo 11 were used for data analysis. The findings show that for all the three teacher participants, there was a significant difference in the mean score of the pre-test and the post-test. In order to learn about the students' metaphoric production ability and cultivate their therapeutic use of metaphors, ten students from each instructor were required to write a short essay according to the given three case scenarios relating to the nervous system, the cardiovascular system and the immune system. After the exercise, both the student and the teacher participants gave valuable feedback on supplementary materials and teachers' instruction.

This book aims to develop the MEELI supplement through preparation, implementation and feedback. This will provide the use of supplementary materials, supplement implementation, and metaphoric competence. It tries to effect teacher professional development for teachers who face the same situation and help researchers in the related field. At the end, recommendations for future research are also made for teachers and researchers.

Zhang Ran
May 2023

Contents

Chapter 1　Introduction ·· 1
  1.1　Background of the Study ·· 1
  1.2　Statement of the Problem ·· 5
  1.3　Rationale of the Study ··· 7
  1.4　Research Objectives ··· 8
  1.5　Research Questions ··· 9
  1.6　Significance of the Study ··· 9

Chapter 2　Literature Review ·· 12
  2.1　Traditional View of Metaphor ··· 12
  2.2　The Contemporary View of Metaphor ·· 14
  2.3　Metaphor Identification Procedure ·· 22
  2.4　Metaphoric Competence ··· 23
  2.5　Conceptual Metaphor and College EFL Teaching ························ 25
  2.6　Metaphor and Medical English ··· 28
  2.7　Conceptual Framework for the Research ····································· 28

Chapter 3　Research Methodology ·· 31
  3.1　Research Paradigm ··· 31
  3.2　Research Design ··· 33
  3.3　Supplementary Materials ·· 36
  3.4　Research Setting ··· 37
  3.5　The Study Population and Sample ·· 38
  3.6　The Research Instruments ·· 41
  3.7　Pilot Study ··· 48
  3.8　Data Collection ··· 56
  3.9　Data Analysis ··· 57

  3.10 Ethical Considerations ·· 58

Chapter 4 Implementation of Metaphor Enriched English Language Instruction ··· 60

  4.1 Preparation, Implementation and Feedback for Metaphor Supplements of Unit 2 ·· 60

  4.2 Preparation, Implementation and Feedback for Metaphor Supplements of Unit 3 ·· 74

  4.3 Preparation, Implementation and Feedback for Metaphor Supplements of Unit 5 ·· 85

Chapter 5 Findings and Discussion ··· 98

  5.1 Research Question 1: What is Students' Current Metaphoric Cognition with the First-year College Students at Xinxiang Medical University China? ········· 98

  5.2 Research Question 2: What is the Effect of Metaphor Enriched Language Instruction on First-year Medical Students' Metaphoric Competence? ·········· 109

  5.3 Research Question 3: What are the Teachers' Performance and Reflection on the Metaphor Enriched Language Instruction? ·· 150

  5.4 Research Question 4: What are the Students' Feedback on the Metaphor Enriched Language Instruction Supplementary Materials? ···················· 179

Chapter 6 Conclusions and Recommendations ······························· 190

  6.1 Implications ·· 190

  6.2 Recommendations ·· 196

  6.3 Suggestions for Further Research ··· 197

References ·· 199

List of Abbreviations ··· 206

Appendices ··· 207

  Appendix A Semi-structured Interview Protocol ····································· 207

  Appendix B Metaphor Cognition Questionnaire ·· 210

  Appendix C Metaphoric Competence Test ·· 213

  Appendix D Classroom Observation Checklist ·· 217

  Appendix E Student Feedback Questionnaire ·· 220

  Appendix F The Transcript of Students' Role Play on Heart Problem (Ms Liu's Class) ·· 222

  Appendix G The Transcript of Students' Role Play on Heart Problem (Ms Wang's Class) ·· 223

List of Figure

Figure 2-1	Metaphor Identification Procedure (MIP)	23
Figure 2-2	Conceptual Framework of Metaphor Enriched English Language Instruction	29
Figure 3-1	Convergent Design	34
Figure 3-2	Metaphor Enriched Supplement	36
Figure 3-3	Triangulation of Data Source	47
Figure 3-4	Triangulation of Research Instruments	47
Figure 3-5	Frequency of Students' MCT (pilot)	54
Figure 3-6	Data Analysis for Qualitative Research	58
Figure 4-1	Classification of Conceptual Metaphor	66
Figure 4-2	The Tenor and Vehicle of the Metaphor	68
Figure 4-3	The Tenor and Vehicle of the Metaphor	70
Figure 4-4	A Screenshot of Students' Role Play on Heart Problem	88
Figure 4-5	The Tenor and Vehicle of the Metaphor	69
Figure 5-1	Percentage of Items on Metaphor Cognition (Ms Wang's Class)	102
Figure 5-2	Percentage of Items on Medical Metaphors (Ms Wang's Class)	103
Figure 5-3	Percentage of Items on Metaphor Cognition (Ms Liu's Class)	107
Figure 5-4	Percentage of Items on Medical Metaphors (Ms Liu's Class)	108
Figure 5-5	The National College Entrance Examination (Ms Wang's Class)	111
Figure 5-6	Pre-test and Post-test Metaphoric Competence Test Marks (Ms Wang's Class)	112
Figure 5-7	The Source-Path-Goal Schema	115
Figure 5-8	Categories Generated in the Pre-test and the Post-test on LOVE IS A JOURNEY (Ms Wang's Class)	116
Figure 5-9	Categories Generated in the Pre-test and the Post-test on IDEAS ARE FOOD	

	(Ms Wang's Class)	119
Figure 5-10	Categories inthe Pre-test and the Post-test on DEPRESSION IS FALLING INTO AN ABYSS (Ms Wang's Class)	122
Figure 5-11	Categories Generated in the Pre-test and the Post-test on HUMAN BODY IS A BATTLEGROUND (Ms Wang's Class)	125
Figure 5-12	Categories Generated in the Pre-test and the Post-test on BRAIN IS A MACHINE(Ms Wang's Class)	127
Figure 5-13	The National College Entrance Examination (Ms Liu's Class)	134
Figure 5-14	Pre-test and Post-test Metaphoric Competence Test Marks (Ms Liu's Class)	134
Figure 5-15	Categories Generated in the Pre-test and the Post-test on LOVE IS A JOURNEY(Ms Liu's Class)	136
Figure 5-16	Categories Generated in the Pre-test and the Post-test on IDEAS ARE FOOD(Ms Liu's Class)	138
Figure 5-17	Categories Generated in the Pre-test and the Post-test on DEPRESSION IS FALLING INTO AN ABYSS (Ms Liu's Class)	140
Figure 5-18	Categories Generated in the Pre-test and the Post-test on HUAMAN BODY IS A BATTLEGROUND (Ms Liu's Class)	141
Figure 5-19	Categories Generated in the Pre-test and the Post-test on BRAIN IS A MACHINE(Ms Liu's Class)	142
Figure 5-20	Metaphors between Mountain and Human Body	154
Figure 5-21	Metaphors of the Nervous System in Prezi	157
Figure 5-22	A Picture of Grenade and Its Origin	171
Figure 5-23	Project Map of Comments on MEELI (Ms Wang's Class)	180
Figure 5-24	Project Map of Comments on Instruction (Ms Wang's Class)	183
Figure 5-25	Project Map of Comments on MEELI (Ms Liu's Class)	185
Figure 5-26	Project Map of Comments on Instruction (Ms Liu's Class)	188

List of Table

Table 2-1	Metaphoric Mappings Between "LIFE" and "PLAY"	15
Table 2-2	Metaphoric Mappings Between "LIFE" and "JOURNEY"	16
Table 2-3	Ontological Metaphor	21
Table 3-1	Labels Commonly Associated with Four Major Paradigms	32
Table 3-2	Student Respondents to Metaphor Cognition Questionnaire	40
Table 3-3	Student Respondents to Metaphoric Competence Test	40
Table 3-4	Student Respondents to Student Feedback Questionnaire	40
Table 3-5	Marks of Items in Metaphor Recognition	43
Table 3-6	The Criteria of Scoring of Part C	44
Table 3-7	The Result of "KMO and Bartlett's Test" on Metaphor Cognition Questionnaire	48
Table 3-8	Pattern Matrix^a of Items	49
Table 3-9	Reliability Statistics of Metaphor Cognition Questionnaire	50
Table 3-10	Age of Respondents (Pilot Study)	50
Table 3-11	Gender of Respondents	50
Table 3-12	English Achievement of Respondents	51
Table 3-13	Percentage of Items on Metaphor Cognition	51
Table 3-14	Percentage of Items on Metaphors and Medical English	52
Table 3-15	The Result of "KMO and Bartlett's Test" on Metaphoric Competence Test	53
Table 3-16	Correlation Coefficient Between NCEE and MCT	54
Table 3-17	Metaphors Generated in Part C: "Learning English is…"	55
Table 3-18	Metaphors Generated in Part C: "Treating illness is…"	56
Table 4-1	Time Arrangement for Unit 2	62
Table 4-2	Linguistic Metaphors in Unit 2	64

Table 4-3	Patterns of Metaphors	65
Table 4-4	The Mapping Between ANGER and FLUID	66
Table 4-5	Metaphors of the Nervous System	68
Table 4-6	The Mapping of BRAIN IS A COMPUTER	69
Table 4-7	Metaphors of the Peripheral Nervous System	70
Table 4-8	Metaphors of the Autonomic Nervous System	71
Table 4-9	Metaphorical Words that Originated from Greek	72
Table 4-10	Metaphorical Words that Originated from Latin	73
Table 4-11	Time Arrangement for Unit 3	75
Table 4-12	Metaphors and Their Metaphorical Descriptions	77
Table 4-13	The Metaphors of Neuron	77
Table 4-14	The Metaphors of Dendrite	78
Table 4-15	The Metaphors of Axon	78
Table 4-16	The Metaphors of Myelin Sheath	78
Table 4-17	The Metaphors of Synapse	79
Table 4-18	Metaphorical Meanings of Heart and Examples	79
Table 4-19	Metaphorical Expressions of Heart that are Unique to Chinese	81
Table 4-20	Metaphors in the article "Heart"	82
Table 4-21	Metaphorical Sentences in the Extract of *I am Joe's body*	82
Table 4-22	Time Arrangement for Unit 5	85
Table 4-23	Metaphors in Text: The Battle Against AIDS	91
Table 4-24	The Mapping of TREATING ILLNESS IS FIGHTING A WAR	92
Table 4-25	Scenario of War Metaphor: TREATING ILLNESS IS FIGHTING A WAR	93
Table 4-26	Supplementary Metaphorical Words	93
Table 4-27	Metaphorical Expressions of Health and Medicine that are Unique to Chinese	94
Table 5-1	Age of Respondents (Ms Wang's Class)	99
Table 5-2	Gender of Respondents (Ms Wang's Class)	100
Table 5-3	English Achievement of Respondents (Ms Wang's Class)	100
Table 5-4	Percentage of Items on Metaphor Cognition (Ms Wang's Class)	101
Table 5-5	Percentage of Items on Metaphors and Medical English (Ms Wang's Class)	102
Table 5-6	Age of Respondents (Ms Liu's Class)	104
Table 5-7	Gender of Respondents (Ms Liu's Class)	104

Table 5-8	English Achievement of Respondents (Ms Liu's Class)	105
Table 5-9	Percentage of Items on Metaphor Identification (Ms Liu's Class)	105
Table 5-10	Percentage of Items on Metaphors and Medical English (Ms Liu's Class)	108
Table 5-11	Descriptive Statistics of MCT and NCEE (Ms Wang's Class)	110
Table 5-12	Average Score of Each Part in the Pre-test and the Post-test (Ms Wang's Class)	113
Table 5-13	Paired Samples Correlations Between the Pre-test and the Post-test (Ms Wang's Class)	113
Table 5-14	Metaphoric Mappings Between Source Domain and Target Domain	114
Table 5-15	Similarities of Sub-category of LOVE IS A JOURNEY in the Pre-test and the Post-test (Ms Wang's Class)	117
Table 5-16	Similarities of Sub-category of IDEAS ARE FOOD in the Pre-test and the Post-test (Ms Wang's Class)	120
Table 5-17	Similarities of Sub-category of DEPRESSION IS FALLING INTO AN ABYSS in the Pre-test and the Post-test (Ms Wang's Class)	123
Table 5-18	Metaphoric Mappings Between Source Domain and Target Domain	124
Table 5-19	Similarities of Sub-category of BRAIN IS A MACHINE in the Pre-test and the Post-test (Ms Wang's Class)	127
Table 5-20	Metaphors Generated on "Learning English is…" (Ms Wang's Class)	129
Table 5-21	Metaphors Generated on "Treating illness is…" (Ms Wang's Class)	131
Table 5-22	Descriptive Statistics of MCT and NCEE (Ms Liu's Class)	133
Table 5-23	Average Score of Each Part in the Pre-test and the Post-test (Ms Liu's Class)	135
Table 5-24	Paired Samples Correlations Between the Pre-test and the Post-test (Ms Liu's Class)	135
Table 5-25	Metaphors Generated on "Learning English is…" (Ms Liu's Class)	144
Table 5-26	Metaphors Generated on "Treating illness is…" (Ms Liu's Class)	147
Table 5-27	Metaphor Enriched Class Structure for Unit 2	150
Table 5-28	Teaching Strategies for Unit 2	153
Table 5-29	Teacher's Use of Materials for Unit 2	155
Table 5-30	Nervous System Metaphors in Prezi	157
Table 5-31	Teacher's Use of Language for Unit 2	159
Table 5-32	Metaphor Enriched Class Structure for Unit 3	161

Table 5-33	Teaching Strategies for Unit 3	163
Table 5-34	Teacher's Use of Materials for Unit 3	164
Table 5-35	Teacher's Use of Language for Unit 3	165
Table 5-36	Metaphor Enriched Class Structure for Unit 5	167
Table 5-37	Teaching Strategies for Unit 5	169
Table 5-38	Teacher's Use of Materials for Unit 5	171
Table 5-39	Teacher's Use of Language for Unit 5	174
Table 5-40	Percentage of Part Ⅰ: Your Learning Experience of the MEELI (Ms Wang's Class)	179
Table 5-41	Percentage of Part Ⅱ: Teacher's Instruction of the MEELI (Ms Wang's Class)	181
Table 5-42	Percentage of Part Ⅰ: Your Learning Experience of the MEELI (Ms Liu's Class)	184
Table 5-43	Percentage of Part Ⅱ: Teacher's Instruction of the MEELI (Ms Liu's Class)	186

Chapter 1

Introduction

This thesis focuses on applying the metaphor enriched instruction supplement to the College English (CE) class to facilitate the language proficiency of students and the learning of Medical English. The immediate purpose of this study is to gain a broader knowledge of the understanding of college students about metaphors and facilitate their Medical English learning by supplementing the topic-related metaphor-based Medical English knowledge to the College English class. The long-term purpose of this study is to solve the disconnectedness between the EGP (English for General Purposes) learning and ESP (English for Specific Purposes) learning of medical college students.

1.1 Background of the Study

Initiated in 2002, College English Curriculum Requirements (simplified as Requirements) was drawn up as official guideline and in 2007, the revised Requirements was issued. With the particular stress on developing the overall competence of students, Requirements 2007 formulates that individual learning, based on constructivism, enables students to process information in terms of their cognitive style. The objective of the Requirements 2007 is to "develop students" ability to use English in a well-rounded way, especially in listening and speaking, so that in their future studies and careers as well as social interactions they will be able to communicate effectively, study independently and improve their general cultural awareness so as to meet the needs of China's social development and international exchange" (2007).

English Language Teaching (ELT) in China has been criticized for being test-oriented and producing "deaf and dumb" English learners who are competent in grammar but incompetent in communication (Cheng and Wang, 2012). The College English Teaching Reform Project put forward by the Chinese Ministry of Education aims to strengthen practical English instruction and improve the English language proficiency (listening, speaking, reading, and writing) of college students. Although 13 years ago, China's College EFL (English as a Foreign Language) teaching had already brought the language competence into teaching syllabus, the problem of "naturalness" could not be solved in the second language acquisition which is one of the important criteria to achieve successful language acquisition. College EFL learners blindly apply sentence patterns and expressions in the textbooks to the written or oral environment. In addition, vocabulary teaching is a crucial step in the process of foreign language teaching. The whole vocabulary in college should be at least 4,795 words and 700 phrases (Ministry of Education, 2007). While traditional College English vocabulary teaching is less efficient, the poor vocabulary hinders college students in improving their English. Furthermore, as one of the compulsory subjects of medical colleges, Medical English is characteristic of its huge amount of vocabulary with the fast development of the medical science. How to effectively improve the English vocabulary of Medical English for medical students is a difficult problem in the process of the College English instruction.

Although China's College EFL (English as a Foreign Language) teaching has already brought the language competence into its curriculum, it still cannot solve the problem of naturalness in the second language acquisition which is one of the important criteria to achieve successful language acquisition. College EFL learners blindly apply sentence patterns and expressions in the textbooks to written or oral environment. Although they have learned morphological characteristics of the target language, their thinking is still in the Chinese conceptual system. They tend to use some words and structures of the target language as a "carrier" to transfer the concept of native language. When concepts of native language do not match with those of the target language, imbalance will result between the language form and the concept which result in some unnatural expressions.

On the other hand, one kind of ESP curriculum, Medical English, is known for its vast vocabulary as there is a continuous advancement of medical science. There are more than 1,500 new medical words being created every year. Therefore, in medical universities, Medical English vocabulary instruction occupies an important position in English teaching. The current teaching approaches of Medical English vocabulary mainly focus on word-formation, memory skill and other functions of medical vocabulary. Students memorize the sound, form and meaning by repetition. Although students can use short-term memory by memorizing medical vocabulary, they will soon forget them due to their relatively limited general English. How to effectively expand Medical English vocabulary is the concern of the teachers. One approach is to apply conceptual metaphor theory to the Medical English vocabulary instruction process to facilitate the students' metaphor awareness and metaphorical thinking ability.

Metaphor accounts for around ten percent of everyday speech, says James Geary (2011). According to George Lakoff and Mark Johnson's (1980) *Metaphors We Live By*, metaphor is not simply a matter of word or linguistic expressions, but of concept, of thinking of one thing in terms of another. Examples of this include when we talk and think about life in terms of journey, about argument in terms of war, about ideas in terms of food, about social organizations in terms of plants, and many others. Lakoff and Johnson claim that since the concept and activity are structured metaphorically, the language is structured metaphorically (1980). The cognitive theory of metaphor shows that the abilities of interpreting and producing metaphor in the target language are vital for language learning. As a ubiquitous phenomenon in language, metaphor is the motive power of the language system's development and change, and a leading way to close the gap between the old and new knowledge of students. For College EFL (English as a Foreign Language) students, metaphors enable students to recognize word formation rules and develop their metaphor analysis competence regarding medical terms. From the teacher's point of view, it is better to offer the method of fishing rather than the fish itself. Teachers should help the students master the rules to learn Medical English vocabulary by raising the students' metaphor awareness of Medical English vocabulary and cultivating their metaphoric competence.

Besides, metaphors can facilitate communication by using familiar concepts to describe abstract and complex concepts in medicine. Suitable metaphors can bridge the understanding between the known and the unknown. Hence it can be used as an effective tool to enhance the understanding of diseases which are complex and abstract. Good metaphors can vividly describe the medical knowledge and help patients understand their diseases or treatments easily.

In Medical English, the formation of most vocabulary is influenced by metaphorical thinking. In vocabulary teaching, teachers can trace the etymology of words and develop the metaphorical thinking of students to enhance their understanding and memory of vocabulary. First, teachers can apply the metaphor theory to medical terminology. Due to its historical origins in the process of medical development, medical vocabulary absorbs a large number of foreign words, especially Greek and Latin words, which constitute a large number of complex vocabulary terminology. During the learning process, students do not understand their medical meanings. In fact, understanding the characteristics of word formation and full use of metaphorical thinking, students can achieve twice the result with half the effort; in addition, the root of medical vocabulary usually comes from Greek or Latin, representing a part of the body. Like "gastr" (stomach), different words contain the same root. The core meanings of words such as gastritis, gastrotomy, gastrilgia, and gastroscope are from "gastr" which means stomach. Thus, mastering a root using analogy and other metaphorical thinking, we can derive the basic meaning of a certain type of words. It can be seen that the composition of Medical English terminology is metaphoric in nature, and it is necessary to understand them by metaphoric thinking, that is, to perceive as many morphemes as possible from the existing Medical English terms, and remember these concepts in relation to their forms. Secondly, we should apply the metaphor theory to the interpretation of amphibious vocabulary. A large part of medical vocabulary is General English words. This vocabulary has specific medical implications and hence called amphibious vocabulary. During the learning process, students do not understand their medical meanings. In fact, although these words are different in meaning from the original words, they do have an inner connection. For example, "labour" means "work" especially physical work in General English; it means "the process of childbirth" in Medical English; "plastic" means "a synthetic material made from a wide range of organic polymers" in General English while it means "the process of reconstructing or repairing parts of the body" in Medical English; "focus" means "the centre of interest or activity" in General English and it means "the principal site of an infection or other disease" in Medical English. As regards these medically specific meanings, even with the aid of a dictionary, it is still difficult to find an accurate explanation. Therefore, teachers can relate their original meanings to their metaphoric meanings, using metaphorical thinking to reason and associate, and finally get the accurate meanings. Thirdly, teachers can apply metaphor theory to medical compound words which are often composed of two or more independent words. The meaning of the words is not the simple addition of the original two words as it is also based on its extended meaning. There are a large number of compound words in Medical English. Such as pink-eye, combing "pink" and "eye" which means "the principal site of an infection or other disease". Teachers can analyze vocabulary, generate associations, use metaphorical thinking in vocabulary instruction, and deepen the students' understanding of compound words. Finally, with the continuous development of medical science, new words relating to new diseases, drugs and therapies will come into existence. According to statistics, about 1,500 new words appear every year. These vocabularies use a variety of metaphorical thinking methods such as analogy, association and metonymy in the creative process as in Parkinson disease, rubella, bird flu, rose fever black lung etcetera, involving personal names, place names, animal names, plant names, and color words, which use metaphorical thinking to extend their semantics.

Apart from the problems in learning medical vocabulary, while reading scientific papers, medical students have difficulties in using and understanding the metaphors inside. They always understand metaphors from Chinese concepts and way of thinking. However, sometimes, the Chinese concepts do not have equivalent meanings in English concepts which will generate ambiguous meanings. Hence, strategies of facilitating metaphor comprehension need to be cultivated. When communicating with patients who are less educated, doctors need to use simple and concrete concepts to interpret complex and abstract ones, metaphors are tools in describing the conditions of patients, weapons in treating process, and ties between doctor-patient relationship (Reisfield and Wilson, 2004; Vyjeyanthi, 2008; Casarett, et al., 2010). Serving as the basis for a shared understanding in clinical practice, metaphoric competence does play an important role in the language of the medical context. If the Chinese and English concepts belong to different or non-corresponding conceptual systems, they will have interpretative problems in understanding the contexts. For medical students who are going to frequently use metaphors in learning and working, a metaphor enriched English language instruction is very necessary to be conducted to improve their English for Medical Purposes (EMP) level (Danesi, 1992; Kecskes, 2006) as well as increasing their metaphoric interpretation skills (Johnson and Rosano, 1993; Kanthan and Mills,2006).

1.2 Statement of the Problem

Jin and Cortazzi (2006) state that, although China owns the world's largest educational system due to its largest number of English learners, Chinese students are still far from being adept in English competence (reading,speaking,listening and writing). The cognitive theory of metaphor claims that the abilities of interpreting and producing metaphor in the target language are vital for language learning. However, metaphoric language is often insufficient in college EFL learning and English instruction. Native learners who grow up in the American culture and have immersed in the environment of oral language and schooling, can acquire linguistic competence of metaphoric language easier than L2 learners. However, second language learners are suggested to learn a new language at an early age without cultural references or natural oral environment. Then several years of EFL (English as a Foreign Language) education in high school only prepares them for the surface features of English, providing them with some basic reading and writing skills, but that is hardly adequate for meeting our advanced college English goals. To make matters worse, metaphoric language is seldom taught at the beginning stage of college EFL teaching for fear of overwhelming second language students with the complexity of understanding the multiple layers of meaning.

Comparing with the weakness English proficiency, there is a strong demand of ESP which comes from college students. Cai (2010) suggests that the teaching and learning of a foreign language are to meet the society's need which help learners engaged in international academic and cultural exchange. Comparing with the social need, the learners' needs are far more apparent. A lot of researchers (Yang,2010;Huang,2011;Cai,2012) have proved that what college students earnestly need is not basic General English knowledge but knowledge relating to their majors and future careers. Yang (2010) states that the Chinese learners' major purpose of learning English is to use English as a tool to obtain information in their field and to express their ideas freely. What calls for attention is the disconnectedness between EGP teaching and ESP in some universities. Taking my university as an example, General English course is set up for the first and the second-year college students. There are four semesters for this phase where students mainly study the English skills, including listening, speaking, reading and writing. In the third year, they are going to access the Medical English course. However, they have already learned the professional courses in their first year. Students attach more importance to their professional courses and spend less time on learning English. Many students can understand college English textbook easily due to the same grammar and vocabulary which they had studied in high school. With the increased English language comprehending ability, the first-year students in the medical university call for specialized English as more urgent, since their English College

Entrance Examination scores go higher and higher. A questionnaire survey of 269 college students at Capital Medical University showed that 88.9% of the students strongly demanded to add Medical English content to the General English course (Lu, 2012). In contrast, these students' high English level and their high expectations of the English class, the present college General English phase disconnects with the medical specialty. There is no natural transition from General English to ESP and so it is difficult for students to adapt to. Therefore, metaphor enriched medical knowledge could be supplemented in EGP class to improve the language competence of the students, especially the metaphoric competence, and their professional skills.

Furthermore, metaphors play a large role in many aspects of medicine. Anatole Broyard states, "Metaphors may be as necessary to illness as they are to literature, as comforting to the patient as his own bathrobe and slippers. At the very least, they are a relief from medical terminology…Perhaps only metaphor can express the bafflement, the panic combined with beatitude, of the threatened person" (1990). Danielle Ofri (2010) notes that understanding metaphors is a key clinical skill in diagnosis; the symptoms of patients are often presented in metaphoric manners which require doctors to interpret patients' metaphors skillfully. Casarett (2010) states that metaphors may offer a valuable supplemental strategy that physicians could use to enhance communication. Therefore, metaphor can be viewed as a tool for relating one's past experiences as well as present knowledge to the unknown things. Clinicians are able to help patients attach the things they have already known or experienced to the existing "schema" in their mind and then connect the schema to the information about their illnesses in terms of metaphor. While discussing the complex and the risky situations, in an indirect manner, metaphors are always used euphemistically. For example, the war metaphor is usually adopted in cancer therapy, all the knowledge that involves warfare are applied to the desire to "fight to the bitter end" (as cited in Vyjeyanthi, 2008). On the other hand, metaphors can explain an abstract domain in terms of a specific domain which is based on body experiences. These body experiences make metaphors universal and trans-cultural. In many languages, "good" is associated with warm, bright and positive features while the bad or difficult things are often associated with cold, dark and negative features. These metaphors can simulate the experiences of the human body in the mind of the patients. Kövecses (2000) has thoroughly investigated the metaphors of emotions in different languages. He came up with a conceptual metaphor on anger THE ANGRY PERSON IS A PRESSURIZED CONTAINER (small capital letters are used to distinguish conceptual metaphors from linguistic metaphors). Wickman and Campbell (2003) highlight that the understanding and development of a client's metaphor can help the therapist follow the client's line of thought, improve rapport, reveal a deep sense of empathy, and can be a catalyst for change of self-perception. McLeod and Cooper (2011) claim that using metaphors to illuminate and develop understanding of clients' processes characterizes the nature of their professional work and is indicative of their pluralistic approach. Hence, metaphor is very important for the professional study of the medical college students. However, college freshmen do not know how to communicate with patients in terms of metaphor. Sometimes, it is difficult or impossible to express their emotional experiences in a literal language. Using a metaphor can connect the relational new experience with a familiar one, a contextual road map can be created by doctors in order to understand and thus process a complex pattern of feelings.

The problems with metaphoren riched English language instruction aroused great attention and concern of scholars at home and abroad, such as Danesi (1986,1992), Cameron (1999), Low (1997,1999), Littlemore (2001), Yan Shiqing (2001), Dong hongling (2003), Wang Yin (2007), and Hu Zhuanglin (2020). Littlemore and Low state that since metaphors are often hard to treat in a clear, rule-governed way, language instructors are inclined to using few metaphors in their classroom discourse (2006). With the development of the metaphor cognitive theory, all of them turned to metaphor for help. However, when teaching metaphors, teachers always take metaphor as a figure of speech that we can do and as a rhetorical device which can be used for special effects. As a result, teachers tell the students the meaning of metaphors without any further elaboration. In the long run, instructors will realize that limited metaphoric language study may severely affect the reading and writing abilities of students. Without acquiring the English conceptual systems which are mostly manifested by the metaphoric linguistic expressions, the students tend to speak English with the logic of their mother tongue. For example, understanding English in the Chinese thinking pattern, their English outputs are unnatural and are with thick Chinese flavour. Furthermore, although some scholars have done some empirical studies to demonstrate the positive effects of metaphor enriched teaching on language study, few suggestions about how to effectively teach metaphors in an English as a Foreign Language class have been advanced. Therefore, it is necessary for this thesis to try to use an experimental research as an inspection tool to find out the effective teaching methods of conceptual metaphor in the EFL class in addition to proving that the conceptual metaphor does have a positive effect in enhancing the English competence and medical vocabulary of students.

1.3 Rationale of the Study

Although there are anumber of articles or researches related to the importance of metaphors both for students and teachers, there are only a few articles explaining how to use metaphors to improve the students' metaphoric competence and how to implement metaphor instruction in detail. The previous researches mainly focus on the analysis of some specific metaphors and the professional belief of teachers, reflected in their metaphors. This study offers students the very basic theory of conceptual metaphors and helps them identify metaphors in the text which is beneficial for their English learning.

Additionally, supplementary materials are offered for the added understanding of medical knowledge which is a creative effort benefiting College English instruction. In this study students are encouraged to create metaphors both in written and oral forms in English which is to aid suitably in their metaphoric production.

This research tried to stimulate the interest of first-year students in English learning and metaphoric expressions in daily English and Medical English via supplementing medical knowledge to their English course. It tried to assess how the metaphor enriched English language instruction supplements the selected units of the current textbook via the classroom observation of teachers, feedback, interview and questionnaires of students after collecting them from teachers and students. The thesis proposes to refine the metaphor enriched English supplementary materials to help students smoothly transit from College English to Medical English and lay a good foundation for their future careers.

As a teacher of English as Second Language (ESL) with 11 years of experience, the researcher finds that metaphor is like an active elf existing in the thoughts and practices of instructors, which has not attracted enough attention from the ESL researchers. As a basic approach to education and teaching, metaphor exists in many contemporary education and teaching theories. In educational courses, if the teaching theories and a teacher's individual teaching methods are discussed together in the classroom via metaphor, it will benefit the teacher's reflective and introspective teaching ideas. During this process, teachers can better understand the functions of the metaphor and apply it to his or her own teaching methods.

1.4 Research Objectives

This research aims touse the qualitative research as an inspection tool to find out the effective teaching methods of metaphor enriched supplement in the EGP class. The main research objectives are as follows.

(1) To investigate the metaphor cognition of the first-year medical students at Xinxiang Medical University, China.

(2) To implement the Metaphor Enriched English Language Instruction supplementary materials with the first-year medical students during their first semester at Xinxiang Medical University, China.

(3) To monitor and observe if the students' metaphoric competence has improved or not after implementing the Metaphor Enriched English Language Instruction supplementary materials.

(4) To collect the feedback of teacher participants on Metaphor Enriched English Language Instruction and supplementary materials.

(5) To collect the feedback of student participants on Metaphor Enriched English Language Instruction and supplementary materials.

1.5 Research Questions

It is not difficult to find out that many students consider metaphor as a rhetorical device and it means that they lack the metaphoric competence, compared to the native English users. Although the texts, produced by the Chinese college students have high verbal fluency, they still lack the conceptual fluency of the native speakers. The literalness of textbooks written by the Chinese scholars is inadequate in conceptual metaphor compared to the target language text. As a result, students often work hard in reading and writing of English but the result is far from satisfactory. Some students are not satisfied with the present college English for General Purposes (EGP) teaching and wish there is more professional knowledge and skills in classrooms. The present research aims to supplement metaphor enriched college EGP teaching for the first-year college non-English majors and is going to address the following questions.

(1) What is the current metaphor cognition of the first-year college students at Xinxiang Medical University, China?

(2) What is the effect of metaphor enriched language instruction on first-year medical students' metaphoric competence?

(3) What is the feedback of teachers regarding the metaphor enriched language instruction supplementary materials?

(4) What is the feedback of the students' on the metaphor enriched language instruction supplementary materials?

1.6 Significance of the Study

As a global language, millions of people are learning English in China. But the biggest problem is that though they spend much time on learning English, they do not benefit enough from their hard work. Students still cannot get out of the dilemma of "deaf-mute" English because of their weak metaphoric competence. They always make an impression on others with their stiff and humourless expressions. As a language tool, metaphoric competence, linguistic competence, and communicative competence constitute the fundamental ability of language proficiency. Consequently, attention should be paid in cultivating the metaphoric competence and language proficiency of students in foreign language instruction. It can enrich the language expressions in the linguistic cognitive process of students. Learners can understand the implications of metaphor exactly and reasonably, thus achieve the purpose of improving their English language proficiency in listening, speaking, reading, and writing. Furthermore, metaphor enriched English language instruction can improve the language skills, promote creative thinking, stimulate the interest in language learning, strengthen the self-confidence and form a habit of

English thinking in students. Consequently, it is necessary to lay emphasis on adopting the metaphor enriched English language instruction in college while teaching English as a Foreign Language (EFL).

College English teaching in China is in an important transition period. On the one hand, due to the increasing English competency level of high school graduates, many universities are compressing their English courses and credits. On the other hand, with the economic globalization and internationalization of higher education, students urgently need the knowledge of professional English. They need to concentrate and master the academic course, search the English literature, participate in the international conferences and work extensively in English. Metaphor teaching can improve the English competence as well as the medical knowledge of students. Introducing the medical vocabulary into the General English course via metaphor will meet the requirements of students, make them learn about the universality and features of English, blend General English and Medical English, improve their listening and writing ability related to their professional materials, and in the long run, achieve a higher competency level in English.

The pedagogical potential of metaphors has been claimed (Ortony, 1979; Pugh, 1989; Williams, et al., 1992), but not empirically demonstrated (Duit, 1991). This thesis is going to contribute some pedagogical evidence that might enhance the conceptual claims and the theoretical rationale. The results will be relevant for practical application if it is able to demonstrate that metaphors are a readily accessible means of making abstract content more memorable and meaningful. At the same time, metaphors do influence the ways of thinking about learning, the perceptions of the links between teaching and learning, and the modeling by the tutor for learners. Metaphor enriched instruction can help teachers to plan and deliver courses, and track professional development. It also will facilitate a "critical and creative-thinking" education system that both empowers and supports and teachers to engage within a forward-looking knowledge economy (Zhao, et al., 2010).

According to Pena and Andrade-Filho (2010), over the past century, there are over 450 metaphors used in the medical literature which relate to fruit, vegetables, cereals, seafood, dairy products, fauna, flora, astronomical bodies, weapons, dining table utensils, laboratory equipment, drinks and colours. These metaphors continue to be in use today. Chinese medical students come from the backgrounds which are culturally and geographically different. Most of them have had no experience of the British culture and hence find the use of some metaphors rather complex and inappropriate with their culture, especially when the analogues in English are not familiar with their mother tongue environment.

Stephen Lankton (2002) claims metaphors work due to the mind being metaphoric. He claims the profound effect of stories and metaphors on listeners: they can teach, inspire, guide, communicate, be remembered, and, most of all, are everywhere (as cited in George, 2007). Metaphors are ubiquitous in our everyday conversations. They not only make ordinary language more vivid, but also add colour to our communication. However, metaphors exist so commonly in the language that they frequently go unnoticed. It does play an important role in the communication between patients and doctors. If patients use such figurative language to express their experience, doctors need to use an appropriate and practical language to join the conversation, to meet the patients in their mode of communication, then to bring changes in both figurative and pragmatic processes. Unlike in other lectures in which the lecturer is active and the listener may be passive, metaphor requires an active involvement on the listener's part. If the listener wants to find the meaning, he/she has to engage with the lecturer, and the interactive communication is established between both the lecturer and the listener. Everyone loves a good story. As attractive as stories, the messages embedded in metaphors can draw the attention of the listeners. They are also helpful in transmitting the sound and helpful advice, especially when patients are generating the therapeutic metaphors, they will not resist the ideas, metaphors, or analogy which emerge from their own story. Mikaela Hildebrandt, Fletcher, and Hayes (2010) describe metaphors as "a bridge between the world created by language and the experience of the world that transcends language". In a good story, the main character often faces a problem or challenge, and tries to find the methods to reach a solution. When engaging with the main character or the problem, listeners also become involved in how to solve the problem, or how to develop the problem-solving skills which they do not have. A metaphoric story owns the power to allow listeners to get out of the frame of reference in which they have been stuck by a different experience.

Chapter 2

Literature Review

This chapter reviews the related literature of different metaphor theories and proposers from the perspectives of traditional views and contemporary views. Due to the importance of the conceptual metaphor theory, three types, namely, structural metaphor, orientational metaphor and ontological metaphor will be discussed in detail. In orde to avoid the sensitivity in metaphor identification process, the Pragglejza Group's Metaphor Identification Procedure (MIP) will be adopted in this study (2007). The previous studies of conceptual metaphor and EFL (English as a Foreign Language) instruction will be discussed. Further, the relation between metaphors and Medical English will be mentioned. The conceptual framework of metaphor enriched English language instruction will be presented in this chapter.

2.1 Traditional View of Metaphor

The term "metaphor" is directly derived from the Greek "metaphora" which is made up of two semanteme, the first semanteme "meta" means "across", the other one "pherein" means "carry". Therefore, "metaphor" essentially means "carrying across". The definition of metaphor can be generalized. In a narrow sense, metaphor is a term in traditional rhetoric which is different from other figures of speech. It is also known as linguistic metaphor. The interpretation of metaphor in *A Dictionary of Current Chinese* (2012) is: "a kind of metaphor without 'like', 'as if' but with 'become', 'be' and often compares something with another thing which has a similar relationship". The definition in *A Dictionary of Literary Terms and Literary Theory* (2013) is: "A figure of speech in which one thing is described in terms of another. A comparison is usually implicit; whereas in simile it is explicit". In a broad sense, Aristotle once took all the rhetoric phenomena as metaphoric language.

Among the metaphor theories, two outstanding ones are Aristotle's comparison theory and

Quintilian's substitution theory and both viewed metaphor as a figure of speech. An ancient Greek philosopher, Aristotle did the earliest study of metaphor. In his book *Rhetoric and the Poetic* (1954), he proposed the definition of metaphor and explicitly expounds the formation as well as the rhetoric function of metaphor. He claims that metaphor is the application to one thing of a name belonging to another thing. He believes the main function of metaphor is for decorative use. He has said that the greatest thing by far is to be the master of metaphors and he considered those who can use metaphors freely and properly as language genius. Aristotle's view of metaphor has dominated western rhetoric for nearly two thousand years (as cited in Eduard, 2019).

The comparison view of metaphor focuses on the fact that the two components of metaphor can successfully build the metaphoric relationship which is decided by the speaker who can find the similarities between them through the comparison of their semantic characteristics. Ortony views metaphor as a literal simile with "like" or "as" deleted and the respect of the similarity left unspecified (1979). Take the metaphor THE MAN IS A WOLF as an example, in essence, this metaphor is equal to the simile "The man is like a wolf". People behave like wolves in some unspecified aspects. The reason why speakers and listeners can understand such metaphors is because they own the common background knowledge (common sense) or life experience. People sometimes show some vicious and greedy behaviors like wolves, so it is a similein its essence. The comparison view regards metaphor as a rhetorical flourish that surprises or delights the audience rather than the traditional view of a linguistic adornment. Hu Zhuanglin (2004) claims the comparison view of metaphor confines metaphor within the rhetorical field. It is regarded as a figure of speech.

In 1936, for the definition of metaphor, I. A. Richards sparked a twentieth-century debate in his famous lectures "The Philosophy of Rhetoric" and put forward the interaction view. In this lecture, Richards (1936) claimed a completely new view about metaphor, "Thought is metaphoric, and proceeds by comparison, and the metaphors of language derive there from…" Suggesting that thought itself is partially constituted by metaphors. He also pointed out that one cannot speak three sentences without employing some kind of metaphoric phrase. Richards sought to put metaphor into an important place in language studies by combining with Freud's psychological theories of interpretation (as cited in Berthoff, 1991). According to Richards, the metaphor can create meaning by bringing two thoughts, a tenor and vehicle, into contact with one another, in other words, causing the distinct meanings to "interact" and to create a new meaning which cannot be paraphrased into its literal terms in the listener's mind. Moreover, his approach views this interaction between the tenor and vehicle as the essential defining quality where the comparison view of metaphor focuses on the fact that whether the two components of metaphor can successfully build the metaphoric relationship which is decided by the speaker who can find the similarities between them through the comparison of their semantic characteristics. In other words, metaphor is a real literal simile with "like" or "as" deleted and the respect of the similarity left unspecified (Ortony, 1979). Black (1962) further develops the interaction view by turning to cognitive psychology and schema theory to illustrate how metaphors work. Black argues that metaphors contain a cognitive content which is produced by the interaction of schema and cannot be expressed in literal terms. He claims that the metaphorical statement contains a principal subject and a subsidiary subject which are viewed as "systems" rather than isolated words. Black states that the principal subject is "projected upon" the field of the subsidiary subject in understanding a metaphor. By emphasizing that metaphor is a prevalent phenomenon of language, and by highlighting the cognitive interaction between the tenor and the vehicle, the interaction view of metaphor has already begun to realize the cognitive value of metaphor. It also has paved the way for the coming of a new cognitive approach.

2.2 The Contemporary View of Metaphor

With the cognitive study of metaphor, several influential theories appeared, among which the conceptual metaphor theory has unanimously been recognized as the outstanding one of the contemporary views of metaphor. Lakoff and Johnson (2003) in an afterword to their 1980 book, *Metaphors We Live By*, described the theory of metaphor as having several key components. First of all, metaphors are conceptual and are not just a function of language. These conceptual metaphors are grounded in our experiences. In other words, the experiences we have in life shape the metaphors that we hold about various concepts. In addition, Lakoff and Johnson assert that metaphoric thought is unavoidable in our lives and is largely unconscious. Though abstract thoughts have a literal core, they are extended by metaphors; our understandings of them are deepened by metaphors. We live our very lives every day on the basis of inferences we derive through metaphors.

2.2.1 Conceptual metaphor theory

A completely new view of metaphor, which is different from all traditional viewpoints of metaphor was first put forward by George Lakoff and Mark Johnson in their book published in 1980, *Metaphors We Live By*. Their conceptual metaphor has come to be known as "Conceptual Metaphor Theory" which exerts great influence upon the cognitive study of metaphor and also is one of the central researches in the field of cognitive linguistics. In Lakoff and Johnson's view, metaphor is not simply a matter of words or linguistic expressions, but a matter of concepts, even of thinking one thing in terms of another (1980). For example, the abstract concept like "life" is usually talked through a concrete concept "play". For the conceptual metaphor theory, metaphor becomes a valuable cognitive tool which poets as well as ordinary people rely on; metaphor is conceptual in nature.

Lakoff (1993) defines conceptual metaphor as "mapping from a source domain to a target domain". The formula "Target Domain is Source Domain" (A IS B), or "Target Domain as Source Domain" (A AS B) was used into mapping. For example, for the conceptual metaphor LIFE IS PLAY, "LIFE" is the target domain and "PLAY" is the source domain (Lakoff, 1993). The use of capitalised letters is due to Lakoff and Johnson's conventional use of mnemonics for labelling conceptual metaphors. Mappings are sets of systematic correspondences between the source domain and the target domain, Kövecses(2002) states it is "where constituent conceptual elements of the source correspond to constituent elements of the target". The following example which is taken from Lakoff shows a typical conceptual metaphor.

> All the world's a stage,
> And all the men and women merely players.
> They have their exits and their entrances;
> And one man in his time plays many parts.
>
> (Lakoff, 1993)

These sets of correspondences between the source domain and target domain are both ontological and epistemic. The mapping relations are shown in Table 2-1.

Table 2-1 Metaphoric Mappings Between "LIFE" and "PLAY"

Target domain	Source domain
Life	Play
World	Stage
All the men and women	Players
One's birth and death	One's exit and entrance (of the stage)
Duties	A player should play many parts

Another metaphor related to LIFE, LIFE IS A JOURNEY is another conceptual metaphor. In this metaphor, "LIFE" is the target domain and "JOURNEY" is the source domain. The mapping relation between the two domains are shown in Table 2-2.

Table 2-2　Metaphoric Mappings Between "LIFE" and "JOURNEY"

Target domain		Source domain
Life	→	Journey
Travelers	→	People
Start	→	Birth
Conditions	→	Talents
Obstacle	→	Outside difficulties
Distance	→	Length of time
Destination	→	Life goal
Terminal point	→	Death

In conclusion, in the early period of the contemporary theory, conceptual metaphors are conventional mappings from the source domain to the target domain and are activated constantly and automatically with neither effort nor awareness (Lakoff, 1993). The mappings are based either on conceptual knowledge or the image schema of the source domain: the former entails ontological and epistemic correspondences between the source and the target domains, and the latter is the basis of image-schema metaphor. The conventional mappings across domains do not only help us understand one thing in terms of another, but also allow us to make appropriate inferences. The everyday metaphorical expressions we are used to, are nothing but the linguistic manifestations of conceptual metaphors.

2.2.2　Conceptual metaphors and linguistic metaphors

According to Lakoff and Johnson (2003), understanding metaphor from a cognitive linguistic perspective requires us to distinguish conceptual metaphors from linguistic metaphors. Conceptual metaphors refer to a connection between two semantic areas which is at the level of thought, while linguistic metaphors are the spoken or written realizations of conceptual metaphors. For the cognitive approach to metaphor, more metaphor analysis is given to conceptual metaphors rather than the linguistic level. For instance, the concept ARGUMENT is generally viewed in terms of the conceptual metaphor ARGUMENT IS WAR which entails a wide variety of expressions, these expressions are regarded as linguistic metaphors.

> AGRUMENT IS WAR
> Your claims are indefensible.
> He attacked every weak point in my argument.
> His criticisms were right on target.
> I've never won an argument with him.
> If you use that strategy, he'll wipe you out.

He shot down all of my arguments.

(Lakoff and Johnson, 1980)

Lakoff and Johnson hold the idea that people understand the abstract domain ARGUMENT in terms of their knowledge of WAR, which is a more concrete domain. They remark, "It is in this sense that the AGRUMENT IS WAR metaphor is one we live by in this culture; it structures the actions we perform in arguing" (1980). The conceptual metaphor is realized by the linguistic metaphors linguistically. Metaphor is not in the words, it is in the ideas; it is part of ordinary language, not only of poetry; it is used for reasoning. They also mention language instruction and learning, for example, the language people use to talk about the concept is systematic because the metaphorical concept people live by is metaphoric. Besides the systematicity found in the reasoning of abstract concepts, there is also a systematicity in the usage if conventional expressions and novel language constructions. Therefore, linguistic expressions are ultimately grounded in experience: bodily, physical, social and cultural (Popova, 2003).

2.2.3 Main features of conceptual metaphor

Metaphor is an essential tool to structure and represent many concepts, especially the abstract ones in our conceptual system. Metaphor is not only a way of expression, but also a way of conceptualization. It means "a cross-domain mapping in the conceptual system" (Lakoff, 1993). The conceptual systems of human beings are rooted and shaped in the environment where people live as well as the physical and psychological experiences people have experienced. It is well acknowledged that all humans share the same physical experiences such as the same physical attributes. Everybody has the same organs to see, to speak and to feel, to have the same functions to use and create conceptual metaphors as well. Hence, there is no doubt that people's experiences are universal, and also the metaphor based on them should be universal in nature. That is why there are so many identical conceptual metaphors in different languages and cultures, which show the great resemblance in people's universal experiences and thinking modes. Kövecses and Ning Yu consider that there are some universal metaphors, such as happiness is up, happiness is light, happiness is a fluid in a container, anger is a pressurized fluid or gas in a container (Kövecses, 2002; Ning, 1998).

The relation of linguistic metaphors and conceptual metaphors is that the former is governed in a systematic way by the latter due to each linguistic metaphor is a particular linguistic manifestation of its corresponding conceptual metaphor. The system of metaphor is highly structured by its ontological and epistemic correspondence operating across conceptual domains. Lakoff and Johnson both consider that the conceptual metaphors do not operate in isolation from each other, rather "metaphorical entailment can characterize a coherent system of metaphor concepts and corresponding coherent system of metaphorical expressions for the concept" (1980). An example is given as follows.

SOCIAL ORGANIZATIONS ARE PLANTS
She works for the local branch of the bank.
Our company is growing.
They had to prune the workforce.
The organization was rooted in the old church.
Employers reaped enormous benefits from cheap foreign labor.

(as cited in Kövecses, 2002)

As is shown in the above example, readers can observe that elements of plants systematically correspond to elements of social organizations, such as companies, organizations and so forth. Notice that in the case as well, words that are used to describe plants are employed systematically in connection with social organizations. Words involved are branch, is growing, prune, root, blossom, reaped. Similar to the former discussion, people are inclined to talk about an abstract concept in virtue of a concrete one, and usually the concrete function is viewed as the source domain and the abstract one as the target domain. We understand a concept well by the systematic set of correspondence between these two conceptual domains.

Lakoff (1993) claims that the systematic governance of metaphorical expressions, conceptual metaphors also systematically relate to each other and form a hierarchical structure, "metaphorical mapping do not occur isolated from one another, they are sometimes organized in hierarchical structures, in which 'lower' mappings in the hierarchy inherit the structure of the 'higher' mappings". For example:

IDEAS ARE FOOD
There are too many facts for me to *digest*.
I just can not *swallow* that claim.

IDEAS ARE PLANTS
Her ideas finally came to *fruition*.
He has a *fertile* imagination.

IDEAS ARE COMMODITIES
That idea just won't *sell*.
There is always a *market* for good ideas.

IDEAS ARE BUILDINGS
This idea is carefully *constructed*.
This idea *collapsed* after she obtained the new data.

(as cited in Lakoff, 1993)

In conclusion, systematicity exists not only within the metaphor but across the metaphor. It shapes various kinds of metaphorical expressions, and helps to manifest that the language and the thought of human beings are metaphoric in nature. Hence the systematicity of conceptual metaphor can facilitate the language study. Lakoff(1980) considers that because metaphorical expressions connect to metaphorical concepts which are systematic, metaphorical linguistic expressions can be used to study the nature of metaphorical concepts as well as understanding the metaphorical nature of our activities. From this point, the systematicity of conceptual metaphor makes it possible to learn and create metaphor in the process of language teaching and learning.

2.2.4 The classification of conceptual metaphor

Three kinds of conceptual metaphor are talked of in Lakoff and Johnson's book *Metaphors We Live By*, they are structural metaphor, orientational metaphor and ontological metaphor. In the following sections, these three types of metaphors which are classified based on their cognitive functions will be discussed.

2.2.4.1 Structural metaphor

Structural metaphor refers to constructing one concept (target domain) through another one (source domain). The cognitive domains of these two concepts are certainly different, but they keep their structure unchanged, namely, their constitutional components have an orderly corresponding relation. A comparatively rich knowledge structure will be provided by the source domain to the target domain, namely, conceptual mappings between these two conceptual domains can promote people's understanding. It is the cognitive functions of metaphors that enable speakers to understand the target domain by way of the structure of the source domain (Kövecses, 2002). Mostly, target A is a relatively abstract and inherently unstructured concept, while the source B is a more concrete and highly structured one. Here is an example of structural metaphor TIME PASSING IS MOTION OF AN OBJECT.

> Time is flying by.
> Thanksgiving is coming up on us.
> The time for action has arrived.
> I'm looking ahead to Christmas.
>
> (as cited in Kövecses, 2002b)

In these examples, words normally used to talk about the motional object are now applied to describe time passing. What is more, they talk about the motional aspect of passing time in a systematic way: time can fly and move as an object. This structural metaphor explicates a large amount of linguistic metaphors in English. Not only explaining particular metaphors' meanings, but the mappings also provide an overall structure in the process of understanding of time notion. Without metaphors, it will be very difficult for people to understand the abstract concept of time. Most structural metaphors can provide such understanding and structuring for their corresponding abstract target concepts. Yan Shiqing says that structural metaphors are a much more exquisite and sophisticated cognitive process (2001).

2.2.4.2 Orientational metaphor

Orientational metaphor derives from the fact that most metaphors that serve this function have to do with the basic human spatial orientations. The space orientations are rooted in the interaction between human beings and nature. Furthermore, they are the basic concepts that people live by, such as UP-DOWN, FRONT-BACK, CENTER-PERIPHERY. People use these concrete concepts to project into some abstract concepts like health status, quantity, emotion, social class. The cognitive function of such kind of metaphors lies in the coherence between the target concepts and our conceptual system. This kind of metaphor is usually so common in our language that speakers do not have the awareness of their existence as orientational metaphorical expressions. Here are some examples.

> MORE IS UP; LESS IS DOWN
> Speak up, please. Keep your voice down, please.
>
> HEALTHY IS UP; SICK IS DOWN
> Lisa rose from the dead. He fell ill.
>
> HAPPY IS UP; SAD IS DOWN
> She is feeling up today. He was really low those days.
>
> CONSCIOUS IS UP; UNCONSCIOUS IS DOWN
> Wake up. She sank into a coma.
>
> VIRTUE IS UP; LACK OF VIRTUE IS DOWN
> He is an upstanding citizen. That is a low-down thing to do.
> (as cited in Kövecses, 2010)

The above examples demonstrate that the concrete orientational concepts UP and DOWN are mapped onto the abstract concepts MORE and LESS, HEALTHY and SICK, HAPPY and SAD, CONSCIOUS and UNCONSCIOUS, VIRTUE and LACK OF VIRTUE, which have no orientations by themselves. These mappings are rooted in our physical experiences, which lies in the fact that upward orientation goes with positive evaluation, while downward orientation goes with a negative one. These metaphorical orientations have a basis in human physical and cultural experiences which are not arbitrary. And they will vary in different cultures.

2.2.4.3 Ontological metaphor

According to Kövecses, ontological metaphor simply means that we conceive of our experiences in terms of objects, substances, and containers, in general, without specifying exactly what kind of object, substances, and container is meant (2002). Their cognitive job seems to be to "merely" give an ontological status to general categories of abstract target concepts. In general, ontological metaphors enable people to see a more sharply delineated structure where there is very little or none. Table 2-3 shows the two conceptual domains of ontological metaphors.

Table 2-3 Ontological Metaphor

Source domain	Target domain
Physical object	Nonphysical or abstract entities (e.g., the mind)
	Events (e.g., going to the race)
	Actions (e.g., giving someone a call)
Substance	Activities (e.g., a lot of running in the game)
Container	Undelineated physical objects (e.g., a clearing in the forest)
	Physical and nonphysical surfaces (e.g., land areas, the visual field)
	States (e.g., in love)

From the perspective of cognitive linguistic, it is very important to connect a basic status, like objects or substances with human experience which are not clearly depicted or abstract. For example, we can imagine the mind which we cannot clearly depict as an object to understand more about the mind, such as the metaphor MINDS ARE MACHINES. The source domain is the physical object MACHINE and the target domain is the abstract concept MIND. If we conceptualize MIND as an object, we can easily find more structures by the MACHINE metaphors. For example, there are metaphorical linguistic expressions in English such as "His mind is rusty recently". The next example in the above table is "going to the race" and here the source domain RACE can be understood as a physical object ROOM which people can go in, so there is a linguistic expression in English like "Tom is going to the race now". In these two examples, we treat the abstract target domain MIND and RACE as a concrete physical object like MACHINE and ROOM. Of ontological metaphor, the most representative one is the container metaphor. Every individual can be seen as a container, with a bounding surface and in-out orientation. Our own orientation can be projected onto other objects, like house, forest, field and even some abstract and intangible things and events. Let's consider the following examples.

The ship is coming into view.
We are in trouble now.
Is she in the race on Sunday?

In these sentences, the words "view" "trouble" and "race" are conceptualized as a container, therefore the ship can "come into" it, people are "in" trouble, and a person is "in" the race.

From this perspective, personification can be regarded as a form of ontological metaphor. In personification, human qualities are given to non-human entities, as the following examples show.

Life has cheated me.
Inflation is eating up our profits.

(Kövecses, 2002)

Theoretically, life, theory and inflation are not human, but they are endowed with the qualities of cheating, explaining and eating. Thus we can have a better understanding in the process of personifying non-human entities as humans.

2.3 Metaphor Identification Procedure

A group of scholars called Pragglejaz Group (a combination of 10 name initials) provides a prescriptive approach of identifying metaphors in a written material in 2007. This approach gives a way of identifying metaphors without the involvement of the investigator's sensitivity and avoids the investigator's lack of metaphor knowledge. It is almost mechanical, for, its identification of each word is checked against a dictionary definition. The literal meanings of the words come from the dictionary, and if the meaning in the written material is not the same as the literal meaning given in the dictionary, this word can be viewed as a metaphor. The Pragglejaz Group summarizes that there are six steps in finding metaphorical words and phrases. Figure 2–1 states the detailed procedure.

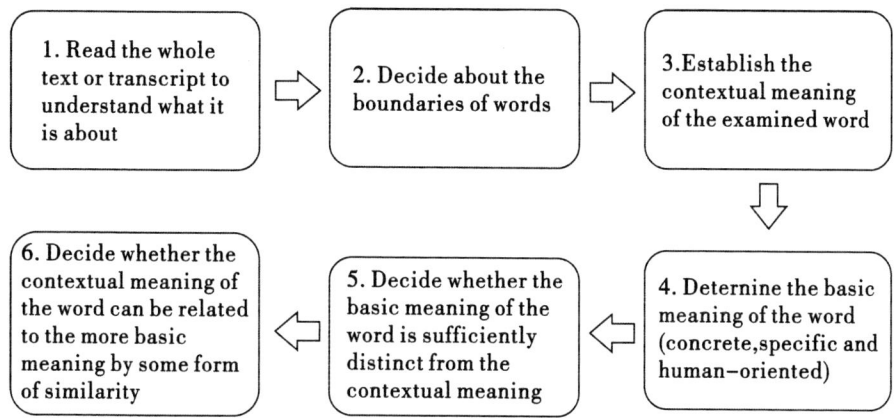

Figure 2-1   Metaphor Identification Procedure (MIP)

This procedure divides the written text into individual words and compares each one's contextual meaning with its dictionary meaning. According to the result, if the contextual meaning can be related to its basic meaning by similarity, a decision can be made that this word is used metaphorically. This research adopted the MIP which is convenient to confirm the suitability of uncertain metaphors. It also provides the decision-making records and the reasons for them.

2.4 Metaphoric Competence

In order to improve second language learners' proficiency in the target language, grammatical or communicative competence has been emphasized in L2 teaching (Danesi, 1988). Metaphoric Competence (MC), following Chomsky's linguistic competence and Hymes' communicative competence (1972), drew the interest of a number of L2 researchers like Gardner and Winner (1978); Low (1988); Danesi (1993); Littlemore (2001); Littlemore and Low (2006).

In 1986, linguist Danesi brought "metaphorical competence" into the field of second language acquisition and foreign language teaching. Danesi used MC as a component of communicative competence and one of the important signs of language proficiency. He believed that the competence to recognize and use novel metaphors, including the appropriateness of context and instrumental strategies is a sign of successful communication of second language learners. The appropriateness of context is manifested in the competence to recognize metaphorical images, while instrumental strategies refer to the competence to correctly use conceptual schema in communication (1988). Low (1988) also discussed the notion of MC in his article emphasizing the presence and effects of conventional metaphors as well as pedagogical approaches in English Language Teaching contexts. He also came up with a series of real skills that L2 learners need to master as MC. Tóth (1999, as cited in Berendi, 2005) defined metaphoric competence based on the appearance and continuous change of the range of conceptual metaphors, saying that it is a complex competence that develops gradually and change constantly.

In 2001, Littlemore proposed that in addition to the eight multiple intelligences proposed by Gardner, there is a ninth one, metaphorical intelligence. Littlemore (2001) pointed out that metaphoric competence depends on analogy reasoning and divergent thinking. In the same year, Littlemore (2001) proposed that metaphoric competence consists of four aspects: originality of metaphor production, fluency of metaphor interpretation, ability to find meaning in metaphor, and speed in finding meaning in metaphor. The originality of metaphor production refers to the ability to innovate conventional metaphors; the fluency of metaphor interpretation refers to the ability to understand multiple meanings; the ability and speed in finding meaning in metaphor refer to understanding metaphorical meanings accurately and quickly. Littlemore believed that these four aspects are indispensable and is a sign of success in second language communication. Another Scholar Nacey claims that MC is "a production and interpretation of metaphorical expressions which is often considered more challenging in an L2 than an L1" (2010). Nacey defines MC as "the ability to understand and produce metaphor". In other words, metaphoric competence is an ability of a person who is able to understand metaphors generated by others and who can use metaphors to communicate with others.

Moreover, metaphoric competence plays a vital role in achieving fluency of L2, and the ability of generating metaphors in L2 is a sign of the learners' communicative fluency (Danesi, 1994). Danesi noticed that when foreign learners speak, they are not as natural and authentic as native speakers. He believed that this phenomenon of learners' discourse literalization is because they cannot use metaphors well to construct the conceptual system of the target language. An important sign of people's language proficiency is metaphoric competence. Although foreign language learners may have achieved high levels of grammar and communicative skills, they lack the conceptual accuracy of the target language. They can use the language form and structure of the target language country, but they use the language concept of their mother tongue, that is, they use foreign language vocabulary and grammatical structure to express concepts. As there are many inconsistencies in the expression structure of various nationalities, it will produce an asymmetry between the learner's discourse and the conceptual system, which leads to a lack of conceptual fluency in foreign language learners. Foreign language learners must understand how the language they learn reflects concepts on the basis of metaphorical reasoning. Only by understanding can they achieve the level of conceptual fluency of native speakers. Cooper (1999) states that students with metaphoric competence can interpret idiomatic expressions in L2 successfully. Lack of this competence, will result in a breakdown in communication. It should be highlighted that successful interpretation of figurative language is closely linked to the learners' cultural knowledge, the literal meaning of expressions, as well as the context in which it is used. Linguist Kecskes (2000) proposed that conceptual fluency is the ability to understand and use foreign language concepts similar to that of native speakers. Kecskes (2000) further pointed out that conceptual fluency means the ability to process meaning first. Andreou and Galantomos (2009) further regarded conceptual fluency as an important part of second language communicative competence. Therefore, if a foreign language learner wants to learn a foreign language well, he must achieve conceptual fluency, that is, first deal with the most prominent meaning of the language like native learners. However, traditional classroom teaching can only cultivate the learners' basic grammatical and communicative skills.

Although the importance of metaphoric competence in L2 learning and instruction is emphasized these days, it is still not viewed as an essential ability which must be developed and there are still many students who cannot understand and generate metaphors in L2 language. Some do not know how to use metaphors appropriately. Therefore, more attention should be paid to the improvement of metaphoric competence of L2 learners as well as L2 practitioners. Littlemore and Low once stated that "control over metaphor is one of the essential tools for empowering learners to cope successfully with native speakers" (2006). They believe that metaphoric competence is very important for communicative competence. In a word, metaphoric competence, not only promotes human thinking and behavior, but also fosters communication which takes conceptual system and metaphors as basis. And it is a vital feature of one's language competence.

2.5 Conceptual Metaphor and College EFL Teaching

Herronstates that what we teach (or think we are teaching) and how we teach, along with the complementary perceptions of value, are intimately linked to metaphor(1982).

2.5.1 The conceptual metaphor instruction

The conceptual metaphor instruction is different from the traditional metaphor instruction. The former is based on the conceptual metaphor theory while the latter is based on the traditional metaphor theory. Therefore, the main difference between them is that the former teaches metaphor in a cognitive way by studying the underlying conceptual systems of the metaphorical linguistic expressions while the latter teaches metaphor in a rhetoric way, only studying the surface meaning of metaphor.

The most obvious and most frequently used examples of how to apply the conceptual metaphor instruction to the college EFL class can be based on metaphoric prepositions and adverbials such as over, up, down, on, in. For example, the word "up" has many meanings. The following are two examples.

He went up the stairs, so that we could see him.
He spoke up, so that we could hear him.

In the first sentence, "up" means "upward", while in the second sentence, it means "more intensity". We wonder how these two meanings of "up" are related to each other. They can be explained in terms of a conceptual metaphor: MORE IS UP. In the second example, more intensity of sound is understood as being physically higher to some extent. Therefore, the two very different meanings of "up" are linked by this metaphor. In the traditional metaphor instruction, as there is no mention of conceptual metaphors, this explanation cannot be made and instructors can only say that there is some kind of pre-existing similarity between the two. Hence, the traditional method gives no room for a deep study of the underlying conceptual system of the two examples.

2.5.2 Previous studies of the relationship between conceptual metaphor and EFL teaching

The application of metaphor in EFL (English as a Foreign Language) instruction is still a new and tentative area and the complexity of metaphor makes it a rather challenging job. It is necessary to review the previous studies and know what have been done and what have not been done in this field.

In the Western countries, many scholars have realized the importance of comprehending and producing metaphors in the target language. It is necessary to introduce metaphor in college EFL (English as a Foreign Language) classroom. Only in this way can we make the students aware of the conceptual metaphors of English which they can employ in their native speech. Danesi (1994) claims that to use a language metaphorically is a key characteristic of the native speaker's display. He ascribes the literalness of the learners' discourse for providing little or no chance for students to access the metaphorically structured conceptual domains inherent in L2 discourse (1994). In 1999, English scholars Cameron and Low compiled and published a book *Researching and Applying Metaphor*, which indicates the metaphor research has already stepped into the applied research phase. Those abroad who have researched in metaphor teaching and learning in applied linguist field include Danesi (1995), Littlemore (2001), Gardner (1979), Kecskes (2000). In China, there are some scholars such as Lin Shuwu (1997), and Yan Shiqing (2001). In 2002, our first national cognitive linguistics seminar was held where, some related papers that outlined the keystone and future development of metaphor research were published. As far as the application of conceptual metaphor theory is concerned, Shu Dingfang says, "...the Conceptual Metaphor Theory has an active instruction and application function to language teaching. Language teachers can use this theory to illustrate the evolutive process of language meaning and the correlation of lexical meanings; at the same time, they can use this theory to explain the systems and interrelations of different metaphors" (2002). Based on Shu's viewpoints, it can be said that Conceptual Metaphor Theory has an application value in language instruction.

According to the retrieval results from China National Knowledge Infrastructure (CNKI), there are 16,246 papers about metaphor research from 2000 to 2019, but there are only 127 papers on the function of conceptual metaphor theory to language teaching. However, this issue has already drawn more and more attention of researchers nowadays. It has been applied to language teaching, especially second language teaching, mainly focusing on vocabulary teaching, cultural introduction, and cultivation of students' language proficiency. Recently, the article "Metaphoric Competence and Foreign Language Instruction" by Yan Shiqing (2001) has discussed the relation between metaphoric competence and language learning. Of late, as a core competence in language learning, metaphoric competence has grasped the attention of many scholars. Zhenhua's (2007) Conceptual Liu zhenqian and Shi Xiaoying (2002) explored the relationship between culture and metaphor from the aspects of cognitive science, linguistics, and psycholinguistics. They stated that metaphor is not only a linguistic phenomenon, but also a cultural phenomenon. The interpretation depends to a large extent on the understanding and grasp of the target language culture. Wang Shouyuan and Liu Zhenqian (2003) explored it is a feasible way to teach culture from the aspect of metaphor in foreign language teaching. Wang Yin and Li Hong (2004), based on contemporary metaphorical cognitive theory, emphasized metaphoric competence and language proficiency. They believed that metaphoric competence, language competence, and communicative competence together constitute the basic language use. It has an important cognitive function for innovative thinking and broadening of ideas. Zhu Wei (2005) made an attempt of a new English vocabulary teaching approach which is under the guidance of the prototype category theory, and proposed attention should be paid to the learning of basic category words, the explanation of polysemous words, and the recognition of metonymy and metaphor to enhance students' interest in learning, improve the classroom atmosphere and the quality of teaching. Zhou Honghui (2006) discussed metaphor from a cognitive perspective and its role and significance in teaching. Taking conceptual metaphor as a way of thinking to improve students' metaphorical thinking, vocabulary learning, pragmatic competence and cross-cultural communicative competence in English teaching. Wei Jing (2006) discussed the metaphors of "death" and believed these metaphors help students understand the cognitive thinking characteristics of the target language and culture which could be used to understand vocabulary more effectively. Zhao's *Metaphor and Metaphor Teaching*, Liu Chang's (2007) *Conceptual Metaphor and EFL Learning in China: an Empirical Study*. These dissertations make a detailed research of metaphoric competence and introduce it into language teaching and study.

However, there are few articles talking about the application of metaphor enriched materials in English for Specific Purposes (ESP) curriculum. Little has been done in putting forward some Medical metaphors to better the current Medical English teaching and learning. Therefore, further researches still need to be conducted on metaphor enriched ESP instruction in China.

2.6 Metaphor and Medical English

Since English is a very important international language, non-native English speakers, attending medical schools have to deal with the difficulty of translating and interpreting metaphors in oral and written contexts. In the existing research, Roche (2002), Gibbs and Franks (2002), Semino, et al. (2004), Pena and Andrade-Filho (2010), Gwinyai and Zumla (2012) studied metaphors in oral usage; Calsamiglia and Dijk (2004), Knudsen (2005), and Divasson and León (2006) studied metaphors in written usage. Although metaphors are pervasive in our language, not much attention is paid on metaphors in medicine, leave alone applying metaphors to Medical English instruction. There are quite a few reasons for including metaphor instruction in Medical English.

Metaphor is an important way of language generation, as well as a way to develop word meanings. In medical vocabulary instruction, metaphor makes the abstract concepts more concrete due to its cognitive features. Most Medical English vocabulary, including common English words and medical terms, are influenced by metaphorical thinking. Instructors can trace back their etymology and guide students to use metaphorical thinking to understand and memorize medical vocabulary.

Therefore, the metaphor-based instruction should be implemented in EFL curricula, providing medical students with an appropriate approach in order to improve their English proficiency (Danesi, 1992; Kecskes, 2006), to increase their skills in the interpretation of metaphors (Johnson and Rosano, 1993; Kanthan and Mills, 2006) and to read and evaluate medical literature and answer their patients' queries (Mungra, 2007; Shokoui and Isazadeh, 2009).

2.7 Conceptual Framework for the Research

This research is based on the conceptual metaphor theory and aims to pave the way for the transition of students from General English to Academic English via the metaphor enriched approach. The ADDIE model was adopted in metaphor enriched English language instruction. "ADDIE" stands for analysis, design, development, implementation and evaluation (Morrison, et al., 2011). The instructional design was considered from the five aspects to promote the effective learning. Metaphor enriched supplement instruction not only involves the implementation of materials, but also the analysis of students' needs, time arrangement, selection of materials and evaluation of materials. Figure 2-2 shows the conceptual framework of this research.

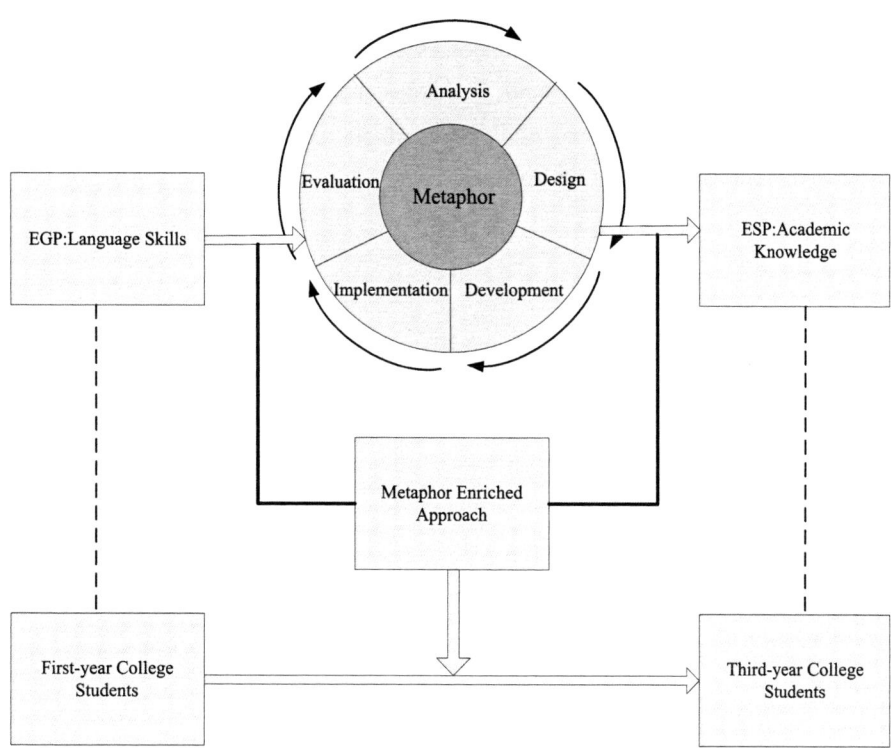

EGP. English for ceneral purposes; ESP. English for specific purposes.

Figure 2-2　Conceptual Framework of Metaphor Enriched English Language Instruction

According to Figure 2-2, the analysis phase involves participant teachers' understanding of metaphor and metaphor instruction, students' cognition on metaphors in General English and Medical English and participant students' metaphoric competence. The results played a role in the selection of supplementary materials and how to design and implement metaphor enriched instruction. In the design phase, a target teachers' and students' description was made as well as learning objectives. The supplement materials was chosen by discussion with an anatomy professor and teacher participants. In addition, the sequence of the instruction was confirmed. In the development phase, lesson plans were generated and the media for the instruction, including hardware and software, was confirmed. In the implementation phase, the conceptual metaphor and metaphorical mapping were supplemented at the beginning of selected unit to pave the way for the follow-up activities. Metaphor Identification Procedure (MIP) was adopted in identifying metaphors in text. Combined the topic of selected unit, medical knowledge, including medical vocabulary and expressions, was supplemented via metaphors. There is metaphor enriched assignment after each lecture and various media were adopted in this process. In addition, the whole process was recorded in the form of classroom observation. Observation checklist was distributed to participant teachers and a feedback questionnaire was distributed to student participants after each unit. In the evaluation phase, the feedback of observation checklist and questionnaire were collected to measure the effectiveness and efficiency of metaphor enriched instruction. This systematic process promoted the implementation smoothly. This process improved students' language skills and medical knowledge, which did help first-year college students' transition to their third-year academic learning.

Chapter 3

Research Methodology

This chapter is devoted to the methodology of applying metaphor enriched language instruction material to college EFL (English as a Foreign Language) classroom to facilitate the English proficiency of Chinese college freshmen. With the aim to test the effectiveness proposed in the research and fulfill its goals, an convergent mixed methods research was implemented. In this research, two EFL teachers and their non-English major class of Xinxiang Medical University of China participated. There are 200 students for each large class. A qualitative research was conducted via semi-structured interviews, classroom observations, and a quantitative data were collected in terms of the pre-test and the post-test and were analyzed via NVivo 11 and SPSS 22.0. In addition, in order to test the validity and reliability of these instruments, a pilot study was implemented as described in this chapter.

3.1 Research Paradigm

According to Mertens (2010), a paradigm is a way of looking at the world. It is composed of certain philosophical assumptions that guide and direct thinking and action. A paradigm consists of ethics (axiology), epistemology, ontology, and methodology (Denzin, 2011). Cube and Lincoln (2005) came up with four questions which help define a paradigm: the axiological question that what is the nature of ethics, the ontological question that what is the nature of reality, the epistemological question that what is the nature of knowledge and the relationship between the knower and the would-be known and the methodological question that how can the knower go about obtaining the desired knowledge and understandings (as cited in Mertens).

According to Mertens (2010), who makes an adaptation and extension of paradigms discussed by Lather (1992) and Guba and Lincoln (as depicted in their writings that span from 1994 to 2005), there are four major paradigms: postpositivism, constructivist, transformative and pragmatic one. Table 3-1 contains the four paradigms with labels commonly associated with them. This table is adapted from Creswell's classification (2014).

Table 3-1 Labels Commonly Associated with Four Major Paradigms

Postpositivism	Constructivist	Transformative	Pragmatic
Experimental	Naturalistic	Critical theory	Mixed methods
Correlational	Phenomenological	Feminist theories	Mixed models
Causal comparative	Hermeneutic	Participatory	Participatory
Quantitative	Symbolic interaction	Postcolonial	
Randomizedcontrol trials	Ethnographic	Action research	
	Qualitative		
	Participatory action research		

The pragmatic mixed methods study was adopted in this study, since researchers focus on the research problem and use all approaches available to understand the problem (Rossman and Wilson, 1985). As a philosophical underpinning, Morgan (2007), Patton (1990), and Tashakkori and Teddlie (2010) convey its importance for focusing attention on the research problem in social science research and then using pluralistic approaches to derive knowledge about the problem. Besides, the selection of a research paradigm is determined by the factors connected to the characteristics of the research problems and the research environment (Trauth, 2011). Tashakkori and Teddlie (2003) identify pragmatism as one of the paradigms that provides an underlying philosophical framework for mixed methods research. In a pragmatic mixed methods study, for the axiology, researchers hold the view that the ethical goal of research is to gain knowledge in the pursuit of desired ends (Morgan, 2007). For the ontology, the pragmatists emphasis on creating knowledge through lines of action points to the kinds of "projects" that different people can accomplish together (Morgan, 2007). Effectiveness is the criteria for judging research value research (Maxcy, 2003). For the epistemology, researchers are free to study what interests them and is of value, study it in the different ways and utilize the results in ways that can bring about positive consequences within their value system. (Tashakkori and Teddlie, 1998). For the methodology, method should be decided by the aim of the research (Patton, 2002), which means qualitative and/or quantitative methods are compatible with the pragmatic paradigm. Pragmatism allows the researchers to choose the methods (or combination of methods) that work best for answering their research questions (Johnson and Onwuegbuzie, 2004).

3.2 Research Design

Creswell states that mixed methods research is an approach to inquiry involving collecting both quantitative and qualitative data, integrating the two forms of data, and using distinct designs that may involve philosophical assumptions and theoretical frameworks (2014). The core assumption of this form of inquiry is that the combination of qualitative and quantitative approaches provides a more complete understanding of a research problem than either approach alone. Qualitative data are open-ended without predetermined responses while quantitative data includes closed-ended responses such as found on questionnaires and instruments (2014).

There are three primary models found in the social sciences today (2014), convergent parallel mixed methods, explanatory sequential mixed methods and exploratory sequential mixed methods. Convergent parallel mixed methods refers to a design in which the researcher converges two forms of data to provide a comprehensive analysis of the research problem. The researcher collects both forms of data at almost the same time and integrates the information in the process of interpreting the results as well as explains the contradictions findings. For explanatory sequential mixed methods, the quantitative research was conducted first, the results were analyzed and more detail with qualitative research were then explained on the basis of the former results. It is considered sequential because the initial quantitative phase is followed by the qualitative phase which is popular in fields with a strong quantitative orientation, that is why it begins with quantitative research, but it has challenges of identifying the quantitative results which require a further exploration and the sample sizes for each phase are unequal. For exploratory sequential mixed methods, which is the reverse sequence from the explanatory design, the researcher first conducts a qualitative research to explore the views of participants, analyzes the data and use the information to build into the followed quantitative phase. The qualitative phase can be used to build an instrument and to find appropriate instruments for the follow-up quantitative phase. It has challenges on the use of appropriate qualitative findings and the sample selection for both research phases.

This study aims to explore the effectiveness of Metaphor Enriched English Language Instruction (MEELI) supplement for first-year college students in a selected university by using the convergent design. The purpose of this design is to merge the results of the quantitative and qualitative data analyses which can provide both a quantitative and a qualitative picture of the research problem. The qualitative method was used in the process of implementing the metaphor enriched English language materials which could present a clear instruction to others, and it was used in the interviews for both teachers and students to better understand their opinions through inquiry. It was also used to generalize the categories of the students' metaphorical sentence through the Metaphor Cognition test. The quantitative method was used to collect the data of multiple-choice questions in the test, SPSS 22.0 was used to find whether there was a significant difference in the pre-test and the post-test of the students from which we can learn further about the effectiveness of implementing this method. Integration of data involved merging the results from the quantitative and qualitative data so that a comparison could be made and a more complete understanding emerge that what was provided by the quantitative or the qualitative results alone. In this research, the combination of these two forms of data contributed to seeing the effectiveness of MEELI from multiple perspectives and both are useful for this study. This is the logic behind a convergent design. Besides, the researcher can validate one database with the other. Figure 3-1 shows a convergent design which is adapted from Creswell (2015).

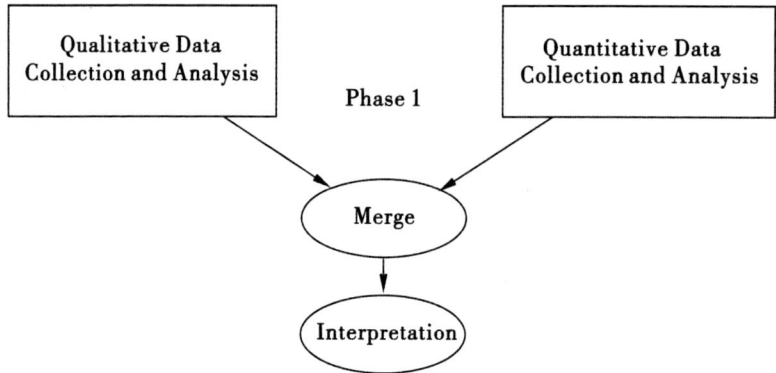

Figure 3-1 Convergent Design

The procedures for using the convergent design are presented as follows.

At the beginning of the metaphor enriched English language instruction, the significance and implementation plans were discussed with the other two teachers (Ms Wang and Ms Liu). In order to investigate EFL teachers' application of metaphor and their attitude toward this approach, an interview was conducted in July, 2017. This semi-structured interview (Appendix A) aims to find out the metaphoric competence of teachers and their attitude towards metaphor-enriched English instruction. Data collected from the interview were analyzed. According to the result, this researcher drafted a detailed plan to discuss the metaphor theories with the teacher participants in the form of group discussion.

In order to learn about students' understanding of concepts of metaphor and its cognition roles in English as a Foreign Language (EFL) teaching, a pilot study was conducted with 30 non-English major students at Xinxiang Medical University (Appendix B). The questionnaire was the modification of Wei Yaozhang's questionnaire on investigating the influence of cognitive competence on students' understanding and generating of metaphors (Wei, 2007). It included 20 questions involving the understanding and application of metaphors and medical metaphors in the process of learning English. The appropriate supplementary materials were discussed by teacher participants as well as the metaphor theories.

At the beginning of the first semester (09/2021), one class from each teacher participant was chosen to implement the metaphor enriched supplements during this semester. According to the teaching program, six units were delivered in the first semester (09/2021-12/2021). Three units were chosen from the text book *New Horizon College English Reading and Writing* by the three teacher respondents as selected units which were supplemented with metaphor enriched medical knowledge. The details of these three units are listed in Chapter 4.

Before implementing eachselected unit, there was a discussion among the two teacher participants and researcher. The themes of the discussion are finding out the metaphors in the text, how to introduce the supplementary materials, how to instruct with the supplementary materials and how to arrange the assignment. The suggestions discussed were adopted in further sessions and recorded by this researcher with their permission for further analysis.

During the sessions, the two teacher participants applied metaphor related knowledge when interpreting the selected units of the textbook, supplemented medical metaphor words and expressions related to the topic. This researcher observed Ms Wang's and Ms Liu's classroom sessions and recorded the detailed process in the form of classroom observation checklist (Appendix D).

After introducing each metaphor enriched unit, a student feedback questionnaire was distributed to the 30 students to learn about their understanding and feedback of metaphor enriched instruction and supplement. A qualitative analysis was conducted with the collected data from student participants. In addition, to test whether there was improvement on the students' metaphoric competence and related medical knowledge, a pre-test and a post-test respectively were conducted at the beginning and the end of the selected units (Appendix C).

The metaphor enriched supplement consists of conceptual metaphor theory, metaphors identified in the three selected units and supplementary medical knowledge. As for the metaphor theory, the metaphoric mapping from the source domain to the target domain were interpreted in detail and the image schema was mentioned for students' further understanding. As for the text metaphor identification, metaphoric words both in General English and Medical English were explained. The medical knowledge supplement involves in the nervous system, the cardiovascular system and the immune system which are corresponding to the unit themes. Figure 3-2 shows the categories of supplementary materials.

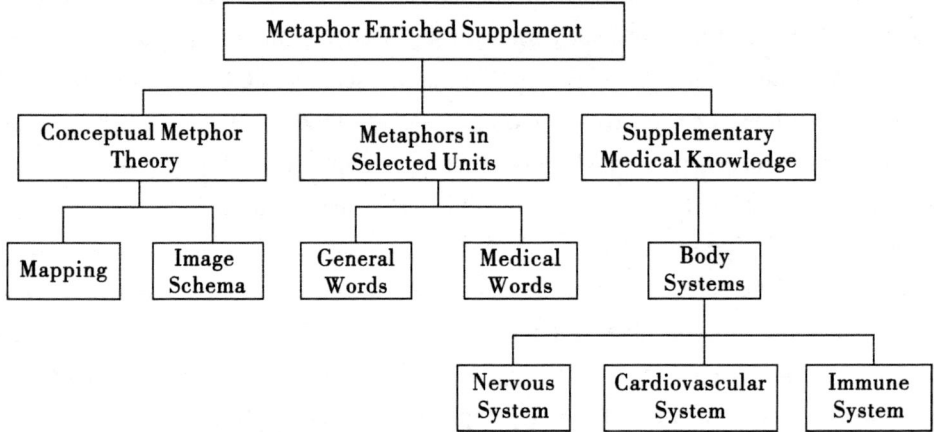

Figure 3-2　Metaphor Enriched Supplement

Note. According to the topics of three selected units, medical knowledge of three body systems were supplemented to the instruction.

3.3　Supplementary Materials

The teaching material is the *New Horizon College English* which was compiled and published by Foreign Language and Research Press (Zheng, 2015). The selection of this textbook can be justified by the following reasons. Above all, this textbook has already been chosen as the teaching material for the first-year students for ten years, and so it is easily available to all the students. What is more important is that using this textbook in the research will not interfere with the normal work of English teaching. This textbook has two reading passages in each unit with an abundance and variety of reliable metaphors. They make it a suitable teaching material for the metaphor teaching research. All the passages in the textbook were written by native English speakers who study linguistics. Therefore, both the language and thinking modes are authentic.

According to the teaching syllabus, students have to study six units for each semester. This researcher and two teacher participants discussed in detail which units were suitable to be supplemented at the beginning of the new semester. Due to the limitation of unit topics, three units, namely "Deep Concern" "A Good Heart to Lean On" and "The Battle Against AIDS", were chosen eventually as these topics could be connected with medical knowledge better than other three topics. Among them, "Deep Concern" portrays the anxiety of Cindy's parents which can be associated with the Nervous System; "A Good Heart to Lean On" shows the kindness and warm heart of the hero of the story which can be associated with the Cardiovascular System; "The Battle against AIDS" details the present condition of the disease which can be linked with the Immunological System.

Then time for each selected unit was arranged according to the content and three teachers' office was chosen to be the venue for discussion.

Apart from the teaching materials, the researcher also consulted some indispensable sources for metaphor teaching, such as Lakoff and Johnson's *Metaphor We Live By* (1980), Kövecse's *Metaphor* (2002), Ning Yu's *The Contemporary Theory of Metaphor: A Perspective from Chinese* (1998), Sommer's *Metaphor Dictionary* (1996) and related papers. There are abundant underlying metaphorical concepts of English being talked about as well as many conventional metaphors being discussed in these books and papers. Ning Yu (1998) in his book has elaborated many English conceptual metaphors and Chinese conceptual metaphors and he has also analyzed the conceptual differences between English and Chinese. Therefore, the examples in those books are all perfect choices for the teaching materials and tests in this research.

3.4 Research Setting

The research was conducted at Xinxiang Medical University which is located in the Xinxiang city, Henan Province of China. It is a provincial public medical University which has been in operation since 1950 and been granted recognition by the World Health Organization (WHO) since 1958. There are over 40,000 students, among them there are over 12,000 undergraduates, over 500 postgraduates, over 15,000 adult education students, and over 200 foreign students. Presently there are over 8,366 staff including 939 professionals and 19 departments, which cover medicine, literature, science, technology, management and so on. 23 specialties, namely surgery, psychiatry, pediatrics, applied psychology, mental illness, mental health, etc., are available. In order to meet the demands of this University, 5 affiliated hospitals were built with a total 8,000 beds, and 14 teaching hospitals and more more than 50 teaching intern bases as well.

In this research, one non-English major class from each teacher participant was chosen to implement the supplement. The study was implemented at the very beginning of the school year so as not to interfere with the momentum of the regular instructional sequence and to limit prior exposure to the material. The participant students were native speakers of Chinese and none of them had the experience of studying abroad. Before their first year of English study in college, they did not receive any systematical instructions of conceptual metaphor teaching (neither English conceptual metaphors nor Chinese conceptual metaphors).

3.5 The Study Population and Sample

Students from two classes (288) and 3 teachers who are in charge of their EGP curriculum were chosen as the sample for the study. The details of teachers sample and students sample are as follows.

3.5.1 Teachers sample

3.5.1.1 The profile of teacher respondent 1: Ms Wang

Starting her teaching career shortly after she graduated from Henan Normal University, Ms Wang has been teaching for almost 20 years. She is a cheerful and enthusiastic teacher with her own unique teaching style. Her classroom atmosphere is always active and she often applies current affairs and personal life experiences to her classroom teaching. In the year 2005, she received her master's degree in Tourism and Hospitality Management in Australia and got a glimpse of the cultural difference between China and the West. Her study experience in Australia had furthered her understanding of Chinese and Western cultures which broadened students' horizons.

3.5.1.2 The profile of teacher respondent 2: Ms Liu

Ms Liu is a teacher with a wide range of knowledge and has been teaching college English for 16 years. She graduated from Henan University majoring in English Linguistics and Literature department. In 2012, she obtained her master's degree from Henan Normal University. During her class, she places more emphasis on enhancing of the students' basic skills, including listening, speaking, reading and writing competence. In her classroom the atmosphere is relaxed and enjoyable. Most of her research is about the reform of College English teaching and she has already published 7 related papers. In her daily life, she usually likes watching American TV series, like Dr. House (Medical theme). She is very interested in medicine as her husband is a military doctor.

3.5.1.3 The profile of the researcher: Ms Zhang

The researcher is also a teacher with 16 years of teaching experience and has been doing the research on teaching methods for many years. She began her study metaphor from the year of 2012. After more than 10 years of College English teaching, she found that there were some comprehension obstacles not only in the students' College English textbooks, but also in medical textbooks due to the use of metaphors. Metaphor comprehension is so important in the students' understanding of the western culture and their medical study. It can be a boost to their future academic study. In the researcher's university, students study Medical English in their third year which is a big challenge for them due to the difficulty of the medical terminology. Therefore, the researcher tries to connect College English learning with Medical English learning in terms of metaphors, and assumes that students can foster their learning interests and enhance their creativity in the long run.

All the three teacher participants who took charge of their EGP curriculum in the sample collectionmet the following specific criteria.

(1) Have adequate time to learn and acquire metaphor related knowledge and medical English.

(2) Have background knowledge of English instruction.

(3) Be willing to participate.

3.5.2 Students sample

Participant students are Chinese students who had already participated in the College Entrance Examination. The reason to choose non-English majors as subjects rather than the English majors is that the former have more time and opportunities to learn English than the latter. Moreover, the English majors are familiar with rhetoric and literature courses, and hence not suitable for the research. The reason to choose first-year college students as subjects is that they seldom studied metaphors in their high school rather than the sophomores. Their need to improve their medical knowledge was urgent which are more suitable for the research.

This study was introduced in two classes of teacher participants. The target population was the first-year college students who majored in Medical Rehabilitation and Preventive Medicine, Psychiatry and Paediatrics in Xinxiang Medical University. The details of each specialization are as follows.

Medical imaging is a study of interaction with the human body by means of a medium, such as X-rays, electromagnetic fields, ultrasonic waves, which expresses the structure and density of the internal organs and organs of the human body in an image format for the diagnostician, who based on the information provided by the image has to evaluate the health status of a person.

Psychiatry is a branch of clinical medicine. It is a clinical discipline that studies various human psychological disorders, the etiology, pathogenesis, clinical features and preventive methods of mental illness. It aims to explore the mysteries of the human spiritual world and promote human mental health. Students are requested to master the basic theories and diagnosis and treatment skills of basic medicine, clinical medicine, clinical psychology and mental illness, and they are supposed to master general medical skills and the ability to deal with common psychological, behavioral, mental and related diseases. It aims to cultivate the students' basic theoretical knowledge and the ability in basic medicine, clinical medicine and modern medical imaging for future engagement in medical imaging, medical intervention, radiology and medical imaging technology. After graduation, students can work in clinical medical imaging diagnosis, radiotherapy work, medical education, or medical research work. They can also do medical imaging diagnosis, interventional radiology, and nuclear medicine imaging technology in medical units.

Paediatrics is a secondary discipline of clinical medicine which studies the growth and development of children and adolescents, and improves their physical and mental health. It aims to promote the growth of physical and mental health and disease prevention from fetus to adolescent children. At present, it refers to children's health, respiratory, cardiovascular, blood, kidney, nerve, endocrine and metabolic, immune infection and digestion, first aid and paediatric surgery. Each professional discipline is closely related to certain disciplines of basic medicine, such as physiology, biochemistry, pathology, genetics, and molecular biology.

The students in the test group met the following criteria. ①Be first-year college students who have not majored in English. ②With no experience studying abroad. ③Be willing to participate.

3.5.2.1 Student respondents to Metaphor Cognition Questionnaires

The Table 3-2 shows information of student respondents to Metaphor Cognition Questionnaire (Appendix B).

Table 3-2 Student Respondents to Metaphor Cognition Questionnaire

Lecturers	Students' specialization	Participant numbers
Ms Wang	Medical imaging	158
Ms Liu	Psychiatry and pediatrics	130

The Table 3-3 shows information of student respondents for Metaphoric Competence Test (Appendix C).

Table 3-3 Student Respondents to Metaphoric Competence Test

Lecturers	Students' specialization	Participant numbers	
		Pre-test	Post-test
Ms Wang	Medical imaging	158	158
Ms Liu	Psychiatry and pediatrics	130	130

3.5.2.2 Student respondents for Student Feedback Questionnaire

The Table 3-4 shows information of student respondents for Student Feedback Questionnaire (Appendix E).

Table 3-4 Student Respondents to Student Feedback Questionnaire

Lecturers	Students' specialization	Participant numbers		
		Unit 2	Unit 3	Unit 5
Ms Wang	Medical imaging	30	30	30
Ms Liu	Psychiatry and pediatrics	30	30	30

Detailed information about the research instruments used in this study will be introduced in this section.

3.6 The Research Instruments

3.6.1 Instruments for teacher interview

Qualitative data were collected in the study in order to understand and possibly better explain reasons which might not have been received from the questionnaire. In order to investigate teachers' understanding of metaphor and metaphor enriched instruction, a semi-structured interview protocol was designed by the researcher and was distributed to seven teachers in the pilot study (Appendix A). There are six questions with four probes under each question which focus on the main challenges in their English as General Purposes (EGP) teaching, the problems they found in the students' EGP learning, teachers' understanding of metaphor and their metaphor teaching practice, as well as the benefits and challenges in the process of metaphor enriched instruction. All these questions were designed in terms of research questions and teachers' opinions in accord with the problem statement and inspired more consideration in the researcher. According to the respondents' understanding of metaphor, the metaphor related theories was taught in class.

Besides, during the process of conducting the study, the researcher interviewed the two participant teachers about their reflection on their instruction after each metaphor enriched unit. In addition, before each selected unit, the research discussed with the two teacher participants about the set induction, the time arrangement, the supplementary materials and collected their suggestions.

3.6.2 Instruments for metaphor cognition

A questionnaire is a written list of questions, the answers to which are recorded by respondents. The respondents read the questions, interpret what is expected and write down the answers. It has two advantages: on one hand, you can save time, and human and financial resources unlike interviewing the subjects. It is comparatively convenient and inexpensive when it is administered to students. On the other hand, it provides greater anonymity when sensitive questionsare asked and it helps to increase the likelihood of obtaining accurate information. In order to investigate students' metaphor cognition ability, a metaphor cognition questionnaire was used to collect students' opinions on metaphor cognition and medical metaphors (Appendix B). It was the modification of Wei Yaozhang's questionnaire on investigating the influence of cognitive competence on students' understanding and generating of metaphors (Wei, 2007). Students were asked to write down the marks of their National College Entrance Examination (NCEE) to learn whether there is any difference among different levels of students and their understanding of metaphor. As a standardized test, NCEE is a prerequisite for entrance into almost all higher education institutions at the undergraduate level. It represents a student's English competence. The student participants were required to complete it within 20 minutes. At the very beginning of the test, there was a rubric in native language Chinese, briefly explaining what a metaphor was like with simple examples. 18 items were kept under two dimensions after the pilot study. Part 1 refers to the metaphor cognition and part 2 refers to medical metaphors. Students were required to mark the most appropriate answers range from strongly disagree to strongly agree.

3.6.3 Instruments for metaphoric competence

A metaphoric competence test was used as the pre-test and post-test to investigate whether there is significant difference on test results. The testing materials were composed of 20 metaphorical sentences. The resources of the test were adopted from Jiao Weida's (2007) metaphoric competence test which consists of three parts.

3.6.3.1 Part A: Metaphor recognition (40%, 15 minutes)

Materials for metaphor comprehension were collected on the principle that a sentence is regarded as metaphorical if it contains a comparison between two or more entities from different domains. The examples in the test were adapted from the following works: Ning Yu's (1998) *The Contemporary Theory of Metaphor — A Perspective from Chinese*, Chen Jaxu's (2007) *A Contrastive Study of Metaphor between English and Chinese*, Lu Guoqiang's (2008) *A Contrastive Analysis of English-Chinese Conceptual Structures* and Oxford Advanced Learner's *English-Chinese Dictionary*.

If students thought a sentence was obviously a metaphor, it belonged to The Same or Nearly the Same Concepts or Conceptual Systems (SCS), they needed to write down the number 4 within the brackets; if they thought the sentence was a metaphor, but not very convincing, it belonged to Different Concepts or Conceptual Systems (DCCS), they needed to write down the number 3; if they thought the sentence might contain some kind of metaphorical expression, but could not find it, they needed to write down the number 2; if they thought that the sentence was obviously not a metaphor, they needed to write down the number 1. The details of scores are as follows as Table 3-5.

Table 3-5 Marks of Items in Metaphor Recognition

The Same or Nearly the Same Concepts or Conceptual Systems (SCS)	Marks
1. I'm feeling down	4
2. My job is a jail	4
3. He led a dog's life when he was young	4
4. Speech is silver, silence is gold	4
5. From the plane we had a bird's eye view of London	4
6. Is her husband a man or a mouse? (brave or cowardly)	4
7. He has learned that happiness is gold. (valued)	4
8. Unfortunately their relationship turned sour after one waspromoted. (turn out badly)	4
9. That event was the spark that started the war. (cause)	4
10. He was in a dark mood after the examination. (sadness is dark)	4
Different Concepts or Conceptual Systems (DCCS)	
11. I couldn't see my own flesh and blood insulted in this way	3
12. It might make him embarrassed if you pull his leg in the meeting	3
13. The death penalty for murder works on the principle of an eye for an eye	3
14. You must be green to believe that! (inexperienced; easily fooled)	3
Non-metaphorical expression	
15. Music is death	1
Non-corresponding Concepts or Conceptual Systems (NCCS)	
16. Their marriage was on the rocks	2
17. He dived right into the problem	2
18. The two contestants are neck and neck	2
19. The gold medal has become a white elephant for him	2
20. She is the apple of her father's eye	2

3.6.3.2 Part B: Metaphor interpretation (30%, 20 minutes)

This part required students to list the interpretation of 5 conceptual metaphors as much as possible, what were the similarities between the source domain and the target domain and the more the explanation, higher the scores. If students had a limited English vocabulary, Chinese answers were acceptable. Because the focus was how students understood and interpreted these metaphors rather than the language itself. There were 6 marks for each sentence and each similarity under the same metaphor got 2 marks.

3.6.3.3 Part C: Metaphor production (30%, 15 minutes)

There are 2 unfinished sentences for this section. They are "Learning English is..." and "Treating illness is..." Students were requested to complete the sentence in English by using imagination. For each answer, 3 marks could be received for the production of one novel metaphor. 2 marks for the conventional metaphor completion. 1 mark for the literal completion. 0 for the inappropriate completion. A high mark indicates that the student participants had a preference for original metaphor production. The Table 3-6 shows the scoring criteria adapted from the test from Littlemore (2010).

Table 3-6 The Criteria of Scoring of Part C

Marks	Criteria	Examples
0. Inappropriate completion	Nothing meaningful can be found	Agnes is always knocking things over. You might say that it's a bit for her
1. Literal completion	The adjective remains in its customary domain	What a beautiful day! The clear sky reminds me of...my home country
2. Conventional metaphor completion	The resulting metaphor is a familiar English or Chinese saying	It's true that now she's old and ugly, but when she was young, she had skin like a bean curd
3. Novel metaphor completion	At least one of the following:	
	a. The topic is projected onto a sensory domain, where it is not literally applicable, and the resulting metaphor is not a familiar English or Chinese saying	Dr. Livingstone had been walking across the Sahara for 5 days without any water. His throat was beginning to feel as dry as a sheet of paper in Moses' bible
	b. The topic, which is typically associated with the physical world, is projected onto a psychological state, and the resulting metaphor is not a familiar English or Chinese saying	We could tell by the look on the teacher's face that his anger was like a rocket searching its target
	c. The topic remains in its customary domain (sense modality or physical reference), but a radical shift in perspective is required, and the resulting metaphor is not a familiar English or Chinese saying	When I was a child, I was frightened of my grandma's teeth soaking in the glass in the bathroom. They made me think of an old wreck forgotten in the sea

3.6.4 Instruments for metaphor identification

Metaphor Identification Procedure (MIP) was adopted to identify metaphors in the textbook. Detailed steps of MIP will be interpreted by analyzing one sentence which was separated in terms of lexical units. The basic meaning of each lexical unit was compared with its contextual meaning to identify whether there is similarity or not. A metaphor can be identified by this procedure. The following is the detailed steps for this procedure. Take the sentence "Acquired Immune Deficiency Syndrome (AIDS) was diagnosed in the United States in the late 1970s" as an example.

Step 1: Read the entire text ("The Battle against AIDS") to establish a general understanding of the meaning.

Step 2: Determine the lexical units in the text/discourse.

Acquired /Immune/ Deficiency/ Syndrome/ (AIDS)/ was/diagnosed/ in/ the/United States /in/ the /late /1970s/. Since then/, AIDS/ has/ killed/ more than/ 204,000 /Americans — half/ in/ the past /few/ years/ alone/. Another/ 185,000/ of /the /one/ million /infected/ with/ the /HIV/ virus/ are /also/ expected/ to/ die/.

Step 3: For each lexical unit in the text, establish its meaning in context.

Step 4: For each lexical unit, determine its basic meaning.

Step 5: Decide whether the basic meaning of the word relates to the contextual meaning.

Step 6: Decide whether the contextual meaning of the word is related to the basic meaning by some form or similarity.

In conclusion, in the sentence "Acquired Immune Deficiency Syndrome (AIDS) was diagnosed in the United States in the late 1970s", the word "Deficiency" is a metaphor.

3.6.5 Instruments for classroom observation

Observation is an ideal form of qualitative data when the qualitative inquirer can actually visit the site where the central phenomenon is being talked about. It can also be a good adjunct to interviewing because they enable a researcher to compare the codes and themes from the observation with findings from the interviews. It can also yield detailed information that may not be divulged during discussions.

In this study, two EFL (English as a Foreign Language) English teachers, Ms Wang and Ms Liu, were observed during the research. They voluntarily participated in the training of metaphor related knowledge before the beginning of the first semester. Research venue is the classroom assigned by the university. The researcher obtained permission for entering the venue and conducting an observation. A classroom observation checklist, including descriptive and reflective notes was designed as a method for recording the observational notes in the field (Appendix D). It was adapted from Echevarria's *The Sheltered Instruction Observation Protocol* (2008). Appropriate information, including the date, place, and time were provided. The researcher observed 3 units (about 6 weeks) and 90 minutes for each observation. The observation focuses on the teachers' delineation while applying the metaphor enriched teaching approach and the students' reactions.

3.6.6 Instruments for students feedback

In order to collect the feedback of the students on MEELI and the supplementary materials, 30 students from the class of each teacher were chosen to form a focus group. The researcher asked about their comments and distributed them a feedback questionnaire on each selected unit. The data of the students' feedback were collected from the Student Feedback Questionnaire (Appendix E). Part Ⅰ is about Metaphor Enriched English Language Instruction (MEELI) which consists of 6 items relating to metaphor theories, metaphoric competence, medical knowledge, and the effect of MEELI, as well as 2 open-ended comments. The first one is "What aspects of MEELI are most useful to your learning?" The second one is "How could the MEELI be improved for your better learning?" The answers of the students were fed into NVivo and a project map was drawn to show the related themes. The students' opinions for each unit are put together to study about their overall opinions. Part Ⅱ deals with opinions about the teachers providing Metaphor Enriched English Language Instruction (MEELI). There are 6 items relating to the materials, language, questioning and coaching, and the effect of instruction, as well as 2 open-ended comments. The first one is "What aspects of teacher's instruction are most useful to your learning?" The second one is "How would you like the teaching be changed (if at all), for your better learning?" This questionnaire was adapted from Polytechnic's (2017) *The Hong Kong Polytechnic University Student Feedback Questionnaire.*

3.6.7 Reliability

Polit and Hungler (1993) refer to reliability as the degree of consistency with which an instrument measures the attribute it is designed to measure. Therefore, internal consistency procedures were used in determining the reliability of the questionnaire. The internal consistency procedure was conducted to measure whether the questionnaire is reliable.

Further, an audit trail was used to describe in detail how data were collected and how decisions were made throughout the inquiry. The researcher kept the research records, memos, etc., for the ongoing process of conducting the research. The researcher's reflections, questions, decisions were made by her with regard to problems, and ideas she encountered when collecting data.

To increase the reliability of the research, the researcher considered whether there was consistency in test administration and scoring. The same instructor administered the pre-test and the post-test and the scoring criteria was discussed with colleagues, including one who is skilled in language testing.

3.6.8 Validity

Validity is one of the strengths of qualitative research and is based on determining whether the findings are accurate from the standpoint of the researcher, the participant, or the readers of an account (Creswell and Miller, 2000). He recommends the use of multiple approaches which will enhance the researcher's ability to assess the accuracy of findings as well as convince readers of that accuracy. There are three primary strategies which are most frequently used and easy to implement.

Firstly, triangulate different data sources of information by examining evidence from the sources to build a coherent justification for themes. If themes are established based on converging several sources of data or perspectives from participants, then this process adds validity to the study. This study used the method of triangulation by data source and triangulation by methods. The researcher collected data from teacher colleagues, student participants combined with her own observation (Figure 3-3).

The researcher collected data through different methods. In this study, the researcher mainly adopted interviews, questionnaire, observation and documents to ensure the validity of the study. Look the Figure 3-4.

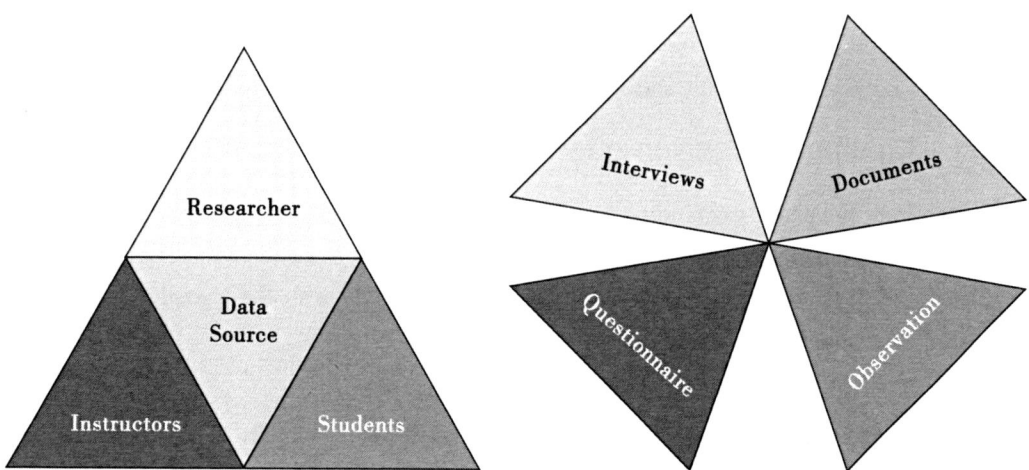

Figure 3-3 Triangulation of Data Source   Figure 3-4 Triangulation of Research Instruments

Secondly, member checking was used to determine the accuracy of the qualitative findings through taking the final report or specific descriptions or themes back to participants and determining whether these participants feel that they are accurate. The researcher conducted a follow-up interview with participants in the study, providing an opportunity for them to comment on the findings.

Thirdly, negative or discrepant information that run counter to the themes was also presented. Real life is composed of different perspectives that do not always coalesce, discussing contrary information adds to the credibility of an account. The researcher accomplished this by discussing evidence about a theme. By presenting this contradictory evidence, the account became more realistic and more valid.

Establishing validity through logic implies justification of each question in relation to the objectives of the study, whereas the statistical procedures provided hard evidence by way of calculating the correlations between the questions and the outcome variables. Content validity refers to the extent to which an instrument represents the factors under study.

3.7 Pilot Study

In order to identify the reliability of the questionnaire and deficiencies in the instruments, and to learn about the procedures of the research project before the full study a pilot study was conducted in 2 weeks. The pilot study included teachers' interview, students' Metaphor Cognition Questionnaire and Metaphoric Competence Test. 5 teachers and 90 students participated in it. The details are presented as follows. For the teacher interview, opinions of 5 interviewees are listed in a table. For the students' questionnaire, demographic profile of respondents, reliability test and descriptive analysis of items were analyzed. For students' metaphoric competence test, descriptive analysis of test result and types of metaphors generated by students are listed.

3.7.1 Metaphor cognition questionnaire

The pilot Metaphor Cognition Questionnaire was distributed to 90 first-year college students of researcher's class. All the student participants major in medical imaging. 86 of them completed and returned questionnaires. The recovery rate was 95.6%. Demographic information for this questionnaire is presented as follows.

3.7.1.1 The reliability of metaphor cognition questionnaire

Factor analysis was conducted by the researcher to check the KMO (Kaiser-Meyer-Olkin) value and the result is as follows (Table 3-7).

Table 3-7 The Result of "KMO and Bartlett's Test" on Metaphor Cognition Questionnaire

Kaiser-Meyer-Olkin measure of sampling adequacy		0.743
Bartlett's Test of sphericity	Approx. Chi-Square	684.139
	df	190
	Sig.	0.000

The KMO value is 0.743 which belongs to 0.7–0.8 group. It indicates the relationship among the items is medium (0.70–0.79 middling). In order to do a further check of relationship of all the items, Pattern Matrix was conducted to find out the unrelated items. Table 3–8 shows the details.

Table 3-8   Pattern Matrix[a] of Items

Items	Component 1	Component 2	Items	Component 1	Component 2
2	0.797		5		0.730
14	0.752		12		0.730
17	0.709		4		0.692
7	0.681		6		0.522
1	0.616	-0.449	11		0.509
8	0.559		3		0.450
20	0.525		19		
13	0.524				
16	0.504				
10	0.477				
18	0.468				
9	0.445				
15					

After analyzing the Pattern Matrix[a] of 20 items, item 15 and item 19 are not close to other items of the two dimensions, so they will be deleted from the metaphoric cognition questionnaire.

3.7.1.2 Reliability analysis

Reliability test is a paramount test to acquire measurement of standardization. It is used to examine whether all variables are reliable. Cronbach's alpha value represents the correlation and standardization of elements in the questionnaire and reflects the reliability of the data collected (Table 3–9).

Table 3-9 Reliability Statistics of Metaphor Cognition Questionnaire

Cronbach's α	N of items
0.866	20

Note. If 0.80<α<0.89, it means the implied reliability is good.

The Cronbach's α is 0.866 (between 0.80 and 0.89), which means its reliability level is good.

(1) Demographic profile of respondents from questionnaire

The demographic information of 86 respondents includes age, gender, major and NCEE scores. The main age groups are as follows (Table 3-10).

Table 3-10 Age of Respondents (Pilot Study)

Age	Frequency	Percent/%	Valid percent/%
18	25	29.0	29.0
19	45	52.3	52.3
20	14	16.3	16.3
21	1	1.2	1.2
22	1	1.2	1.2
Total	86	100.0	100.0

The total number of respondents is 90, including 86 valid questionnaires and 4 invalid ones. There are 20 males ($n = 86.23\%$) and 66 females ($n = 86.77\%$). The percentage is presented in Table 3-11.

Table 3-11 Gender of Respondents

Gender	Questionnaire	
	Frequency	Percent/%
Male	20	23.3
Female	66	76.7
Total	86	100.0

During the 86 respondents, 66 respondents (76.7%) are female and 20 respondents (23.3%) are male. The English achievement of respondents is presented as follows (Table 3-12).

Table 3-12 English Achievement of Respondents

English achievement (NCEE English score)	Questionnaire	
	Frequency	Percent/%
< 90	3	3.5
91-100	9	10.5
101-110	36	41.9
111-120	33	38.4
121-130	5	5.9
> 130	1	1.2
Total	86	100.0

Note. The full score of NCEE is 150.

For the English achievement, 86 respondents were required to write down their National College Entrance Exam (NCEE) English scores which are divided into 6 groups. The 101-110 group takes the largest percentage (41.9%); then the 111-120 group is the second which takes 38.4% of all respondents; the 91-100 group takes 10.5%; the 121-130 group takes 5.9%; the less than 90 group takes 3.5%; the more than 130 group takes the smallest percentage (1.2%). From the percentage, it is easy to find the English scores of most respondents are belong to 101-110 group and 111-120 group which means their English level are relatively good.

(2) Percentage of items on metaphor cognition

This part involved 10 items and the details of each item are listed as follows (Table 3-13).

Table 3-13 Percentage of Items on Metaphor Cognition

Questionnaire items	SD/%	D/%	A/%	SA/%
1: I know that there are many metaphors in General English	7.0	17.4	54.7	20.9
2: I know that metaphors in English articles can make language more vivid	2.3	4.7	45.3	47.7
3: I find teachers always use metaphors in their instruction	3.5	22.1	65.1	9.3
4: I know that some conceptual metaphors in English are different from those in Chinese	12.8	51.2	32.6	3.4
5: I know that some metaphorical expressions in English are different from those in Chinese	9.3	52.3	34.9	3.5
6: The image of the compared object will immediately flash in my mind when I find metaphors	10.5	56.9	25.6	7.0
7: I will understand metaphors in the context of the texts	7.0	16.3	61.7	15.1

Continue to Table 3-13

Questionnaire items	SD/%	D/%	A/%	SA/%
8: I will consciously apply metaphors which I have learned in the classroom in my writing	4.7	12.8	59.3	23.2
9: When communicating with English native speakers in English, I often discuss metaphors with them	7.0	47.7	32.6	12.8
10: I often try to express my ideas through new metaphors	2.3	12.8	54.7	30.2

Note. N=86.

Item 1 showed that 75.6% respondents knew that there were many metaphors in general English which indicates the majority of the respondents knew the existence of metaphor, while there were still 24.4 respondents who did not know it. Item 2 presented 93.0% respondents affirmed the vividness of metaphor, only 7% respondents disagreed with its function. Item 3 stated that 74.4% student respondents thought their teachers often used metaphors in their instruction while 25.6% respondents disagreed. This showed a relatively considerable difference in the teachers' metaphor instruction. Items 4 and 5 relate to the difference between English metaphors and Chinese metaphors. 36.0% respondents realized the difference while 64.0% respondents did not. For metaphorical expressions, 38.4% respondents realized the difference while 61.6% respondents did not. Items 6 and 7 concern the understanding approaches of metaphors. 32.6% respondents could associate the images of compared objects, while 76.8% respondents could not. 23.2% respondents could understand metaphors in the context of the texts, while 76.8% respondents could not. Items 8, 9 and 10 relate to the application of metaphors. 82.5% respondents would use metaphors in their writing, while 45.4% of them would not use metaphors to communicate with English native speakers, 84.9% of them did not think of creating new metaphors to express their ideas.

(3) Percentage of items on metaphors and Medical English

This part involved 10 items and the details of each item are listed as follows (Table 3-14).

Table 3-14 Percentage of Items on Metaphors and Medical English

Questionnaire items	SD/%	D/%	A/%	SA/%
11. I know that there are many metaphors in Medical English	12.8	30.2	45.4	11.6
12. I am sensitive to metaphors in the articles in medical journals	17.4	58.1	18.7	5.8
13. I find teachers always use metaphors in their instruction	5.8	22.1	57.0	15.1
14. I know that metaphors help me to memorize medical words	3.5	20.9	58.1	17.4

Continue to Table 3-14

Questionnaire Items	SD/%	D/%	A/%	SA/%
15. The image of the compared object will immediately flash in my mind when I find metaphors	5.8	18.6	50.0	25.6
16. I think it is interesting to understand medical articles from the perspective of metaphors	2.3	11.6	60.5	25.6
17. I realize that using metaphors can express the phenomenon that some non-metaphorical languages cannot express	9.3	50.0	34.9	5.8
18. I will use metaphors to explain conditions of illness to my patients in future	9.3	24.4	47.7	18.6

Note. $N = 86$.

Items 11 and 12 relate to the respondents' cognition of medical metaphors. Item 11 showed that 57.0% of the respondents knew that there were many metaphors in Medical English, while nearly a half of them did not know. Question 12 stated that only 24.5% respondents were sensitive to medical metaphors, which indicates 75.5% respondents could not identify medical metaphors. Item 13 presented that 72.1% respondents realized the use of metaphors in teacher's instruction. Item 14 showed 75.5% of the respondents knew that metaphors contributed to the understanding of medical words. 75.6% respondents affirmed that they would have the image in their minds when encountering a metaphor. 86.1% respondents thought it was an interesting approach to understand medical articles and 59.3% respondents believed metaphor could express the phenomenon that some non-metaphorical languages could not. Item 18 involved the future application of metaphor in explaining conditions of illness to patients. 66.3% respondents chose to apply it in future which implies that most respondents had realized the importance of metaphor.

3.7.2 Metaphoric competence test

3.7.2.1 The reliability of metaphoric competence test

A factor analysis was conducted by the researcher to check the KMO value and the result is as follows (Table 3-15).

Table 3-15 The Result of "KMO and Bartlett's Test" on Metaphoric Competence Test

Kaiser-Meyer-Olkin measure of sampling adequacy		0.762
Bartlett's Test of sphericity	Approx. Chi-Square	320.242
	df	21
	Sig.	0.000

The KMO value is 0.762 which belongs to 0.7–0.8 group. It indicates the relationship among the items is medium (0.70–0.79 middling).

3.7.2.2 Descriptive analysis of results of metaphoric competence test

118 student participants of the researcher's class participated in the pilot test. 110 of them completed and returned the questionnaires. The Figure 3–5 shows the frequency of their scores.

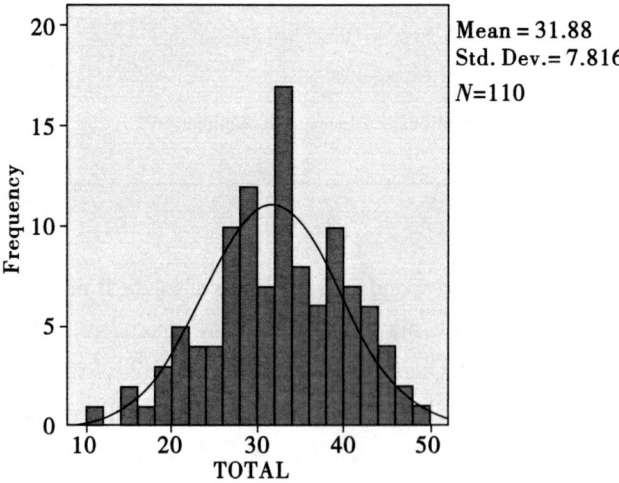

Figure 3–5   Frequency of Students' MCT (pilot)

Figure 3–5 shows that all students did not achieve 60 scores in the pilot test which means the scores on Metaphoric Competence Test (MCT) was poor even though they did well in National College Entrance Examination (NCEE). The researcher did a correlation analysis to investigate the possibility of any correlation between scores on MCT and NCEE.

3.7.2.3 The correlation between the research variables: NCEE and MCT

In order to investigate whether there is correlation between scores on NCEE and MCT, the correlation was run between these two variables. The result of this analyse is set forth in the Table 3–16.

Table 3–16   Correlation Coefficient Between NCEE and MCT

Correlation	NCEE	MCT
Pearson Correlation	1	0.021
Sig. (2-tailed)		0.825
N	86	86

Note. NCEE means National College Entrance Examination; MCT means Metaphoric Competence Test.

The Pearson Correlation evaluates whether there is statistical evidence for a linear relationship among variables. If $P>0.05$, it means there is no linear relationship among variables. In Table 3-15, the correlation coefficient ($r=0.021, P=0.825$) uncovers that there is a no linear relationship between NCEE and MCT. This also explains why the respondents achieve low scores on MCT while they performed well in NCEE.

3.7.2.4 Types of metaphors generated by students

According to the superordinate categories of the metaphors given by students, nine types of metaphors were generalized. Through these types, students showed their understanding of learning English (Table 3-17).

Table 3-17 Metaphors Generated in Part C: "Learning English is..."

Types of metaphor	Example
Journey/Movement	Traveling to America, swimming in the sea, a journey, climbing mountain, dripping water, a running, filling the container with water
Playing/Leisure	Listening to music, dancing, playing (piano, basketball, in the amusement park, toys), watching movies, lying in flowers
Exploration	Hiking, climbing a mountain, finding a gold, finding a new land
Experience	Standing under the sunshine, lying in flowers, communicating with (wisdom, a saint), reading a man's mind, understanding a man, absorbing nourishment, making a friend, talking with a friend, flying in the sky, opening a window
War	Fighting with yourself, a battle
Building	Building a house, dripping water, polishing a sword, filling the container with water, constant dropping wears the stone
Farming/Planting	Planting crops
Food and drinking	Eating (sugar, food, nutrition supplies, ice cream, durian), taking pills, drinking (long island ice tea, bitter beverage, water)
Things	A road, a bottomless hole, wealth, a flying bird, wealth, a weapon, a key, a fine art, oxygen, a bridge, an eagle, a door

According to the superordinate categories of the metaphors given by students, twelve types of metaphors were generalized. Through these types, students showed their perceptions of treating illness (Table 3-18).

Table 3-18 Metaphors Generated in Part C:"Treating illness is..."

Types of metaphor	Example
Journey/Movement	Running race, climbing mountain, walking in the sand, robbing time with death, running with time, cleaning (a house, your body)
Experience	Riding the roller coaster, being put in prison, seeing the sunlight again, crossing the desert, living in the dark, opening a way through thorns
Exploration	Hiking, climbing a mountain, finding a gold, finding a new land
Experience	Seeking the secret of body
Playing/Leisure	A game with foe
War	Fighting a war, defeating (enemy, oneself), fighting with enemy, waging(winning) a war, a war between body and virus, a war between doctor and enemies, a campaign, a fight with monster (enemy)
Building	Building a new house, breaking a blockade
Repair	Checking and fixing bugs in our bodies
Food and drinking	Eating sugar, eating bitter gourds
Things	A boxing match, a tree that a woodpecker cures

3.8 Data Collection

Primary data were collected from questionnaires, observations, interviews for this research. In order to guarantee the credibility and validity of the data in the research, all the data were collected at the same time when the exploratory teaching has been completed. Both the questionnaires and tests were evaluated by a colleague who is an experienced English teacher.

Before the research, an interview was conducted to assess the teachers' capability in cognition and understanding of metaphors. At the same time, a metaphor cognitive questionnaire was distributed to the student participants to learn about their understanding of general metaphor and medical metaphor. This provided the researcher the students' background knowledge of metaphor and it well demonstrated the necessity of the study.

To make sure that all the subjects in the two classes have no significant difference in their metaphor study and knowledge, before the research, the researcher conducted the pre-test on Metaphoric Competence Test. Subjects were informed that the test would have no influence on their English achievements in order to guarantee the authenticity of their answers. During the test, the students were not allowed to discuss with other students and they should complete the questionnaire in 30 minutes. The purpose of the pre-test is to have a good idea about the subjects' current cognition about metaphor. The researcher can find the problems in current metaphor teaching through it in order to solve these problems purposefully.

During the research, the researcher observed the participants' class and record the related documents. The teacher's interview was conducted after the class. Data collected from teachers was the primary source for further analysis.

After the exploratory teaching for 6 weeks, in order to find out if the subjects have made any improvement, a post-test was conducted in the subjects at the end of the first semester. Data collected from the test was analyzed by SPSS 22.0.

3.9 Data Analysis

For the data collected from the interview, observation and documents, a qualitative data analysiswas conducted. Flick (2014) describes the process of data analysis as "the classification and interpretation of linguistic material to make statements about implicit and explicit dimensions and structures of meaning-making in the material and what is represented in it". It is important for the researcher to code the data when collecting it according to whatever scheme is relevant to the study, and according to the theoretical framework that informs the study.

After collecting the raw data, the researcher ensured that the data were free from inconsistencies and incompleteness. Then the researcher checked the contents for completeness and responses for internal consistency. For the collected data which contained some identifying information, the subject were contacted over phone to confirm an answer. The software NVivo 11 was used to analyze the code combining the researcher's coding images and pictures. For analysis of close-ended questions, a computer program called Statistical Package for Social Science (SPSS) was used. Frequency tables were drawn and from these the data were presented in pie diagrams and bar graphs(Figure 3-6).

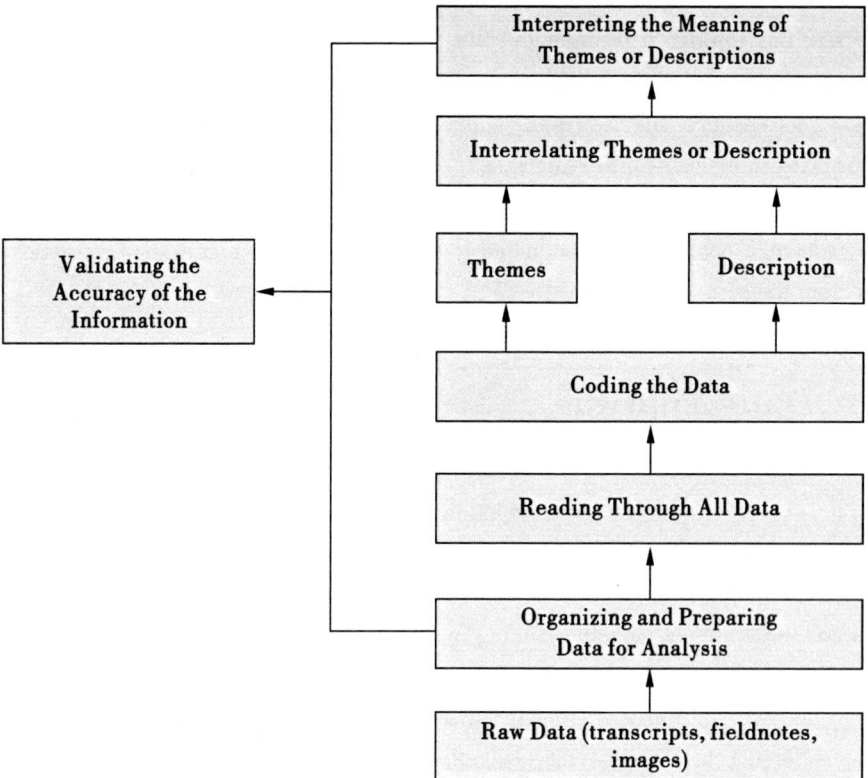

Figure 3-6 Data Analysis for Qualitative Research

For the data collected from the pilot questionnaire, the pre-test and the post-test, the inferential statistics used at this stage involves the Analysis of Variance (ANOVA). On the one hand, descriptive statistics including percentages, mean and standard deviation was used to describe the respondents' understanding of metaphor. On the other, various statistical procedures, including correlation analyse, ANOVA and paired samples correlations were used to answer the research questions.

3.10 Ethical Considerations

In order to recognize and protect the rights of students, honesty and integrity were required during conducting the research. To render the study ethical, the rights to self-determination, anonymity and informed consent were observed. The student's consent was obtained before the conducting the pilot questionnaire. Before the questionnaire, students were told of the content of the study and informed of rights to voluntarily consent or decline to participate. Subjects were informed about the purposes and the procedures of the study. Anonymity was maintained throughout the study and there was no score reduction no matter what opinions they gave. They were treated as anonymous students who need not give their personal information. At the same time, the researcher tried to avoid any form of dishonesty by recording truthfully the answers of subjects and ensured the data to be entered into the SPSS computer software program was true. The open-ended questions to be analyzed were also checked for confirmation of credibility.

Chapter 4

Implementation of Metaphor Enriched English Language Instruction

This chapter introduces the implementation process of Metaphor Enriched English Language Instruction (MEELI) which involves the preparation, implementation and feedback for the selected three units. Preparation phase refers to the learning of metaphor theories, time arrangement for each selected unit, teachers' pre-class discussion and text-based metaphor identification. Implementation phase includes teaching of conceptual metaphor theories, set induction for each selected unit, metaphor enriched assignment, assignment review and supplementary metaphorical words that originated from Greek and Latin. Feedback phase involves to students' feedback data which were collected by the student feedback questionnaire.

4.1 Preparation, Implementation and Feedback for Metaphor Supplements of Unit 2

During the preparation phase, time arrangement, learning of metaphor theories, selection of supplementary units, text-based metaphor identification and text analysis were discussed by the three teachers. The discussion would be presented for three selected units and the reasons for choosing these three units were mentioned in Chapter 3.

4.1.1 Preparation for metaphor supplements of Unit 2

A detailed discussion before the start of a new lesson was conducted by Ms Wang, Ms Liu and the researcher.

4.1.1.1 Metaphor theories learning

Regarding the metaphor theories, this research mainly used conceptual metaphor theories, which include structural metaphor, orientational metaphor and ontological metaphor.

The researcher had recommended several classic books on metaphor to Ms Wang and Ms Liu to enhance their understanding of the metaphor theories. For conceptual metaphor, the researcher cited examples of each type. For the structural metaphor, the researcher cited an example: IDEAS ARE FOOD. The other two teacher respondents could understand it due to the fact that there were so many verbs like "rape" or "digest" can be used to describe ideas. For the orientational metaphor, the researcher cited two phrases from the text, namely, "turn up" and "turn down". Up and down are normally used to describe the orientation of space. However, they are used to describe the volume of the music. Hence these phrasal verbs are orientational metaphors. The third type is the ontological metaphor, in which an abstraction (activity, emotion, or idea), is represented as something concrete (object, substance, container, or person). It contains container metaphor, entity metaphor and substance metaphor, of which the most common one is the container metaphor. When discussing what was container metaphor, the researcher cited the phrase "makes my blood boil" as an example in the text of Unit 2. Here ANGER is compared as a FLUID and we could imagine it vividly. When the fluid reaches the boiling point, steam is generated, and it will exert pressure on the container and it cannot hold the pressure for long and eventually it will explode. Likewise the human body is a container too. In Chinese too there is the same expression which makes it easy to understand. A classic metaphorical expression was summarized: ANGER IS (A HEAT OF) A FLUID IN A CONTAINER. Here is an excerpt on how to understand it.

Ms Zhang: *Since emotion is abstract and the human body is the subject of emotional experience, when people feel angry, the blood circulation will increase and anger can be viewed as a fire which will fill up the body. Then it will break out to certain extent, hence there are such expressions in English. For example, "I had reached the boiling point." or "His behaviour makes my blood boil." People always say that they are going to explode. In these sentences, "anger" can be understood as the increasing gas in the body which is taken as a container.*

Ms Wang: *It's easy to understand because there is a saying in Chinese: To explode in silence, or to die in it.*

From the discussion, the other two teacher participants (Ms Wang and Ms Liu) began to comprehend the features of the metaphor. Next, the time management for Unit 2 was discussed.

4.1.1.2 Time arrangement for Unit 2

According to the academic calendar of Xinxiang Medical University, there were 16 weeks for the fall semester. For freshmen, they received the military training for 2 weeks, so there were 14 weeks for them to study. 6 units were going to be lectured and each unit took 2 weeks. During the 6 units, Unit 2, 3 and 5 were selected, for the titles of each unit can be found in Table 3-3. For each week, there are two successive periods for English learning and each period takes

40 minutes. Unit 2 was conducted from week 6 to week 7. In the first period of Unit 2, teachers cited and explained metaphors and metaphorical expressions in the text. During the second period, the definition of metaphor, as well as linguistic metaphor and medical metaphor were introduced to the students. The topic of Unit 2 is about the parents' anxiety for their teenaged girl. In order to deepen the students' understanding of anxiety, teachers supplemented metaphors of anxiety and connected them with the nervous system which students were going to learn in their systematic anatomy during the same term. The assignment was to watch a video *The Nervous System* and completed the corresponding exercises.

During week 7, at the beginning of the lecture, the teacher participant reviewed the video and interpreted new words and phrases in the text. As the content of the English video was a little difficult to understand for students, the teacher participants spent more time on the understanding of brain which was also the difficult point in the video. During period 4, after summarizing the main idea and analyzing the writing technique, metaphoric affix were supplemented in the class to enhance the students' understanding of the nervous system. Further, the assignment was another video *The Structure of a Neuron* which consisted of personification and metaphors. The details of time arrangement are as follows (Table 4–1).

Table 4–1 Time Arrangement for Unit 2

Periods	Arrangement	Time/min
Period 1	Set induction	10
	To listen to the text record	5
	Role play	5
	To explain the main idea and sentence pattern	10
	To cite the metaphor and metaphorical expressions in text	5
	To explain these metaphor and metaphorical expressions	5
Period 2	The definition of metaphor	10
	Linguistic metaphor and medical metaphor	10
	To identify mother's anxiety and father's anxiety	5
	To supplement metaphors of anxiety	10
	To connect anxiety with nervous system	5
	Assignment: To watch the video *The nervous system*	
Period 3	To review the video of nervous system	10
	To explain the exercises	5
	To interpret new words and phrases in text	20
	To supplement metaphors of brain	5
Period 4	To summarize the main idea and analyze the writing technique	20
	To supplement medical affix which are metaphorical	20
	Assignment: To watch the video *The structure of neuron*	

Note. Each period takes 40 minutes. Words in bold are metaphor enriched supplements.

4.1.1.3 Pre-class discussion on Unit 2

When the teacher participants discussed how to present the supplementary video *The Nervous System*, Ms Liu suggested that students could try to produce the metaphoric sentences after learning this unit. For example, after learning about the nervous system, students were asked to describe the brain's function in terms of metaphors. The title of Unit 2 is *Deep Concern* which mainly focused on the generation gap. The readers could feel the parents' anxiety about Sandy who was a teenager girl.

When the question of how to lead in the nervous system when teaching this unit, the researcher thought that the word "anxiety" could be a key word which would connect the text to it. The teacher suggested students to find out the parents' anxious behavior in the text, and would then ask the students to consider which body part is related to anxiety. Since the nervous system controls our emotions, teachers can show students a video of the nervous system. While watching the video, teachers can pick some metaphor pictures to let students find the similarities and differences between the picture and the function it implies to improve the students' metaphor comprehension and analogy ability. For example, "My stomach feels upset-like it's full of knots." The researcher had stated that the uncomfortable feeling in the father's stomach was the external manifestation of his inner anxiety.

When the question of how to transit from the nervous system to neuron came up, Ms Wang suggested that we could ask the students a question: "Since you have already learned the nervous system, do you know what the medium of information transfer is?" Quite a lot of students might think of cells. Some students would think of nerve cells. Then the teachers could tell the students that the answer was neuron. Then the video of neuron would be shown to them before the next lecture and they were required to form metaphoric sentences.

4.1.1.4 Text-based metaphor identification and analysis of Unit 2

During the preparation phase, how to identify the metaphors in the text was the core issue. Conceptual metaphor theory provides a systematic tool to identify the concepts behind the linguistic metaphors. In addition, Metaphor Identification Procedure (MIP) which was introduced in Chapter 3 provides an explicit and reliable instrument for identifying linguistic metaphors. After explaining the MIP to Ms Liu and Ms Wang, each teacher participant identified the metaphors in the text by MIP. For the uncertain ones, three teachers discussed together and came to agreement eventually. Table 4-2 are linguistic metaphors in Unit 2.

Table 4-2 Linguistic Metaphors in Unit 2

Categories	Structural metaphor	Orientational metaphor	Ontological metaphor		
			container	entity	substance
Verbs	Bug				
Nouns	Anchor				
Verbal phrases	Bolt out (of the house)	Turn up Turn down	Make ones blood boil		
Nominal phrases					Knot (in stomach)

For the embodied conceptual metaphors behind these linguistic metaphors, according to the classification of conceptual metaphor, they had been summarized into three types. First, structural metaphor, which used concrete concepts to understand abstract concepts, can be illustrated by the words "bug" "anchor" and "bolt out" (of the house). The original meaning of bug is an insect, while the metaphoric meaning is to annoy. The readers can have a feeling of annoyance when they see a bug; the original meaning of anchor is "a device for securing ships to the ground under the water by means of cables", while the metaphoric meaning is "a reliable or principal support". The similarity between these two meanings is reliable and safe. Another metaphor is the phrasal verb "bolt out" (of the house) whose literal meaning is "a lightning stroke", in the text, its metaphoric meaning is "to leave the house very quickly like a bolt". A visual image is created immediately by this metaphor. Second, orientational metaphor, which was embodied by the verbal phrases "turn up" and "turn down" involves spatial relationships (such as UP-DOWN, IN-OUT, ON-OFF, and FRONT-BACK). The conceptual metaphors embodied by turn up and turn down are MORE IS UP, LESS IS DOWN. Third, ontological metaphor, embodied by the verbal phrase "make one's blood boil" is a container metaphor ANGER IS (THE HEAT OF) A FLUID IN A CONTAINER which is the emphasis of this unit. "knot" (in stomach) is a substance metaphor of upset stomach by which the feeling is represented as knots.

4.1.2 Implementation for metaphor supplements of Unit 2

The implementation of Unit 2 was carried out from week 6 to week 7 and each week consisted of two periods. During the implementation phase, four parts would be discussed in detail, namely, introduction metaphors in Unit 2, explanation metaphor theories to the students, metaphor mechanism analysis and supplementation of metaphoric medical knowledge.

4.1.2.1 Periods 1 and 2 of Unit 2

Since there was no break between periods 1 and 2, the researcher took these two periods, as well as periods 3 and 4 as a whole. In periods 1 and 2, after finishing the text interpretation, students were asked to think about the usage of some metaphor words and phrases in Table 4-2. Then the lecturers came up with the definition of metaphor. Since the students were not familiar with the metaphor and its classification, the traditional view of metaphor and the conceptual metaphor were explained to the students.

(1) The traditional view of metaphor

It refers to a comparison between unlike things without the use of "like" or "as". This comparison is done between two things that are basically different but have something in common in some significant way. Therefore, people view metaphor as a linguistic phenomenon, a figure of speech, to ornament languages (Table 4-3).

Table 4-3 Patterns of Metaphors

Patterns	Example
Noun	Time is money
Verb	My heart was *pumping*
Adjective	The *mountainous* waves swallowed up the ship
"-of-" phrase	A policeman waved me out of *the snake of traffic* and flagged me to stop
Idiom	We mended our fences
	To kill two birds with one stone
	To teach a fish to swim
	To cast pearls before swine

After introducing the traditional view of metaphor, another important metaphor theory in cognitive linguistics is the conceptual metaphor theory. It was illustrated to the students.

(2) Conceptual metaphor theory and its cognitive functions

According to Lakoff and Johnson (1980), metaphor is not simply a matter of words or linguistic expressions but of concepts, of thinking one thing in terms of another. Lakoff (1993) defines conceptual metaphor as "mapping from a source domain to a target domain". For example, there is a metaphor in Unit 2, make one's blood boil, which is the linguistic metaphor of ANGER IS THE FLUID IN A CONTAINER. The researcher had analyzed the mapping between the target domain ANGER and source domain FLUID. The details are in Table 4-4.

Table 4-4 The Mapping Between ANGER and FLUID

Target domain	Mapping	Source domain
Anger	⟶	Fluid
Anger level	⟶	Fluid level
Body container	⟶	
Body pressure	⟶	Container internal pressure
Body agitation	⟶	Container agitation
Body heat	⟶	Container heat

After introducing the mapping process of conceptual metaphor, in order to enhance the students' understanding of this theory, classification of conceptual metaphor also was introduced to them (Figure 4-1).

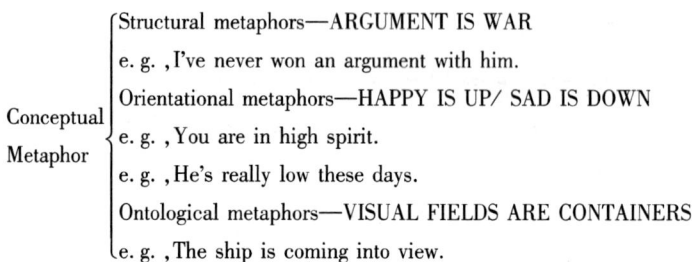

Figure 4-1 Classification of Conceptual Metaphor

Note. Small capital letters are used to distinguish conceptual metaphors from linguistic metaphors.

(3) Set induction for Unit 2

After understanding the functions of a metaphor, the researcher tried to enhance the students' understanding of the topic in terms of metaphors. The students were required to do a brain storming. The questions were "What will the generation gap bring?" "Quarrel?" "Lack of understanding?" "Anxiety?" and so on. After the students answered these questions, the teacher continued to inspire the students by asking them: "Can you feel the anxiety of Sandy's parents?" "How to describe anxiety to others?" Further the students were asked to find out metaphors of anxiety from Emma Ston's words: "I Am Bigger Than My Anxiety". Emma Ston is the heroine of the popular film *La La Land*. She suffered from anxiety for a long time, and from this paragraph, the readers can sense it from her vivid description of anxiety.

Emma Ston

I drewa little green monster on my shoulder that speaks to me in my ear and tells me all these things that aren't true. And every time I listen to it, it grows bigger. If I listen to it enough, it crushes me. But if I turn my head and keep doing what I'm doing—let it speak to me, but don't give it the credit it needs—then it shrinks down and fades away.

(as cited in Allyson Koerner, 2016)

The researcher did another brain storming by asking the students: Since anxiety is a feeling inside, how can you feel it? The students were guided to think about the relationship between anxiety and human body. Another question was "Will anxiety cause change in physical conditions?" If yes, "which body system will be affected by anxiety?" After discussing the answers for these question, the teachers continued to ask: "Do you know which part of the nervous system controls the feeling of anxiety?" They asked the students to find out the answer in the video. That was given as assignment for these two periods of class.

(4) Metaphor enriched assignment

In order to enhance the students' understanding of medical metaphors, a video *Introduction to The Nervous System* was assigned to the students at the end of the second period. It was produced by Career and Technical Education (CTE) skills which specializes in creating customized educational videos for high schools and colleges. It was a quality video meant to complement the classroom instructions. The video lasted for nine minutes and mainly introduced the Central Nervous System (CNS) and the Peripheral Nervous System (PNS) with clear pictures, Standard English pronunciation with English subtitles. It was an integrated video which comprises of the set induction, main content and recaps. Most importantly it contained some metaphorical pictures which could help the students better understand the functions of the components of the nervous system. So, these pictures were chosen to be analyzed by the students to enhance their metaphorical comprehension and medical content comprehension.

4.1.2.2 Periods 3 and 4 of Unit 2

Periods 3 and 4 were conducted on week 7 and the assignment of watching a video was reviewed and related supplementary materials were provided to the students.

(1) Metaphor enriched assignment review

The video *The Nervous System* runs for nine minutes and mainly introduces the Central Nervous System (CNS) and the Peripheral Nervous System (PNS) with clear pictures, standard English pronunciation with English subtitles (Booklet). Therefore, these pictures were chosen to be analyzed by students to enhance their metaphorical comprehension and medical content comprehension. The students were required to watch the video and answered the related questions of three pictures. The first picture of the assignment is shown in link

Link 4–1 A Screenshot of *The Nervous System*

4-1.

There are four questions relating to this picture. Question 1 refers to the exercise in the picture and the implied meaning of this sport in this video. Almost all the students knew the answer "yoga" and it is used to describe the function of the nervous system. Question 2 asks the students to come up with a metaphor, and some students gave the right answer. That is, THE FUNCTION OF THE NERVOUS SYSTEM IS LIKE DOING YOGA (small capital letters are used to distinguish conceptual metaphors from linguistic metaphors). Then the researcher analyzed this metaphor by identifying the tenor and vehicle (Figure 4-2).

THE FUNCTION OF THE NERVOUS SYSTEM IS LIKE DOING YOGA.
⇩ ⇩
Tenor Vehicle

Figure 4-2 The Tenor and Vehicle of the Metaphor

Question 3 refers to the writing down the similarities between the nervous system and yoga. Most frequent answers are both can make balance; both can coordinate all the activities of body; both can regulate heart rate. Question 4 asks the students to come up with their own metaphors of the nervous system. The summary of the students' metaphors are as follows (Table 4-5).

Table 4-5 Metaphors of the Nervous System

Tenor	Vehicles	Similarities
The nervous system	A coordinator/a scale/a band	Both can coordinate all the activities of the body
	A big tree/river/road	Both have many branches
	A CEO/chairman/monitor/manager/administrator/police/leader/commander/big boss/king/president	Both can control our body
	An telephone line/emitter/processor	Both can sent message
	A baby	Both are very fragile
	A riddle/black hole	Both are mysterious
	Sun/water	Both are necessary
	An organization/a railway station	Both have leaders and staff

Since brain is a very important part of human nervous system and its structure and functions are difficult to understand, the researcher supplemented metaphors of brain. The researcher cited a metaphor BRAIN IS A COMPUTER and explained the mapping between source domain and target domain. The details are stated in Table 4-6.

Table 4-6 The Mapping of BRAIN IS A COMPUTER

Target domain	Mapping	Source domain
The brain	⟶	The host
Sensory organs	⟶	Input devices
Neuron	⟶	Transistor

In conclusion, students could deepen their metaphor recognition in terms of the given pictures. By analyzing the tenor and vehicle of the metaphor THE FUNCTION OF THE NERVOUS SYSTEM IS LIKE DOING YOGA, they could enhance their metaphor interpretation; then they tried to come up with new metaphors which were good for their metaphor creation. In addition, they could easily understand the function of the nervous system and brain via metaphors. The second picture of the assignment is stated in Link 4-2.

Link 4-2 A Screenshot of The Peripheral Nervous System

There are four questions relating to the second picture. For question 1, the highway in this picture implies the function of the peripheral nervous system. Question 2 requested the students to come up with a metaphor, that is, THE FUNCTION OF THE PERIPHERAL NERVOUS SYSTEM IS LIKE A HIGHWAY. The analysis of this metaphor is listed in Figure 4-5.

<u>THE FUNCTION OF THE PERIPHERAL NERVOUS SYSTEM</u> IS LIKE A <u>HIGHWAY</u>.
⇩   ⇩
Tenor   Vehicle

Figure 4-5 The Tenor and Vehicle of the Metaphor

For question 3, the similarities between the peripheral nervous system and the highway were found, and the most frequent answers are both have many branches; both can link to different parts; both can deliver information. Question 4 requires the students to come up with their own metaphors of the peripheral nervous system (Table 4-7).

Table 4-7 Metaphors of the Peripheral Nervous System

Tenor	Vehicles	Similarities
Peripheral nervous system	A post officer /mailman/ road/satellite/a keyboard	Both can transport information
	A blood vessel/river/internet	Both have many branches
	Web	Both can connect things
	A receiver/carriage	Both can receiver information
	An interpreter	Both can translate outside information
	A soldier	Both can defend oneself or escape the threat
	A detective	Both can ratiocinate and think
	An ant cave	Both can extend in all directions
	A department manager	Both can manage others

In conclusion, students could deepen their metaphor recognition with the help of the given picture. By analyzing the tenor and vehicle of the metaphor THE FUNCTION OF THE PERIPHERAL NERVOUS SYSTEM IS LIKE A HIGHWAY, they could enhance their metaphor interpretation. Their trying to come up with new metaphors was good for their metaphor production. The third picture is shown in Link 4-3.

Link 4-3 A Screenshot of The Autonomic Nervous System

There were 4 questions relating to the third picture. For question 1, the exercise in this picture is boxing which implies the function of the autonomic nervous system. Question 2 requested the students to come up with a metaphor, namely, THE FUNCTION OF THE AUTONOMIC NERVOUS SYSTEM IS LIKE BOXING. The analysis of this metaphor is stated in Figure 4-3.

THE AUTONOMIC NERVOUS SYSTEM IS LIKE BOXING.
⇩   ⇩
Tenor   Vehicle

Figure 4-3 The Tenor and Vehicle of the Metaphor

Question 3 required the students to write down the similarities between the autonomic nervous system and boxing, and the most frequent answers are both can respond to threat rapidly; both can defend themselves. Question 4 asked the students to make up their own metaphors of the autonomic nervous system (Table 4-8).

Table 4-8 Metaphors of the Autonomic Nervous System

Tenor	Vehicles	Similarities
Autonomic nervous system	A leaf vein/root of tree/branches	Both are intersecting of tree
	A police/lock/house	Both can protect others
	A railway station/phone/conductor/electric wire	Both can deliver information
	An alarm	Both can warn us of the danger
	A traffic intersection	Both have a lot of things to go through
	A regulator	Both of them can adjust something

In conclusion, the students could deepen their metaphor recognition with the help of the given pictures. By analyzing the tenor and vehicle of the metaphor THE AUTONOMIC NERVOUS SYSTEM IS LIKE BOXING, they could enhance their metaphor interpretation. They tried to come up with new metaphors which was good for their metaphor production. In addition, they could easily understand the function of the autonomic nervous system through the metaphor of boxing.

(2) Supplementary materials: metaphoric words on the nervous system

The three main etymologies of Medical English vocabulary are Anglo-Saxon, Greek and Latin. Most of them originated from Greek and Latin, especially clinical Medical English vocabulary is mostly related to Greek, anatomy words are often related to Latin.

1) Metaphorical wordsthat originated from Greek

It is said that about three-quarters of the Medical English vocabulary is from Greek. One reason is that the father of medicine, Hippocrates, was a physician in the ancient Greek Pericles era, and the other reason is that Greek is easy to construct new vocabulary. Whenever a new disease or new methods appeared, Greek was used as basic roots, and prefixes and suffixes were added to form new words. For example, "appendicitis", "-itis" comes from Greek, which means indicating inflammation of a specified part; "appendix" comes from Latin "append", which means a subordinate part attached to something. They combined to form a new medical term. By learning these affixes with metaphorical meanings, the students can increase their interest in learning and deepen their understanding and memory of medical vocabulary. Some metaphorical words, relating to the nervous system, which originated from Greek, are listed in the Table 4-9. Due to the time limitation, the researcher cited some examples from the table and provided the explanation of these words to students for their self-learning.

Table 4-9 Metaphorical Words that Originated from Greek

Terms	Words from Greek	Meanings
Arachnoid mater	Arachn-: spider	Delicate web-like layer of the meninges
Dendrite	Dendron: tree	One of two processes extending from a neuron cell body; the other is the axon
Thalamus	Thalamos: a bed, a bedroom	Part of the brain that processes sensory information
Neuroglia	-glia: glue	Cells within both the CNS and PNS
Synapse	-apse(hapto): to fasten	The connecting point between nerve cells or between a nerve cell and a receptoror effector cell
Astrocytoma	Astro- (astron): star	Star-shaped tumor that usually develops in the cerebrum a somewhat rounded subdivision of a bodily organ or part
Lobe	Lobos: vegetable pod	A part of an organ in the body, especially the lungs or brain

The word "arachnoid" is an ontological metaphor. The root "arachn-" means spider in Greek, in Medical English, it means delicate web-like layer of the meninges.

The word "dendrite" is also an ontological metaphor. The word "dendron" means tree in Greek, in Medical English, it means one of two processes extending from a neuron cell body which looks like a tree.

The word "thalamus" is another ontological metaphor. It comes from Greek thalamus which means a bed or a bedroom. In Medical English, it means the part of the brain that processes sensory information.

The word "neuroglia" is an ontological metaphor which is based on a similar function. It is a connective tissue which can connect and support various nerve components. In Greek, "-glia" means "glue", which also means the connection of two items. This metaphoric meaning does help learners to understand the function of neuroglia.

The word "synapse" is a metaphoric word. "syn-" is a common prefix which means together. "-apse" "hapto" in Greek, means "to fasten". So, synapse means the junction between two nerve cells.

The word "astrocytoma" is an ontological metaphor which is based on similar appearance. Astrocytoma is a star-shaped tumor that usually develops in the cerebrum. In Greek, "astro-" means "star". This metaphoric meaning does help learners to understand the appearance of astrocytoma.

The word "lobe" in occipital lobe is used metaphorically. It originated from Greek "lobos" which means "lobe, lap, slip", use of "lap-" or "slip-like" parts of the body or plants, especially "earlobe". Due to the similar slip-like shape, it was used to describe divisions of the brain in 1670s.

2) Metaphorical words that originated from Latin

Rome established the world's earliest public medical school in 1400 B. C. In the Middle Ages, Latin was the medium of communication between different European countries at that time, and it was also the language for the study of science, philosophy and theology.

In terms of medicine, the Romans also developed their country under the influence of Greek medicine. In 1543, the founder of modern human anatomy Andreas Vesalius (1950) completed the great work "De humani corporis fabrica" (the structure of the human body). This Latin-written book laid the foundation of Latin in Medical English anatomy vocabulary. In 1895, Latin was recognized as the international language of the world's medical community, and it was required that regular prescriptions or drug names be written in Latin, which more and more showed the status of Latin in medical languages.

Therefore, supplementing metaphorical words with Latin etymology can help students understand and memorize medical words. The details of supplement are as follows (Table 4-10).

Table 4-10 Metaphorical Words that Originated from Latin

Terms	Words from Latin	*Meanings*
Cerebrospinal fluid	Cerebro-: the brain	The clear colourless fluid in the spaces inside and around the spinal cord and brain
Dura mater	Hard mother of the brain	Tough outer membrane surrounding the brain and the spinal cord
Pia mater	Tender mother of the brain	Inner layer of the meninges
Parietal (lobe)	Pariet-(parietalis): walls	The part of the brain that processes information from the sense of touch and other sensory and motor tasks
Pons	Bridge	The part of the brain stem that passes information to the cerebellum and thalamus to regulate subconscious somatic activities

The word "cerebrospinal" (fluid) consists two parts, "cerebr-" and "-spinal". The former means brain, while the latter means backbone which meaning is metaphoric. The original meaning of spine comes from Latin "spina" which means thorn or prickle. The metaphorical extension "backbone" developed in Latin, perhaps via "prickle" and "fish bone". It is easy to associate prickle or fish bone with the human spine due to their similar shapes. So, the word "cerebrospinal" is an ontological metaphor.

The word "dura mater" is metaphoric. It originated from Medieval Latin "dura mater cerebri", which literally means "hard mother of the brain". "Mater" means "mother" in Latin which implies the relationship between the two things. In Arabic, the words "father" "mother" and "son" are often used to describe relationships between things. In Medical English, it is used to describe the outer meninges. Its antonym is "pia mater" in which pia means tender and mater means mother, and it is used to describe the inner layer of the meninges.

The word "parietal" (lobe) is from Late Latin "parietalis" which means "of walls". Due to the similar function as regards the wall, it is used metaphorically to refer the part of the cerebral cortex in either hemisphere of the brain lying below the crown of the head.

The word "pons" is from Latin which means "bridge, connecting gallery, walkway", due to the similar functions of the bridge, it is used metaphorically to refer to the part of the brain stem which can pass information to the cerebellum.

(3) Metaphor enriched assignment

Students are required to watch a video *Structure of a Neuron*, and then answer the related questions via computer and submit their electronic edition to the class monitor before the next lecture (Booklet). This assignment contains two parts. Part one is a matching exercise aiming to check the students' understanding of the basic components of the nervous system by matching the metaphorical descriptions given below with the correct terms. The terms are neuron, dendrite, axon, myelin sheath and synapse. Part two is to make up new metaphors of the above mentioned five terms. For example, "A neuron is like a...because..." By making the metaphoric sentence, students can create more metaphors according to the similarities and improve their metaphoric competence.

4.2 Preparation, Implementation and Feedback for Metaphor Supplements of Unit 3

During the preparation phase, time management, pre-class discussion, text-based metaphor identification and analysis were discussed by the three teachers.

4.2.1 Preparation for metaphor supplements of Unit 3

The discussion before the new lesson was conducted on 19th of October. Time management and supplementary materials were discussed by Ms Wang, Ms Liu and the researcher in detail.

4.2.1.1 Time arrangement for Unit 3

According to the academic calendar of Xinxiang Medical University, Unit 3 was conducted from week 8 to week 9. In the first period of Unit 3, the teachers supplemented metaphors of heart which was the topic of this unit and then analyzed the text structure. During the second period, new words and expressions were taught and assignment review (video: *The Structure of Neuron*) was conducted. In order to enhance the students' understanding of the functions of the heart, an excerpt (Booklet) from the book *I am Joe's body* (1986) was assigned to students as homework. The students were required to list the metaphorical words in this excerpt as well as their original and metaphorical meanings. They were also required to find out the metaphorical sentences within the text and translate them into Chinese. There was the conventional teaching during week 9, including text study, critical thinking and writing technique. The details of time arrangement for each step are as follows (Table 4-11).

Table 4-11 Time Arrangement for Unit 3

Periods	Arrangement	Time/min
Period 1	Assignment review: *The structure of neuron* (video)	10
	Set induction: Father in our eyes	10
	Structure analysis	10
	New words and expressions (1)	10
Period 2	New words and expressions (2)	20
	Metaphors about heart	20
	Assignment: Excerpts from the book *I am Joe's body* (J. D. RADCLIFF)	
Period 3	To watch a movie clip and discuss	10
	Text study (1)	30
Period 4	Text study (2)	10
	Reflection: What is a good heart?	10
	Writing technique	20

Note. Each period takes 40 minutes. Words in bold are metaphor enriched supplements.

4.2.1.2 Pre-class discussion on Unit 3

Before the implementation of supplementary materials on Unit 3, a group discussion was conducted. The main topics of this discussion were the understanding of supplementary metaphors (metaphors of heart) and the content of the assignment (excerpt from *I am Joe's body*). For the set induction, the researcher suggested to introduce metaphors of heart since the topic dealt with what was a good heart. Ms Wang suggested to replace the conventional set induction with metaphors of heart so as to stimulate the students' interest and enlarge their horizon. Here is an excerpt from Ms Wang.

Ms Wang: *We can talk about all metaphors of heart. For the usage of heart, we can explain the phrases referring to heart. For example, what is take heart, lose heart, or by heart. Right?*

Ms Zhang: *Then show students some examples.*

Ms Wang: *Right.*

The explanation of new words and expressions was followed by the set induction. Then Ms Wang suggested that teachers should transfer the meaning of a good heart from the moral to physical, and introduce the assignment of a medical passage on heart. Here is another excerpt from her.

> Ms Wang: *After analyzing the structure, I will mention the language points in the text. Then I will discuss what is a good heart. The good heart in the text refers to a virtue. We can say, physically speaking, a good heart means... Then we can ask students what are the functions of heart.*
>
> Ms Zhang: *Right, our hearts work very hard without stop. It beats about* 70 *times per minute. It is natural to shift to the assignment (excerpt from* I am Joe's body) *from this topic.*

4.2.1.3 Text-based metaphor identification and analysis of Unit 3

The following words and phrases are linguistic metaphors in Unit 3.

Nasty weather (para. 3)

A baseball *fan* (para. 8)

...it was the first time any fighter was urged to take a dive before the fight began(para. 10).

In the text, there is a phrase "nasty weather". The word "nasty" is a metaphoric word which original meaning is dirty or unclean. Later it was used to describe something disgusting in point of smell, taste or even moral character. In 1630s, it was employed in describing the weather which implies a stormy weather.

Another phrase is "a basketball fan". The word "fan" also has many metaphoric meanings. For example, it originates from Latin "ventus" which relating to "wind". In 1889, it developed the meaning "devotee" which originally means baseball enthusiasts.

The verbal phrase "take a dive" is also metaphorical. It refers to the act of jumping into water from a height, usually at a swimming pool or beach. However, in the text, this phrase used to describe the fighter who lost a game on purpose in a competitive match.

4.2.2 Implementation for metaphor supplements of Unit 3

The implementation of Unit 3 was carried out from week 8 to week 9 and each week consisted of two periods. During the implementation phase, four parts were to be discussed in detail, namely, assignment review, introduction metaphors in Unit 3, metaphor mechanism analysis and supplementation of metaphoric medical knowledge.

4.2.2.1 Periods 1 and 2 of Unit 3

(1) Metaphor enriched assignment review

The video *Structure of a Neuron* comes from It's AumSum Time on bilibili which provides physics, chemistry and biology educational videos for kids, children, students and teachers. It is an animation without dialogue which is humorous and easy to understand. The time duration is 6 minutes and 14 seconds which is suitable for self-learning. Personification and metaphor are used to help the learners' understanding. After watching it, there are two questions for students. The first question requires matching the metaphorical descriptions of five words with the correct terms. The metaphorical descriptions of these five words are stated in Table 4-12.

Table 4-12 Metaphors and Their Metaphorical Descriptions

Terms	Metaphorical descriptions
Neuron	Like a silicon chip in a computer that receives and transmits information between input and output devices as well as between other chips
Dendrite	Like a tree. Also, each branch is a telephone wire that carries incoming messages to you
Axon	Like an electrical cable that carries information
Myelin sheath	Like the insulation that covers electrical wires
Synapse	Like a railroad junction, where two trains may meet

The second question required students to make five metaphors of the five terms in the first questions. The summary of each term is as follows. Table 4-13 refers to the vehicles and similarities between neuron and its vehicles.

Table 4-13 The Metaphors of Neuron

Tenor	Vehicles	Similarities
Neuron	A signal tower/a tower crane/a transducer/an accepting station	Both can deliver/pass/send/receive information
	A carrier	Both can deliver goods
	A railway station/phone/conductor/electric wire	Both can deliver information
	A bridge	Both can connect the receptor and effector
	A pipeline/an electric wire	Both can conduct impulse/electricity

Most of the students compared neuron as a signal tower, a tower crane, a transducer, an accepting station by which they can receive and send messages to another. Some students thought the function of neuron as a carrier which could deliver goods. Some students took its function as a bridge which could connect the receptor and the effector. Some students compared the neuron to a pipeline or an electric wire which could conduct impulses of electricity. Table 4-14 refers to the vehicles of dendrite metaphors and their similarities.

Table 4-14 The Metaphors of Dendrite

Tenor	Vehicles	Similarities
Dendrite	A broom head /stream/tree	It has many branches
	An antenna/a post office/a radio	It can receive or transmit information

For the metaphors of dendrite, creation of new metaphors by the students was not rich. Some students took the dendrite as a broom head, stream or a tree which had a similar appearance. They might have been affected by the picture of dendrite in the video. Some students imagined it as an antenna, a post office or a radio which could receive or transmit information. The function of delivering information was emphasized. Table 4-15 refers to the vehicles of axon metaphors and their similarities.

Table 4-15 The Metaphors of Axon

Tenor	Vehicles	Similarities
Axon	A datacable/a messenger A transmitting antenna	Both can deliver message or information
	A main stem	Both of them have only one passageway
	A river channel	Both are long

For the metaphors of axon, students' creation of new metaphors could be summarized into three categories. In terms of delivering function, some students took the axon as a datacable, a transmitting antenna or a messenger which could deliver message or information. In terms of the direction, some students took it as a main stem which had only one passageway. In terms of length, some students took it as a river channel which was long in nature.

Table 4-16 refers to the vehicles of myelin sheath metaphors and their similarities.

Table 4-16 The Metaphors of Myelin Sheath

Tenor	Vehicles	Similarities
Myelin sheath	A skin/a bark/a coat/a pipe/a rain coat/a bullet proof vest/a protection suit/an armor	Both can protect the thing inside
	An isolation strip	Both can separate two things
	A snakeskin	Both are transparent
	A plastic film	Both are lucid and colloidal

For the metaphors of myelin sheath, students' creation of new metaphors could be categorized into three groups. In terms of protection function, some students took the myelin sheath as a skin, a bark, a coat, a rain coat, a bullet proof vest, a pipe, a protection suit and an armor which could protect the thing inside. As regards the separation, some students took it as an isolation strip which could separate two things. In terms of appearance, some students took it as a snake skin or a plastic film which was transparent or colloidal. Table 4-17 refers to the vehicles of synapse metaphors and their similarities.

Table 4-17 The Metaphors of Synapse

Tenor	Vehicles	Similarities
Synapse	A crossing/a freight station	Both can deliver information to others
	A transfer station	Both can transform information
	A transportation	Both can exchange the information
	A bridge/a connector	Both can connect one thing with another one

For the metaphors of synapse, the students' creation of new metaphors could be organized into two categories. In terms of the delivering function, some students found the synapse as a crossing, a freight station, a transfer station or a transportation which could deliver or exchange information. In terms of the connection function, some students took it as a connector which could connect one thing with another.

(2) Supplementary materials for Unit 3

1) Metaphorical meanings of heart

The title of Unit 3 is *A Good Heart to Lean On*, mainly emphasizes the good heart of a father. Therefore, the question "What does 'a good heart' mean?" was asked as the set induction. For this question, most students used many adjectives to define the quality of a good heart. While in Medical English, heart is also an important organ which plays a vital role in our body system. Teachers supplemented the metaphorical meaning of heart to the original meaning of heart. In the original sense, heart is an organ in one's chest that pumps and circulates blood in the body. In the Chinese culture, there are many metaphorical meanings related to the heart. Table 4-18 shows metaphorical meanings of heart and corresponding examples.

Table 4-18 Metaphorical Meanings of Heart and Examples

Metaphorical meanings of heart	Examples
Heart	1) A good or bad intention
	e.g., Ted may not be rich but he's got a good *heart*
	2) One's feelings and emotions considered as part of one's character
	e.g., My advice would be to follow your *heart*

Continue to Table 4-18

Metaphorical meanings of heart	Examples
	3) The center or the core of something e. g. , There is a beautiful house deep in the *heart* of the English countryside
Heart-broken	Meaning: feeling sad and unhappy e. g. , If anything happened to the baby you would be *heart-broken*
Heart-warming	Meaning: something seems to be positive and good and causing feelings of pleasure e. g. , It's really *heart-warming* to see such generosity
Big-hearted	Meaning: kind and generous e. g. , The *big-hearted* fighter forgave his opponent and reassured him he was not to blame for the injuries
Faint-hearted	Meaning: someone is not confident or brave and dislikes taking unnecessary risks e. g. , Our groups must be totally self-sufficient. This is not a journey for the *faint-hearted*
Half-hearted	Meaning: showing no enthusiasm or interest e. g. , The celebrations were rather *half-hearted*
Whole-hearted	Meaning: completely enthusiastic e. g. , We would like to express our *whole-hearted* support for the meeting
Break one's heart	Meaning: making people sad, shocked and upset e. g. , You *broke my heart*, you wrecked my life
(one's) Heart goes out to (someone)	Meaning: feel sympathy for someone e. g. , My *heart goes out to* this compassionate man
Change of heart	Meaning: change your opinion or the way you feel about something e. g. , What has brought about this sudden *change of heart*?
Take heart	Meaning: to feel encouraged e. g. , If you *take heart*, you will become more courageous
Lose heart	Meaning: to stop believing that you can succeed e. g. , I think he *lost heart* after losing the first game
Sink of heart	Meaning: suddenly feel worried or disappointed e. g. , I feel a definite *sinking of the heart*

    The teachers listed metaphoric meanings of heart and heart phrases, as well as examples to increase the students' understanding of metaphorical usage of heart. Students felt very interested in the supplementary materials due to the fact that they never considered these heart-related expressions from the point of view of metaphors.

2) Metaphorical expressions of heart that are unique to Chinese

Students could understand the usage of metaphors of heart as there are similar expressions both in English and Chinese. Then teachers made students think whether there were some metaphorical expressions of heart which were unique to Chinese. Most of the students claimed that there were many expressions of heart in Chinese without an equivalent English translation. From discussing these unique Chinese expressions, the students made a comparison between the Chinese idioms with their English translation which enhanced their understanding of heart metaphors as well as translation skills. The details of supplement are stated in the Table 4-19.

Table 4-19 Metaphorical Expressions of Heart that are Unique to Chinese

Chinese	English
不得人心	Not enjoy popular support
粗心大意	Careless
胆大心细	Bold but cautious
得心应手	With facility
掉以轻心	Lower one's guard
焦心	Feel terribly worried
刻骨铭心	Be engraved on one's bone and heart
利欲熏心	Be blinded by greed
心心相印	Have mutual affinity
平心静气	Calmly
收买人心	Buy popular support
死心塌地	Be dead set
枉费心机	Hatch plots in vain
推心置腹	Response full confidence in someone
心潮澎湃	Feel an upsurge of emotion
心花怒放	Burst with joy
心怀鬼胎	Have evil intentions

Note. 心(xin) is the Chinese character of English word *heart*.

(3) Metaphor enriched assignments

There were two assignments for students to complete after the class. The first one was to read an excerpt *Heart* which comes from the book *I am Joe's body*. Students were required to find out the metaphors (words or sentences) and wrote down their original meanings and metaphorical meaning, then translated the metaphorical sentences in the passage into Chinese. This assignment aims to enhance the students' metaphoric comprehension. The second assignment was to watch a video *The Cardiovascular System* which provides a brief introduction to the cardiovascular system and found the metaphors in this video. This assignment aims to supplement their medical knowledge via metaphors.

4.2.2.2 Periods 3 and 4 of Unit 3

(1) Metaphor enriched assignments review

1) Review of assignment 1: Heart (article)

This passage is an extract from the book *I am Joe's body* (1986) written by J. D. RADCLIFF (Booklet). As a popular science book and the most successful series ever printed, over seven million reprints were sold. It comprises of 33 articles and each article introduces the organs and tissues present in the bodies of Joe and Jane (a couple). The assignment adapted from one article *Heart*. Since this excerpt is interesting and not difficult for students, most of the students completed the exercise well. Metaphors in *Heart* and their meanings were summarized in Table 4-20.

Table 4-20 Metaphors in the article "Heart"

Metaphors	Original meaning	Metaphorical meaning in the article
Pump	A machine for forcing liquid or gas into or out of something	To move very quickly up and down (like a pump)
Ignition system	The mechanism that ignites the fuel in an internal-combustion engine	Pumping function of heart
Branching trees brake	Trees with many branches A restraint used to slow or stop a vehicle	Coronary artery vagus nerves

Metaphorical sentences in this passage and their Chinese translation were summarized in Table 4-21.

Table 4-21 Metaphorical Sentences in the Extract of *I am Joe's body*

Metaphorical sentences	Chinese translation
From time to time, my ignition system gets momentarily out of whack—just like the ignition system of Joe's car	我的起搏系统时不时地会少跳动,就像乔的汽车点火系统一样
I am fed by my own two coronary arteries-little branching "trees" with trunks not much larger than soda straws	我通过我自己的两条冠状动脉滋养,这两条冠状动脉就像分叉的树一样,不比汽水吸管大
The vagus nerves act as a brake	迷走神经的作用像刹车

2) Review of assignment 2: The cardiovascular system

The Cardiovascular System is another CTE (Career and Technical Education) video production which had already been mentioned in the introduction of video *The Nervous System*. It runs for about 9 minutes. Its main focus is on heart, blood vessels and blood. The students were asked to find out the metaphors within the article and the teachers explained them in the class. Six pictures which contain metaphors were stated in the following part. The analysis of the pictures and metaphors are provided as follows.

Describing the function of the heart, Link 4-4 shows a metaphor and the transcript can be seen in the following extract.

The heart pumps the blood in order to move nutrients through the blood vessels to nourish and remove the metabolic wastes from the body. The heart is like twin pumps divided by a septum.

Link 4-4 A Metaphor of Heart

Analysis: In this statement, there are several metaphors like "pump" and "septum". The participant teacher explained the original meaning and the metaphorical meaning of them. For example, the pump is a mechanical device, which uses suction or pressure to move liquids, compressed gases, or force air into inflatable objects such as tyres. Metaphorically heart is admired as a super power pump which pumps 6,000-7,500 liters of blood per day. In Medical English, the word "pump" is often used to describe the function of heart.

Another word is "septum" which means a partition separating two chambers, such as that between the nostrils or the chambers of the heart. It originated from Latin "sepes" which means "hedge". The word "wall" is given within brackets for the sake of clarity. This enables the students to immediately understand the function of septum by comparing it with a wall.

When talking about the function of blood vessels, Link 4-5 shows a metaphor of it and there is a sentence: "…but in anatomy and physiology, blood vessels are meant for carrying blood throughout the body."The picture of cargo ship appears in the video when talking about blood vessels which implies both of them have the same function of delivering objects.

Link 4-5 A Metaphor of Blood Vessels

When talking about the function of arteries and veins, Link 4-6 shows a metaphor and the there is a sentence: "The blood vessels are similar to a two-way highway system. One lane or direction is known as the arteries, and the other is called the veins."There are some similarities between the blood vessels and a two-way highway system. First, both are composed of two parts. Second, the directions of arterial blood and vein blood are opposite which is same with a two-way highway.

Link 4-6 A Metaphor of Arteries

When describing arteries, Link 4-7 shows a metaphorical phrasal verb and there is a sentence: "Arterioles are smaller blood vessels that branch out from larger arteries and lead to the arterial capillaries which are the smallest blood vessels in the body." The verb phrase "branch out" is metaphorical. Its implied metaphor is "arterioles are branches." From this metaphor, students can learn about the characters of arterioles: small and numerous.

Link 4-7 A Screenshot of Arterioles

When talking about the function of arterial capillary and venous capillary, Link 4-8 shows a metaphor (network) and the transcript can be seen in the following extract.

Arterial capillary drops off oxygen and nutrients to the body's cells. Venous capillary picks up metabolic waste from the body's cells. Together they form a network, where arteries and veins connect, completing the (closed) circulatory circuit.

Link 4-8 A Screenshot of Arterial Capillary and Venous Capillary

Analysis: according to the description above of arterial capillary and venous capillary, there is a conceptual metaphor THE CIRCULATORY CIRCUIT IS A NETWORK which entails the following sentences.

Arterial capillary *drops off* oxygen and nutrients to the body's cells.
Venous capillary *picks up* metabolic waste from the body's cells.

When describing the basic function of organ system, a traffic metaphor was used in the video. Link 4-9 shows a metaphoric picture (transportation) and the transcript can be seen in the following extract.

The cardiovascular system is an organ system whose purpose is to circulate to and from cells in the body in order to transport nutrients and remove waste.

Link 4-9 A Metaphor of the Organ System

Analysis: there are several pictures of transportation system in this video which imply the function of the cardiovascular system. For this scenario, words like "stations" "transport" "remove" "blockage" are used to make a comparison.

(2) Assignment: A role play on heart trouble

Since the topic of Unit 3 is about heart, the English expressions of heart were compared with Chinese expressions of heart, and a video of the cardiovascular system was added to help the students learn more about the organ, heart. Heart is the most familiar body part which is used a lot in metaphorical terms in daily life. As students who major in medicine, they were supposed to describe the functions of heart and diseases relating to heart clearly to the patients. Therefore, a role play on heart trouble was assigned to students to enhance their awareness of using metaphors in the conversations with patients, to describe their conditions, and to comfort them.

Students were advised to sign up voluntarily for a role play on heart trouble which would be performed in the next lecture. Since it was the first time for the students to perform a Medical English role play, the teacher participants offered some reference conversation on several heart diseases for students to adapt. They had to use metaphors in their conversation. These reference conversations were extracts from the book *English-Chinese Medical Conversation* published by People's Medical Publishing House (Wang, et al., 2010).

4.3 Preparation, Implementation and Feedback for Metaphor Supplements of Unit 5

During the preparation phase, time management, set induction, text-based metaphor identification and analysis were discussed by the three teachers.

4.3.1 Preparation for metaphor supplements of Unit 5

Time management and supplementary materials were discussed by Ms Wang, Ms Liu and the researcher in detail. The main topics of this discussion were time management for Unit 5, understanding of supplementary metaphors and the content of the assignment. The details of each step are as follows.

4.3.1.1 Time arrangement for Unit 5

According to the academic calendar of Xinxiang Medical University, Unit 5 was conducted from week 10 to week 12. During the preparation phase, the three teachers discussed the video *HIV and AIDS* (Simple show foundation, 2014), the supplementary words, the structural metaphor which embodied this unit and its mapping process and the assignment. The details can be seen in Table 4-22.

Table 4-22 Time Arrangement for Unit 5

Periods	Arrangement	Time/min
Period 1	Assignment review: a role play on heart trouble	15
	Lead-in: a story of Greg Louganis	5
	Watch a video *HIV and AIDS*	10
	Text study: structure	10

Continue to Table 4-22

Periods	Arrangement	Time/min
Period 2	Text study: understanding	10
	Identify metaphors in text	10
	Supplementary materials: structural metaphor	10
	Text study: new words and expressions (1)	10
	Assignment: watch a video *The Immune System*	
Period 3	Assignment review: *The Immune System* (video)	10
	Supplementary materials: msetaphorical expressions of health and medicine that are unique to Chinese	10
	Text study: new words and expressions (2)	20
Period 4	Text study: sentence pattern	20
	Writing technique	20
	Assignment: shoot a video of AIDS	
Period 5	Assignment review: play the self-shot video of students	10
	Set induction (Unit 6)	10
	Text study	20

Note. Each period takes 40 minutes. Words in bold are metaphor enriched supplements.

4.3.1.2 Metaphor identification

The three teachers identified metaphors in the text and discussed them in details. The identified metaphorical words and expressions are deficiency, guide, infect, virus, wipe out, undeclared war, AIDS buster, sign up for an undeclared war, win the war against AIDS, battle against AIDS and guide against the virus (see Table 3-18). Here is an excerpt from Ms Wang and Ms Zhang:

Ms Zhang: *When we talk about the metaphorical words and expressions, their original meanings and metaphorical meanings can be introduced to students.*

Ms Wang: *When talking about the phrase wipe out, I asked the students what is the meaning of wipe? They did not know. I said it means clean up. Suppose there are many things on the table, Mom asks you to clean them up, she will say: "Please wipe them out." Then nothing is on the table. Everything is gone.*

Ms Zhang: *Its original meaning is to clean up. The extended meaning is to destroy. Metaphors are pervasive in articles although we didn't pay attention to them.*

Ms Wang: *For the phrase, be immune to something. In the spoken language, it means not affected or influenced by something.*

Ms Zhang: *Yes, its original meaning is not affected (by something) and then it has a new meaning uninfected in Medical English. This material refers to the immune organs, like ap-*

pendix, the word appendix in common English means the supplementary material that is collected and appended at the back of a book, while in Medical English, it means a tube-shaped sac attached to and opening into the lower end of the large intestine in humans and some other mammals. It came from Latin which means attachment. For a book, "appendix" is materials attached to the back of the article. For the body, appendix is something attached to the back of the large intestine. These two meanings have the similarity, namely, attachment.

Ms Wang: *Right.*

After the discussion of metaphors in the text, Ms Wang and Ms Liu had a better understanding of the way to explain metaphors.

4.3.1.3 Supplementary material: A story of Greg Louganis

The objective of learning these materials was on completion of this part, students should be able to identify metaphorically used words or expressions that can be related to a different source domain, understand the formation of metaphoric words related to the immune system.

For theset induction part, there are a large number of materials relating to HIV and AIDS. Ms Zhang told a story of a diving champion Greg Louganis which was related to HIV and a deep discussion among the three teachers ensued (Bill, 2013). Then the three teachers decided to take this story as the set induction. Here is an excerpt.

Ms Zhang: *When introducing Unit 5, I told a story about the former American diving Olympic champion Greg Louganis who won the diving championship in 1984 and 1988. In a game, his head touched the ground and blood flowed out. When the Olympic officials came to help him, he shouted: "Don't touch me." Later he admitted that he was an HIV positive.*

Ms Wang: *Yes, it is a good example. In this story, David is a HIV positive. Then we need to make students realize that HIV positive is different from AIDS.*

Ms Wang emphasized the difference between HIV positive and AIDS which AIDS reminded Ms Wang of one video named *HIV and AIDS*.

The three teachers watched it and found it was suitable for students due to three reasons. First, there are English and Chinese subtitles which are easy to understand. Second, the time duration is about three minutes and the speaker's speed is very suitable. Third, there are many metaphorical words and images in it. The speaker has used the war scenario to describe how the immune system defends the body against diseases. For example:

The immune system uses guards in the blood called T cells which are to recognize any intruders and destroy them. But instead of attacking the body, the human immunodeficiency virus, or HIV, attacks those T cells themselves. It turns them into copy machines to make more copies of itself, then eventually kills the infected T cells.

In these sentences, T cells are viewed as guards in the blood and viruses are viewed as intruders which attack the guards and kill the infected T cells. These metaphors make the whole process more vivid. Therefore, this video was chosen to play in class.

4.3.2 Implementation for metaphor supplements of Unit 5

The implementation of Unit 5 was conducted from week 10 to week 12. During the implementation phase, four parts were discussed in detail, namely, assignment review, set induction, introduction metaphors in Unit 5, metaphor mechanism analysis and supplementation of metaphoric medical knowledge.

4.3.2.1 Periods 1 and 2 of Unit 5

(1) Metaphor enriched assignment review (role play)

The assignment of Unit 3 is to prepare a role play on heart trouble before week 10 in terms of a group of two or three student participants. As there is no oral test in Chinese College Entrance Examination, speaking ability had often been ignored by teachers and students in high school. After entering college, they were eager to practice oral English, their goals of learning English got transferred from passing the CCEE to communicate with foreigners.

Although this task required them to spend more time on preparation, they showed a great interest in the role play. Because it was the first time they had to speak Medical English, the teachers provided the students with conversations from the book *English-Chinese Medical Conversation* (Wang, 2010) and required them to adapt to using metaphors. At the beginning of lectures on week 10, the students were encouraged to perform in front of their classmates. Here is a picture of their role play (Figure 4-4).

Figure 4-4　A Screenshot of Students' Role Play on Heart Problem

There were three selected conversations from the three teachers' classes, the details of which are explained separately. Conversation 1 was conducted in Ms Zhang's classroom and it refers to four actors, a nurse, a patient, patient's friend and a doctor. In the beginning, the nurse inquired the patient, and then the main show focused on the patient's description of her heart problem and the doctor's suggestion for further treatment. The following extract shows the metaphors they used.

> Doctor: *Oh, what's wrong with you?*
>
> Patient: *I felt sick about my heart. Like the ignition system of a car. It seems that it won't be fired as before.*

When explaining the reason for a bypass heart operation, the doctor used a metaphor to describe this operation. The details are as follows.

> Doctor: *Let me see. Frankly speaking, it is necessary for you to do a cardiac bypass surgery.*
>
> Patient's friend: *What's that? Please explain it in detail.*
>
> Doctor: *Let me make a metaphor. There is a traffic jam in your heart blood vessels. All workers have to build a bridge to make the blood vessels move unobstructed.*

Since the patient's friend did not understand what the cardiac bypass surgery mean, the doctor explained it by using a metaphor. He compared the block in the heart blood vessels to a traffic jam which was very harmful. In order to make the road clear, a bridge was necessary to allow more vehicles to pass. The cardiac bypass surgery was like building a bridge in the blood vessel to allow more blood to pass. This metaphor was very impressive and suitable, and by this way, the patient's friend could understand the importance of the operation immediately.

Conversation 2 was conducted in Ms Liu's classroom, which referred to two actors, a patient and a doctor. In the beginning, the patient told the doctor that he got the angina cordis which would cause shortness of breath sometimes and was worried whether he had got a severe heart attack. Then the doctor asked what kind of pain the patient felt and explained the difference between angina cordis and heart attack in terms of metaphors, and then advised further treatment. The following extract was the metaphor the patient used.

> Doctor: *Well, can you describe your symptoms in detail? For example, when did the pain occur? How long did the pain last? How did you deal with the pain?*
>
> Patient: *I found the pain occurring when I was doing household chores or climbing stairs. At that time, I felt tightness, pressure and a squeezing kind of pain like as if a stone on my heart. Sometimes, the pain radiated to my jaw or the arms like having got an electric shock. Usually, the situation lasted for about five minutes and I applied nitroglycerin as a self-treatment.*

The patient used the expression "a stone on my heart" to describe the pressure caused by heart trouble and "having got an electric shock" to describe the radiating pain. In this way, the doctor could make a judgment quickly. Then, to clear the patient's doubt that he had got heart attack, the doctor used a metaphor to explain the symptoms of a heart attack which relieved the patient of his worry. The following extract was the metaphor the doctor used.

>   Patient: *Is the disease serious, doctor?*
>
>   Doctor: *Not too bad. Angina cordis is not as serious as heart attack. A massive heart attack is like the permanent closure of a large road which is going to cause traffic chaos. If there is a long-term blockage of a large artery supplying blood to the heart muscle, it's going to cause damage and death to a large section of the heart muscle. Take it easy. With proper treatment, you will get better gradually.*

The doctor used a metaphor to describe the symptom of massive heart attack which relieved the patient's anxiety effectively.

Conversation 3 was conducted in Ms Wang's classroom, which had two actors, a patient and a doctor. The patient told the doctor that he suffered chest pain and discomfort and the doctor asked for the exact description. When describing the uncomfortable feeling, a metaphor was used. The following extract shows the metaphors the patient had used.

>   Doctor: *By which you mean?*
>
>   Patient: *A strong banging in my chest as if my heart was going to come out. The heartbeat was irregular just like a speeding motorcycle on the midnight street.*

The patient compared the feeling of the palpitations to a speeding motorcycle on a midnight street which emphasized the fast and irregular heartbeats which helped the doctor to judge the exact condition of the illness.

(2) Set induction for Unit 5

Since the topic of this unit is AIDS, a story of Greg Louganis (a former Olympic diving champion) who was a HIV positive was used asthe set induction. A video *HIV and AIDS* was also played to supplement the students' medical vocabulary on AIDS.

1) Supplementary story: Greg Louganis

The real story refers to one athlete Greg Louganis who was known as "American's diving prince". But in 1988 Olympics in Seoul, Korea, when he climbed the ladder, his body lost control and he hit his head on the board. What was worse was he had a cut on his head and was bleeding. When an official tried to examine his head, he pushed him away and screamed: "Don't touch me!"

Then the teachers posed a question: "He was a very modest and a gentle person. Do you know the reason as to why he screamed at people who wanted to help him?" Quite a few students answered that he was an AIDS patient. Thus, the teachers took this story as the set induction for this unit. The students were interested in the story and quite a number of them guessed the answer.

2) Supplementary video: *HIV and AIDS*

The video *HIV and AIDS* was recommended by Ms Liu who downloaded it from bilibili. It ran for 2 minutes and 47 seconds and explained the difference between HIV and AIDS. As students majoring in medicine, they are supposed to know this difference and the relevant medical words. After playing this video, the teachers analyzed the war scenario and summarized the metaphoric words. For example, there were several entailments in the conceptual metaphor: HUMAN BODY IS A BATTLEGROUND, THE IMMUNE SYSTEM IS THE DEFENDER OF THE HUMAN BODY, T CELLS ARE THE GUARDS IN BLOOD, HIV ARE ATTACKERS OF THE HUMAN BODY.

(3) Metaphor identification

During the period 2, teachers discussed the linguistic metaphors in text, the details can be seen in Table 4-23.

Table 4-23 Metaphors in Text: The Battle Against AIDS

Words	Metaphorical meanings	Examples
Cure	A solution to a problem	It's the only possible cure for our chronic trade deficit
	To solve a problem	Better quality control might cure our production problems
	Relieve (a person or animal) of the symptoms of a condition	Nothing seems to cure him of his tension
Disease	A serious problem in society	Greed is a disease of modern society
	A serious problem with someone's attitude	I have yet to meet a single American who automatically thinks any foreign product must be better than his own. The disease seems to uniquely British
Epidemic	A sudden increase in something bad or unpleasant that affects many people	An epidemic of petty crime has hit the area
Fever	Strong excitement and enthusiasm that affects a lot of people	The whole country was in the grip of election fever
Inject	To add something new to a situation	Young designers are injecting new life into the fashion scene

Continue to Table 4-23

Words	Metaphorical meanings	Examples
Symptom	A sign of a larger problem	The fighting is a symptom of growing insecurity in the region
Syndrome	A set of feelings or actions that are typical in a particular situation	Many parents face "empty nest syndrome" when their children leave home

During the second period, the teachers discussed the linguistic metaphors in the prescribed text. Then a structural conceptual metaphor was summarized: TREATING ILLNESS IS FIGHTING A WAR. The teachers explained the mapping from source domain to target domain. The details are in Table 4-24.

Table 4-24　The Mapping of TREATING ILLNESS IS FIGHTING A WAR

Source domain	Mapping	Target domain
War	→	Illness
Field	→	Body
Enemy	→	HIV/bacteria/virus
Arm	→	Medicine
Defense system	→	Immune system
Win	→	Recover
Lose	→	Die

(4) Assignment: A video *Inner World Discovery: The Immune System*

With the 3D effect and bilingual subtitles, students were interested in acquiring the medical knowledge by watching this video. It runs for about 7 minutes which makes it suitable as the supplementary material in the classroom. It mainly explains what are HIV and AIDS; how this virus attacks and spreads in the human body and destroy the immune system; the common AIDS related opportunistic infections, including meningitis, encephalitis, pneumonia and tuber, intestinal diseases and cancers; how one gets HIV; antiretroviral meditations and therapeutic method and ways to avoid a HIV infection. The requirement is to find out the metaphors in it.

4.3.2.2　Periods 3 and 4 of Unit 5

(1) *Inner World Discovery: The Immune System*

The video *Inner World Discovery* (2010) is made by Dr. Phillip Silverstein, who is presently a full-time emergency physician in California. He received his medical degree from State University of New York Upstate Medical University and has been in practice for more than 20 years. He continues his role as an educator through live appearances, internet presentations, and distribution of *Inner World Discovery* published material. This video is from the *Inner World Discovery*. The conceptual metaphor TREATING ILLNESS IS FIGHTING A WAR can be found throughout the whole video, as well as the use of personification, which makes the knowledge of the immune system very attractive and vivid. Through a battle between the immune system with Hepatitis A, the students can learn about the functions of macrophage, T-4 helper cell, Cytotoxic T cell, B cell and antibodies. Their different division of work and cooperation are emphasized. Besides, it can also cultivate the students' metaphoric identification competence. The answers are as follows (Table 4-25).

Table 4-25 Scenario of War Metaphor: TREATING ILLNESS IS FIGHTING A WAR

Tenor	Vehicle	Similarities
Hepatitis A virus	Invader/attacker	Both can attack or invade others
Immune system	Defense system	Both can defense itself from foreign invasion
Macrophage	Captain Mac	Both can spy something suspicious
T-4 helper cell	General T-4	Both can command all the forces
Cytotoxic T cell	Tox team	Both can use chemical agents to destroy enemies on command
B cell	U.S.S. B-142 (aircraft carrier)	Both can carry out attacks at great distances away
Fighter-M/Fighter-G	Antibody	Both can kill foreign invaders

After analyzing the scenario of war metaphor, the teachers explained the metaphoric words in the video to enhance students' medical vocabulary. The details are as follows (Table 4-26).

Table 4-26 Supplementary Metaphorical Words

Word parts (prefix/root/suffix)	Medical terms	Meaning
Anti-	Antibody	A molecule generated in specific opposition to an antigen
	Antigen	Substance that includes sensitivity or an immune response in the form of antibodies
	Antiretroviral	Inhibiting the process by which a retrovirus replicates
	Antibiotics	Medical drugs used to kill bacteria and treat infections
Immun/o	Immune	Safe from a disease
	Immunodeficiency	Impairment of the immune system
	Immunization	Process by which resistance to an infectious disease is induced

Continue to Table 4-26

Word parts (prefix/root/suffix)	Medical terms	meaning
-itis	Immunology	The medical specialty dealing with the immune system
	Immunotherapy	The treatment of disease by stimulating the body's production of antibodies
	Meningitis	A serious illness in which the outer part of the brain becomes swollen
	Thymitis	Inflammation of the thymus
	Encephalitis	Inflammation of the brain usually caused by a virus
Virus	Retrovirus	A virus of a type that includes some cancer viruses and the aids virus
	Virion	A virus in infective form, consisting of an RNA particle within a protein covering

(2) Supplementary materials: Metaphorical expressions of health and medicine those are unique to Chinese

In order to deepen the students' understanding of the difference between English and Chinese metaphorical expressions of health and medicine, some unique Chinese expressions were provided in the class. The details are as follows (Table 4-27).

Table 4-27　Metaphorical Expressions of Health and Medicine that are Unique to Chinese

Chinese	English
边患	Trouble on the frontier (as caused by foreign invasion)
好了伤疤忘了疼	Forget the pain once the wound is healed
换汤不换药	The same medicine with a different name
祸患	Disaster
旧病复发	Relapse into one's old bad habits
无病呻吟	Adopt a sentimental pose (in writing or speech)
心腹之患	Disease in one's vital organs-danger from within
包治百病	Be guaranteed to cure all ills
病急乱投医	Try anything or consult anybody when in a desperate plight
病入膏肓	Beyond cure
不可救药	Hopeless
不治之症	Incurable disease
旧病复发	Have a relapse
灵丹妙药	Panacea
手到病除	Illness departs at a touch of the hand

Note. Words in bold are Chinese characters relating to health and medicine.

The Chinese characters in bold are relating to health or medicine, while there is no English equivalence. Therefore, the question of how to understand and translate these metaphoric expressions aroused the interest of the students.

(3) Metaphor enriched assignment: Shoot a video on AIDS

In order to enhance the students' metaphor production ability, team work, subjectivity and creativity, they were assigned homework: to shoot a video on AIDS in English which should run for less than three minutes. Three topics were recommended to them: diagnosis of AIDS, attitudes towards an AIDS patient, and AIDS education. The students were required to join in groups in terms of dormitory and this assignment was supposed to be submitted before the next lecture.

(4) Metaphor enriched assignment review

After reviewing the students' self-recorded videos, several good ones had been chosen to present in class during week 12 which aroused the students' enthusiasm for watching and discussing.

1) The students' self-recorded videos from Ms Wang's class

The Self-recorded videos of three students were selected to be presented in Ms Liu's class.

The first video: *AIDS education.*

Six students participated in the recording of this video and they had talked about their understanding of AIDS and posed questions for reflection. The characteristics of this video: Six questions were asked by each student. These questions made the audience thoroughly understand the stress and pains of AID patients. A metaphor was used to describe the AIDS patients' inner world. One student used a question: If you are suffering from AIDS, are you willing to be swallowed by the boundless darkness? This sentence implied that the getting of AIDS was like being swallowed by a deep darkness. It belongs to the orientational metaphor, with HAPPY IS UP, SAD IS DOWN as the most frequent metaphor. At the end of the video, people were encouraged to shower love and concern for the patients. Some pictures of red ribbon were shown to attract the people's attention.

The second video: *Diagnosis of AIDS.*

This video did not emphasize the inquiry from a doctor, but the patient's painful narration of the inner feelings. Sometimes, spiritual comfort is as important as drug treatment. The characteristics of this video: The patient feels so miserable that he uses a metaphoric word *monster* to describe AIDS which has destroyed his life. He lives in a world without care, love and trust. His expressions made the audience have empathy. The doctor, by using another metaphoric sentence, encouraged the patient to face life bravely: "If you take drugs on time, you will control it like a trainer who can control a monster". If AIDS is a monster, the patient should actively face and control it like a trainer. This metaphoric sentence could comfort and establish the relationship with the patient. At the end of the video, information of World AIDS Day was given. The theme of 2017 World AIDS Day is "spread our love". Therefore, a good doctor should practice medicine with empathy and care.

The third video: *Encouragement for AIDS patient*.

The topic of this videowas a campus test to assert whether the AIDS patients could get a hug from strangers. It was recorded by six students of a dormitory, in which one acted as the AIDS patient and the others as strangers. The characteristics of this video: The indifference and discrimination towards the patients can be understood from the strangers' reactions. Although there were not many words, the effect was very impressive. Different from many other videos that lecture with turn-taking dialogue, it is more vivid. The storyline is very rich, using a campus test to show people's various reactions towards the hugging of an AIDS patient. At the end of the video, they depicted the process of re-shoot and the resulting tiredness of shooting.

2) The students' self-recorded videos from Ms Liu's class

The first video: *AIDS education*.

The background of this video is the approach of the 30th AIDS Day. Four students talked about the situation of AIDS and appealed for the right attitude towards AIDS patients and the improving of their life conditions. The characteristics of this video: Each student had prepared and found some data about AIDS. Their dialogues were well prepared. There are quite a few metaphors referring to this disease. For example, the words "evil" and "horrible killers" are metaphors of AIDS which emphasize its deadly effect on people.

The second video: *Discrimination against AIDS patients*.

This video consists of three acts which tells a complete story. It is not a mere discussion but a performance based on a real story. At the beginning, there was a brief introduction to the background of the story. A girl who was HIV positive was eating with her father and stepmother. The first act showed a girl asking her father to take a dish she prepared for him which made her stepmother very angry. In the second act the girl requested a kiss but her dad refused and she was told that she would get a kiss after recovery. The third act deals with the main aspects of AIDS and appealed for love and care towards the patients. This video focuses on how to treat children with AIDS. One possible way of transmission of AIDS is from mother-to-child. The children are innocent who should not be shown any discrimination, especially by their parents and relatives. After watching the video, students acquired the right attitude and determined to bekind to the patients.

The third video: *An AIDS patient's diary*.

One group of students shot a special video, named *An AIDS patient's diary*. It is a diary written on a notebook and one student reads it with emotion. Although there was no complex dialogue and a story of interest, the effect was very impressive. The audience seemed to enter the patient's inner world and deeply felt their misery. Though the diary contains a month long entries, only five days' entries were shown in the video. On the first day, after receiving the report of confirmation of AIDS, the hero used "death penalty" to describe his feeling. There is a metaphor: GETTING AIDS IS RECEIVING DEATH PENALTY. Both mean imminent death. On the second day, the hero said he could not find reasons to live. Day three was a nightmare which made the hero feel he has reached the end. On the fourth day, the hero compared his world to a dark world which made the readers sympathize with him. Then on the thirtieth day, the hero changed his pessimistic attitude after seeing his mother's eyes. Though he lived in a dark world, his mother's sad eyes like the stars in the deep dark night gave him hope, solace and courage. This metaphor implies that he wants to change. In the end, he compared his peaceful mind to living in a realm, which was no more dark, guided by the gods.

Chapter 5

Findings and Discussion

This chapter focuses on the students' perspective on metaphor enriched English language instruction with supplementary materials. It discusses the first-year students' metaphor cognition ability according to the result obtained from the Metaphor Cognition Questionnaire. It ascertains as to whether the students' English study has improved after the implementation of the self-designed English conversations, self-recorded videos, and scenario writing. It also ascertained if the students' metaphoric competence has enhanced by using the Metaphoric Competence Test and further by discussing the students' feedback on the metaphor enriched language instruction with supplementary materials. Therefore, research questions one, three and four will be analyzed and answered.

5.1 Research Question 1: What is Students' Current Metaphoric Cognition with the First-year College Students at Xinxiang Medical University China?

Since metaphor was only mentioned as a figure of speech and often compared with simile in high school, many students do not realize that it also can be a cognitive tool in the cognitive language. They do not realize it is pervasive in daily life with a long history, not to speak of the metaphors in medical articles. In order to ascertain the students' metaphor cognition competence in General English and Medical English, a metaphor cognition questionnaire was distributed to the students of three lecturers in class and the details of each part is discussed in detail.

5.1.1 Data analysis of metaphor cognition questionnaire

The Metaphor Cognition Questionnaire (Appendix B) is the modification of Wei

Yaozhang's questionnaire on investigating the influence of cognitive competence on students' understanding and generating of metaphors (Wei, 2007). At the very beginning of the test, there is a rubric in Chinese, briefly explaining what a metaphor is with simple examples. The first part is the demographic information of the respondents. Part two consists of 10 items referring to their identification and understanding of metaphors in General English. Part three is composed of 8 items which refer to the understanding of medical metaphors. Since the purpose of the research is to learn about the participants' understanding of metaphors, the five-point likert scale was adapted to four categories to eliminate the "neutral" option in a "forced choice" survey scale. The four scales were, strongly disagree, disagree, agree and strongly agree. Numbers were assigned to these four scales. Namely, 1 = strongly disagree, 2 = disagree, 3 = agree, and 4 = strongly agree. Participants were required to choose one according to their understanding. The data were analyzed by SPSS(22.0).

5.1.2 Data analysis of metaphor cognition questionnaire on Ms Wang's class

The Metaphor Cognition Questionnaire was distributed to 164 first-year college students of Ms Wang's class. All these students major in Medical Imaging. 158 of them completed and returned the questionnaires. The recovery rate was 98.8%.

5.1.2.1 Demographic profile of respondents

The demographic information of 158 respondents included age, gender, major and their National College Entrance Examine (NCEE) English scores. The ages of the 158 respondents are shown in Table 5-1.

Table 5-1 Age of Respondents (Ms Wang's Class)

Age	Questionnaire	
	Frequency	Percent/%
17	108	68.4
18	41	26.0
19	5	3.2
20	2	1.2
21	2	1.2
Total	158	100.0

According to Table 5-1, in terms of age, 108 respondents (68.4%) were 17 years old, which makes the majority of the 158 respondents; 41 respondents (26.0%) were 18 years old; 5 respondents (3.2%) were 19 years old; there were 2 respondents in 20-year-old group and

21-year-old group which was 1.2% of the 158 respondents. As regards the gender, the detailed percentage is shown in Table 5-2.

Table 5-2　Gender of Respondents (Ms Wang's Class)

Gender	Questionnaire	
	Frequency	Percent/%
Male	56	35.4
Female	102	64.6
Total	158	100.0

Among the 158 respondents, 102 respondents (64.6%) were females and 56 respondents (35.4%) were males. The detailed percentage of English achievement is shown in Table 5-3.

Table 5-3　English Achievement of Respondents (Ms Wang's Class)

English achievement (NCEE English score)	Questionnaire	
	Frequency	Percent/%
< 90	15	9.5
90-100	14	8.9
101-110	41	25.9
111-120	54	34.2
121-130	28	17.7
> 130	6	3.8
Total	158	100.0

For the English achievement, 158 respondents were required to write down their National College Entrance Exam (NCEE) English scores which were divided into six groups. The 111-120 group had taken the largest percentage (34.2%); then the 101-110 group was the second with 25.9%; the 121-130 group was 17.7%; the less than 90 group was 9.5%; the 90-100 group was 8.9%; the more than 130 group had the smallest percentage (3.8%). From the percentage, it was easy to find that the English scores of most of the respondents belonged to 101-110 group and 111-120 group which means their English level was relatively good.

5.1.2.2　Part one: Metaphor cognition

There were ten items relating to students' metaphor cognition and the detailed percentage of each item can be seen in Table 5-4.

Table 5-4 Percentage of Items on Metaphor Cognition (Ms Wang's Class)

Questionnaire items	SD/%	D/%	A/%	SA/%
1. I know that there are many metaphors in General English	3.2	15.8	46.2	34.8
2. I know that metaphors in English articles can make language more vivid	1.9	0.6	30.4	67.1
3. I find teachers always use metaphors in their instruction	0.6	33.5	55.1	10.8
4. I know that some conceptual metaphors in English are different from those in Chinese	1.3	7.0	51.9	39.8
5. I know that some metaphorical expressions in English are different from those in Chinese	1.9	2.5	50.0	45.6
6. The image of the compared object will immediately flash in my mind when I find metaphors	5.7	31.6	44.9	17.8
7. I will understand metaphors in the context of the texts	1.3	15.8	48.7	34.2
8. I will consciously apply metaphors which I have learned in the classroomin my writing	7.6	47.5	34.8	10.1
9. When communicating with English native speakers in English, I often discuss metaphors with them	20.3	50.0	24.7	5.1
10. I often try to express my ideas through new metaphors	11.4	42.4	34.8	11.4

Note. $N = 158$.

Item 1 showed that 81.0% respondents knew that there were many metaphors in general English and 19.0% respondents did not know it. Item 2 referred to the function of metaphor. 97.5% respondents affirmed the vividness of metaphor, only 2.5% respondents disagreed with its function. Item 3 involved in the teacher's usage of metaphors. 65.9% respondents thought their teachers often used metaphors in their instruction while 34.1% respondents disagreed. Items 4 and 5 related to the difference between English metaphors and Chinese metaphors. 91.7% respondents realized the difference while 8.3% respondents did not. For metaphorical expressions, 95.6% respondents realized the difference while 4.4% respondents did not. Items 6 and 7 involved the understanding approaches of metaphors. 62.7% respondents could associate the images of compared objects, while 37.3% respondents could not. 82.9% respondents could understand metaphors in the context of the texts, while only 17.1% respondents could not. Comparing Item 6 with Item 7, it could be ascertained that respondents were more likely to understand metaphors through context rather than the images. Items 8, 9 and 10 relate to the application of metaphors. Although respondents thought that metaphors were important and common in daily life, 55.1% of respondents did not use it in their writing and speaking. 70.3% of them did not use metaphors to communicate with English native speakers, 53.8% of them did not think of creating new metaphors to express their ideas.

The Figure 5-1 is the histogram of the distribution on metaphor cognition.

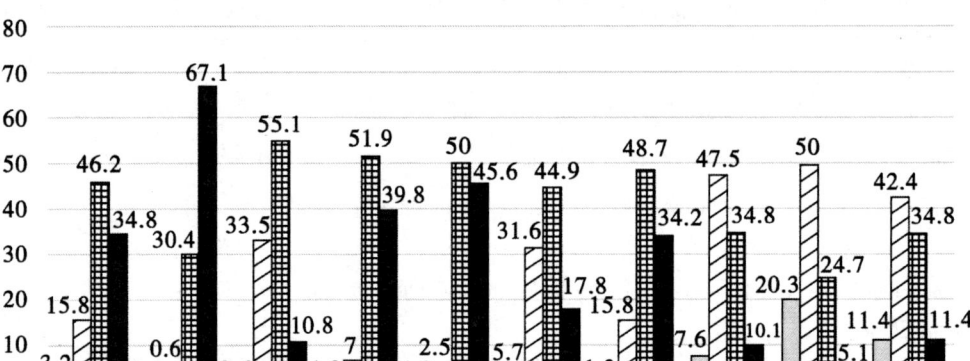

Figure 5-1 Percentage of Items on Metaphor Cognition (Ms Wang's Class)

Note. N=158.

In brief, respondents can realize the existence of metaphors in General English and the teachers' instruction, and they know the function of metaphors, for the understanding approaches, more respondents understand it in terms of context rather than the images. However, less than a half of them only can apply metaphors in their writing and speaking.

5.1.2.3 Part two: Metaphors and medical metaphors

There are 8 items relating to students' understanding of medical metaphor and the detailed percentage of each item can be seen in Table 5-5.

Table 5-5 Percentage of Items on Metaphors and Medical English (Ms Wang's Class)

Questionnaire items	SD/%	D/%	A/%	SA/%
11. I know that there are many metaphors in Medical English	5.1	35.4	41.8	17.7
12. I am sensitive to metaphors in the articles in medical journals	8.9	50.0	31.6	9.5
13. Metaphors help me to memorize medical words	1.3	12.7	56.3	29.7
14. Metaphors help me to understand the medical terms	0.6	12.7	48.1	38.6
15. Metaphorical expressions help me to understand the illness	1.3	11.4	60.1	29.7
16. I think it is interesting to understand medical articles from the perspective of metaphors	1.9	7.6	58.2	32.3
17. I realize that using metaphors can express the phenomenon that some non-metaphorical languages cannot express	0.6	7.0	43.7	48.7
18. I will use metaphors to explain conditions of illness to my patients in future	3.2	15.2	51.3	30.4

Note. N=158.

Items 11 and question 12 relate to the respondents' cognition of medical metaphors. Item 11 shows that 59.5% respondents knew that there were many metaphors in Medical English, compared with 81% in General English, which indicates less respondents knew the existence of medical metaphors. Item 12 shows that only 41.1% respondents were sensitive to medical metaphors, which indicates more than a half of the respondents could not identify medical metaphors. Items 13 to 17 relate to the functions of medical metaphors. 86% respondents knew that a metaphor contributed to understanding medical words, 86.7% respondents believed it contributes to memorizing medical words, 89.8% respondents affirm that it helps to understand the illness, 90.5% respondents thought it is an interesting approach to understand medical articles, and 92.4% respondents believed metaphor can express the phenomenon that some non-metaphorical languages cannot. Item 18 involves the future application of metaphor in explaining conditions of illness to patients. 81.7% respondents chose to apply it in future which implicates that most respondents had realized the importance of the metaphor. The Figure 5-2 is the distribution of students' cognition on medical metaphors.

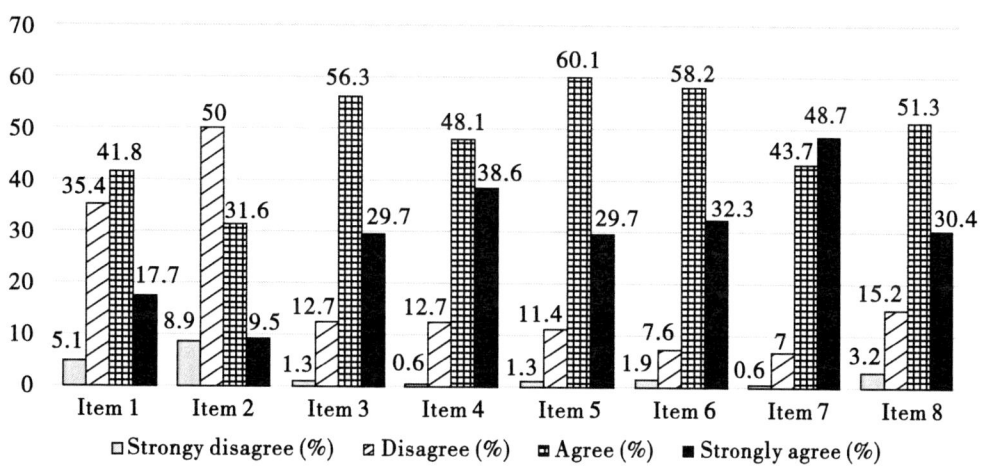

Figure 5-2 Percentage of Items on Medical Metaphors (Ms Wang's Class)

Note. N=158.

In brief, compared with 81% respondents who knew there were many metaphors in general English, 59.5% respondents knew of metaphors in Medical English. There is an obvious difference in the percentage. Only 41.1% respondents were sensitive to medical metaphors, which indicates their ignorance of metaphors in Medical English. Although nearly half of the respondents were not familiar with medical metaphors, they confirmed functions of metaphor in understanding and memorizing medical wordsand illnesses. 81.7% of the respondents would use metaphors in their future careers.

5.1.3 Data analysis of metaphor cognition questionnaire on Ms Liu's class

The Metaphor Cognition Questionnaire was distributed to 140 first-year college students of Ms Wang's class. All these students major in Psychiatry and Paediatrics. 130 of them completed and returned the questionnaires. The recovery rate is 92.9%. Demographic information for this questionnaire is presented as follows.

5.1.3.1 Demographic profile of respondents

The demographic information of 130 respondents is shown in Table 5-6. The age groups are as follows.

Table 5-6 Age of Respondents (Ms Liu's Class)

Age	Questionnaire	
	Frequency	Percent/%
17	78	60.0
18	36	27.7
19	10	14.6
20	4	3.1
21	2	1.6
Total	130	100.0

According to Table 5-6, in terms of age, 78 respondents (60.0%) are 17 years old, which forms the majority; 36 respondents (27.7%) are 18 years old; 10 respondents (14.6%) are 19 years old; there are 4 respondents belong to 20-year-old group and 2 respondents to 21-year-old group which are 3.1% and 1.6% respectively. In terms of gender, the detailed percentage is shown in Table 5-7.

Table 5-7 Gender of Respondents (Ms Liu's Class)

Gender	Questionnaire	
	Frequency	Percent/%
Male	36	27.7
Female	94	72.3
Total	130	100.0

Of the 130 respondents, 94 respondents (72.3%) are females and 36 respondents

(27.7%) are males. The detailed percentage of English achievement is given in Table 5-8.

Table 5-8 English Achievement of Respondents (Ms Liu's Class)

English achievement (NCEE English score)	Questionnaire	
	Frequency	Percent/%
< 90	5	3.8
90-100	4	3.1
101-110	32	24.6
111-120	44	33.8
121-130	38	29.2
> 130	7	5.4
Total	130	100.0

For the English achievement, 130 respondents were required to write down their National College Entrance Exam (NCEE) English scores who divided into six groups. The 111-120 group is the largest (33.8%); the 121-130 group forms 29.2%; the 101-110 group is 24.6%; the less than 90 group takes 3.8%; the above 130 group forms 5.4%; the 90-100 group forms the smallest percentage (3.1%). From the percentage above mentioned, it is easy to find the English scores of most of the respondents belong to the 111-120 group and 121-130 group which means their English level are relatively good.

5.1.3.2 Part one: Metaphor cognition

There were 10 items and each was followed by four choices for the subjects to judge the degree at which that corresponds the most precisely to their actual fact. To avoid ambiguity and for participants to correctly understand the items, the items were described both in Chinese and English (Table 5-9).

Table 5-9 Percentage of Items on Metaphor Identification (Ms Liu's Class)

Questionnaire items	SD/%	D/%	A/%	SA/%
1. I know that there are many metaphors in General English	0.8	13.1	56.2	30.0
2. I know that metaphors in English articles can make language more vivid	2.3	6.2	35.4	56.2
3. I find teachers always use metaphors in their instruction	7.7	43.8	40.8	7.7
4. I know that some conceptual metaphors in English are different from those in Chinese	0.8	21.5	49.2	28.5
5. I know that some metaphorical expressions in English are different from those in Chinese	2.3	16.2	43.8	37.7

Continue to Table 5-9

Questionnaire items	SD/%	D/%	A/%	SA/%
6. The image of the compared object will immediately flash in my mind when I find metaphors	11.5	43.8	32.3	12.4
7. I will understand metaphors in the context of the texts	3.8	10.8	62.3	23.1
8. I will consciously apply metaphors which I have learned in the classroom in my writing	11.5	47.7	34.6	6.2
9. When communicating with English native speakers in English, I often discuss metaphors with them	29.2	55.4	10.0	5.4
10. I often try to express my ideas through new metaphors	11.5	50.8	28.5	9.2

Note. N=130.

Item 1 showed that 86.2% respondents knew that there were many metaphors in General English which indicates that the majority of respondents knew the existence of metaphors, while there are still 13.9% respondents who did not know it. Item 2 was about the function of metaphor. 91.6% respondents affirmed the vividness of metaphors; only 8.4% respondents disagreed with its function. Item 3 stated teacher's usage of metaphors. 48.5% respondents thought their teachers always used metaphors in their instruction while 51.5% respondents disagreed. Items 4 and 5 related to the difference between English metaphors and Chinese metaphors. 77.7% of the respondents had realized the difference while 22.3% respondents did not. For metaphorical expressions, 81.5% of the respondents realized the difference while 18.5% respondents did not. Items 6 and 7 presented the understanding approaches of metaphors. 44.7% respondents could associate the images of the compared objects, while 55.3% respondents could not. 85.4% respondents understood metaphors in the context of the texts, while only 14.6% respondents did not. It could be found that the respondents were more likely to understand metaphors through the context rather than the images. Items 8, 9 and 10 related to the application of metaphors. Although respondents had realized that metaphors were important and common in daily life, more than a half of the respondents did not use it in their writing and speaking. 59.2% respondents did not use metaphors in their writing and 84.6% of them did not use metaphors to communicate with English native speakers, 62.3% of them did not think of creating new metaphors to express their ideas.

The Figure 5-3 is the distribution on metaphor cognition.

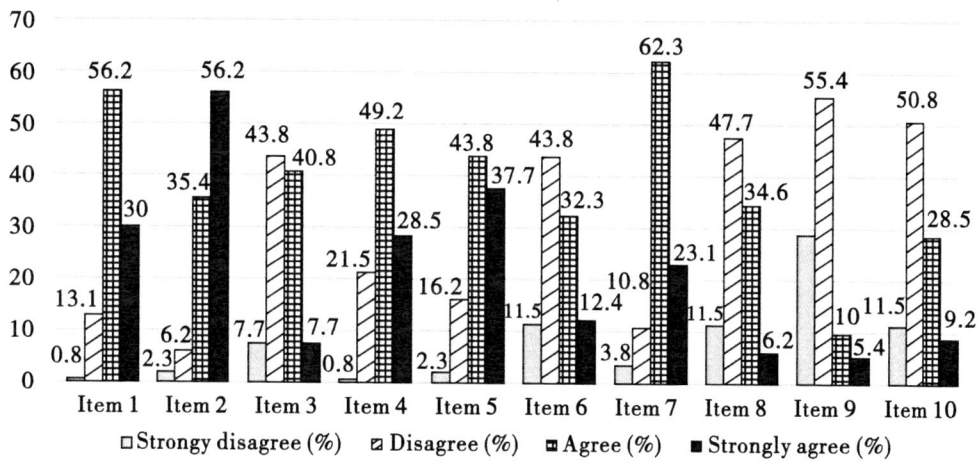

Figure 5-3 Percentage of Items on Metaphor Cognition (Ms Liu's Class)

Note. N=130.

In brief, the respondents could realize the existence of metaphors in General English and the teachers' instruction, and they knew the function of metaphors. As for the understanding approaches, more respondents had understood it in terms of context rather than the images. However, less than a half of them could apply metaphors to their writing and speaking.

5.1.3.3 Part two: Metaphor and medical metaphor

Items 11 and 12 related to the respondents' cognition of medical metaphors. Question 11 shows that 70.0% of the respondents knew that there were many metaphors in Medical English, compared with 86.2% of the respondents of General English, which indicates fewer respondents knew the existence of medical metaphors. Item 12 showed that only 32.3% respondents were sensitive to medical metaphors, which indicates 67.7% respondents could not identify medical metaphors. Items 13 to 17 involved in the functions of medical metaphors. 77.7% of the respondents knew that metaphors contributed to the understanding of medical words, 80.7% respondents believed it contributes to memorizing medical words, 86.2% respondents affirmed that it helps to understand the illness, 83.1% respondents thought it was an interesting approach to understand medical articles, and 93.0% respondents believed metaphor could express the phenomenon that some non-metaphorical languages could not. Item 18 stated the future application of metaphor in explaining conditions of illness to patients. 83.1% respondents chose to apply it in future which implies that most respondents had realized the importance of metaphor(Table 5-10).

Table 5-10 Percentage of Items on Metaphors and Medical English (Ms Liu's Class)

Questionnaire items	SD/%	D/%	A/%	SA/%
11. I know that there are many metaphors in Medical English	4.6	25.4	43.8	26.2
12. I am sensitive to metaphors in the articles in medical journals	16.2	51.5	25.4	6.9
13. Metaphors help me to memorize medical words	5.4	16.9	47.7	30.0
14. Metaphors help me to understand the medical terms	2.3	16.9	46.9	33.8
15. Metaphorical expressions help me to understand the illness	3.1	10.8	56.2	30.0
16. I think it is interesting to understand medical articles from the perspective of metaphors	0.8	16.2	50.8	32.3
17. I realize that using metaphors can express the phenomenon that some non-metaphorical languages cannot express	1.5	5.4	51.5	41.5
18. I will use metaphors to explain conditions of illness to my patients in future	3.8	13.1	56.2	26.9

Note. N = 130.

The Figure 5-4 is the distribution of students' cognition on medical metaphors.

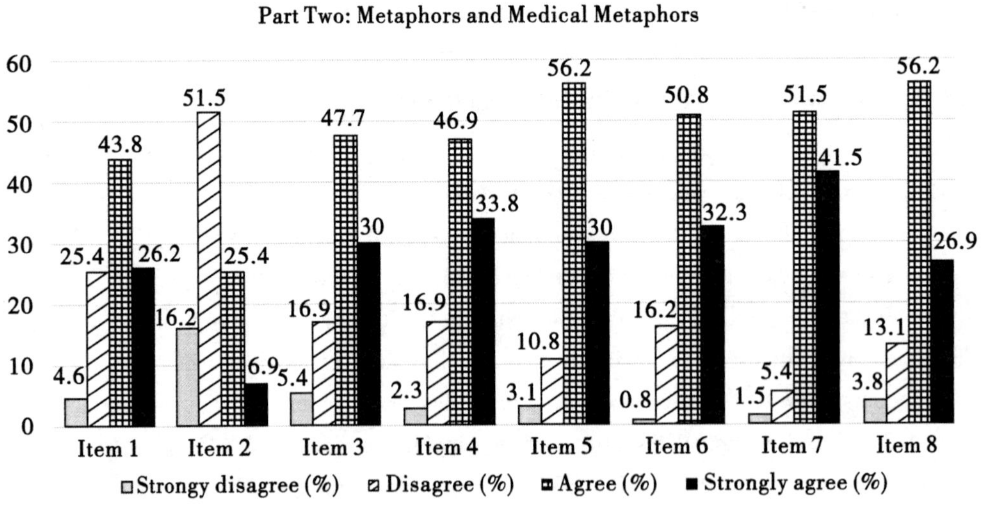

Figure 5-4 Percentage of Items on Medical Metaphors (Ms Liu's Class)

Note. N = 130.

While there are 86.2% respondents who knew there were many metaphors in General English, 70.0% respondents were aware of metaphors in Medical English. Only 32.3% respondents were sensitive to medical metaphors, which also indicates their ignorance of metaphors in Medical English. Although, nearly half of the respondents were not familiar with medical metaphors, they confirmed the role of metaphors in understanding and memorizing medical words as well as illnesses. 83.1% respondents would use metaphors in their future careers.

5.2 Research Question 2: What is the Effect of Metaphor Enriched Language Instruction on First-year Medical Students' Metaphoric Competence?

The importance of metaphoric competence has already been discussed in Chapter two. In order to ascertain the improvement of the students' metaphoric competence, two tests including the pre-test and the post-test were assigned to the students (Appendix C). The full score is 100 and the participants were required to complete it within forty minutes. There was a brief introduction in Chinese at the beginning, which aims to explain what a metaphor is with the mapping process. This test compromises of three parts, metaphor recognition, metaphor interpretation and metaphor production. For metaphor recognition, there were 20 sentences which require the students to judge as to what extent they are metaphoric expressions. For metaphor interpretation, five conceptual metaphors were provided and the students are supposed to write down the similarities between the source domain and target domain. For metaphor production, two sentences were completed by the students, namely, "Learning English is…" and "Treating illness is…" The scoring of the test is presented as follows.

5.2.1 Scoring of metaphoric competence test

5.2.1.1 Introduction of scorers

Scoring is a very essential step in the whole research. A scoring system with a high reliability can ensure the validity of the test. In this empirical research, along with the researcher, two teacher participants (Ms Liu and Ms Wang) were invited and trained in order to achieve this goal. Ms Liu is an instructor with 14 years of college English teaching experience. Ms Wang is an instructor with 16 years of college English teaching experience. She studied and communicated with the local people in Australia for two years. The researcher has studied metaphor theories and the relation between metaphor and culture for five years. Before the valuation took place, all the evaluators had been trained so thoroughly that they fully understood the specific requirements of the test. All the explanations about these items were evaluated independently. Whenever differences arose among the three evaluators in the awarding of marks for the same item, the researcher would organize a discussion in order to reach an agreement.

5.2.1.2 The distribution of scores

A total of 100 marks for all the items is distributed unevenly in the test. Part A refers to the Metaphor Recognition which consists of twenty items of English sentences, each item gets 2 marks. Part B refers to the Metaphor Interpretation which consists of five conceptual metaphors, with each item getting six marks, each correct answer gets two marks. Part C refers to the Metaphor Production which consists of two descriptions of "Learning English is..." and "Treating illness is..." Fifteen marks for each sentence, and each correct answer gets 3 marks. A high score indicates that the participants are more competent in understanding and producing L2 metaphors.

5.2.2 Data analysis on metaphoric competence test (Ms Wang's class)

158 students of Ms Wang's class participated in the pre-test and the post-test. 135 of them completed and returned the questionnaires. For the results of the pre-test and the post-test, the statistic descriptive analysis was conducted.

5.2.2.1 Descriptive analysis of results of MCT and NCEE (Ms Wang's class)

The Table 5-11 shows a statistic description of the participants' scores in the Metaphoric Competence Test (MCT) and the National College Entrance Examination (NCEE). The total marks for NCEE is 150 while for the MCT it is 100. The researcher converted the score of NCEE to the hundred-mark system. As for the first-year college students, they had not attended any other national examination except the NCEE, so NCEE mark is taken as a reference of students' English competence.

Table 5-11 Descriptive Statistics of MCT and NCEE (Ms Wang's Class)

	NCEE	MCT	
		Pre-test	Post-test
Num of valid cases	135	135	135
Mean	74.38	34.76	46.21
Std. Deviation	9.180	11.056	11.005
Range	53	66	59
Skewness	-1.224	0.268	0.197
Kurtosis	2.434	0.636	-0.195
Minimum	39	11	20
Maximum	92	77	79

Note. $N = 135$.

In Table 5-11, the arithmetical average mark of NCEE is 74.38, of the pre-test is 34.76 and of the post-test is 46.21. It is evident that the student participants did not perform well in the pre-test and the post-test compared to their NCEE scores, though their post-test scores have shown marked improvement. In the 135 candidates, the highest score of the NCEE is 92, and the lowest is 39. The range or the spread of different marks from the maximum 92 to minimum 39 is 53. The highest mark in the pre-test (MCT) is 77 and the lowest is 11. The range or the spread of different marks is 66. The highest mark of the post-test (MCT) is 79 and the lowest is 20. The range or the spread of different marks is 59. The standard deviation in NCEE is 9.180, in the pre-test (MCT) 11.056 and in the post-test 11.005. It is obvious that the marks of the CCEE and the two MCT tests are not uniformly distributed.

Figure 5-5 shows the histogram provided by the SPSS, where we can see this central tendency more clearly in the bar chart. Though the curve in the figure is a normal distribution curve, the scores of the two MCT tests are not uniformly distributed. Based on this histogram and the positive skew of 0.268 (pre-test) and 0.197 (post-test) reported in Table 5-11, we can find that it is positively skewed. The kurtosis of the two curves is 0.636 (pre-test) and -0.195 (post-test) which means the curve of the pre-test is leptokurtic and the curve of the post-test is platykurtic. We can see that most of the two MCT scores are centered in the middle and lower part which is quite different from the scores in NCEE. Figure 5-5 is the frequency of NCEE scores.

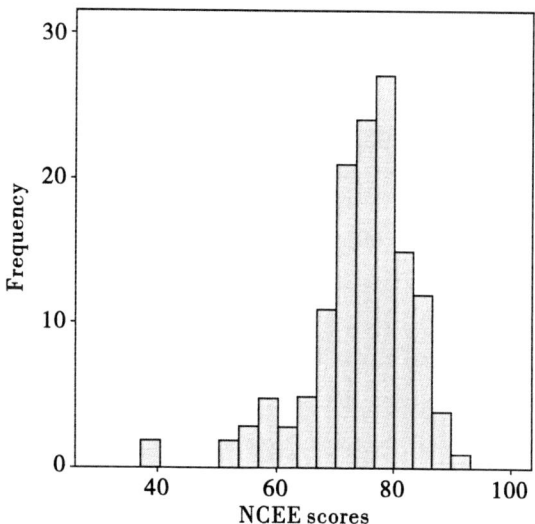

Figure 5-5 The National College Entrance Examination (Ms Wang's Class)

Note. $N = 135$.

Figure 5-5 shows that most of the students' marks is over 60 and more than half of the students marksis over 70, which means they did well in the NCEE examination. Figure 5-6 shows the students' pre-test marks and post-test marks.

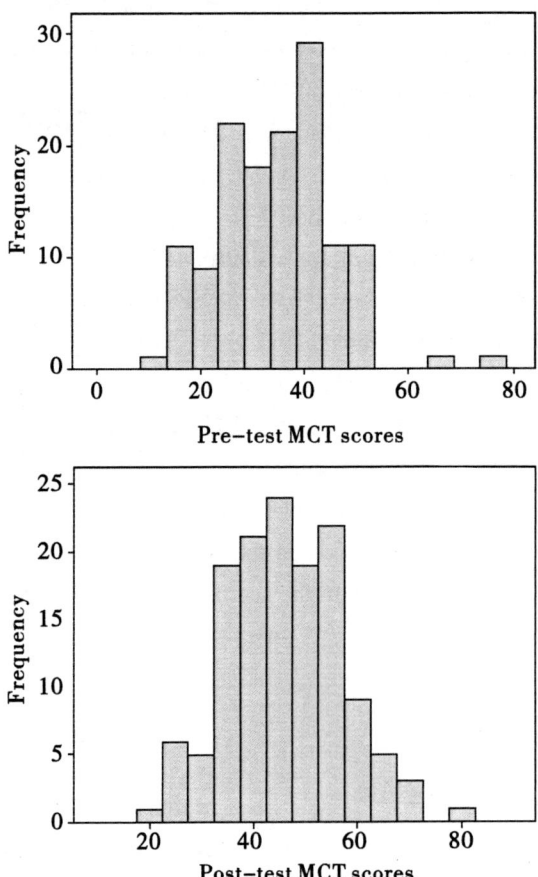

Figure 5-6　Pre-test and Post-test Metaphoric Competence Test Marks (Ms Wang's Class)

Note. N = 135.

　　Figure 5-8 shows the vast majority of the students did not achieve 60 marks in the pre-test and most of them did not achieve even the pass marks in the post-test, though there was an increase on the mean score of the post-test. Comparing the mean of NCEE with MCT, the students' metaphoric competence was poor even though they did well in the NCEE. That is quite different from the performance of the native English speakers.

5.2.2.2　Part A in MCT of Ms Wang's class

　　The researcher did the analysis of each part between the pre-test and the post-test of MCT to compare whether there is an increase on the mean score of the post-test. The details are presented in Table 5-12.

Table 5-12 Average Score of Each Part in the Pre-test and the Post-test (Ms Wang's Class)

	Average score of the pre-test	Average score of the post-test
Part A	18.56	19.89
Part B	10.71	16.23
Part C	5.49	10.10
Total score	34.76	46.21

Note. N = 135.

It is evident that there is increase for each part when comparing the pre-test average score with the post-test average score. The paired samples test is a measurement taken at two different times. It is done in order to get a statistical evidence to learn the difference between the two tests. For example, the pre-test and the post-test with an interval administered between the two time points of the same individual. A paired-samples test is conducted to compare the mean score of the pre-test and the post-test. The result can be seen in Table 5-13.

Table 5-13 Paired Samples Correlations Between the Pre-test and the Post-test (Ms Wang's Class)

N	Correlation	Sig.
135	0.613	0.000

There is a significant difference in the mean score of the pre-test and the post-test with $P = 0$ ($P<0.05$). These results suggest that the Metaphor Enriched English Language Instruction Supplement really does increase the students' metaphoric competence.

5.2.2.3 Part B in MCT of Ms Wang's class

People always use metaphors in their daily lives to show how they perceive the world (Lakoff and Johnson, 1980). People can also use metaphor as a cognitive tool to understand the real world (Nikitina and Furuoka, 2008). As an important part inmetaphoric competence, the first-year students' competence of metaphorical reasoning, in correspondences with the target domain and the source domain is investigated in Part B. The result shows how many categories of similarities of the given metaphors can be associated.

It is worth noting that the metaphoric mappings are partial which means only a part of the source domain is utilized in each conceptual metaphor. This partial structure of the source highlights, that is, provides structure for, only a part of the target concept (Kövecses, 2002). Hence, it is called the metaphorical highlighting which can be easily understood through a good metaphorical reasoning. This explains why the students were required to find the similarities between the source domain and the target domain in Part B. LOVE IS A JOURNEY was analyzed from the metaphor itself, the embodied image schema, and the categories generated in the pretest and the post-test.

(1) Analysis of LOVE IS A JOURNEY

It is a classic structural metaphor which belongs to the conceptual metaphors identified by Lakoff and Johnson in *Metaphors We Live By* (1980). There is a visual metaphor relating to it (Link 5-1).

It belongs to a generic-level metaphor conveying a self-propelled motion. According to Lakoff (1993), EVENT STRUCTURE metaphors means "states, changes, processes, actions, causes, purposes, and means, are characterized cognitively via metaphor in terms of space, motion, and force" (Lakoff). The specific instances of the EVENT STRUCTURE metaphor do not occur in isolation but may be organized in hierarchical structures where the lower mappings in the hierarchy inherit the structure of the higher mappings. Small capital letters are used to distinguish conceptual metaphors from linguistic metaphors. One example of this hierarchy with the three levels is the following.

Link 5-1 A Picture of LOVE IS A JOURNEY

Level 1: The EVENT STRUCTURE metaphor.
Level 2: PURPOSEFUL LIFE IS A JOURNEY.
Level 3: LOVE IS A JOURNEY.

Just as significant life events are special cases of events, so too are events in a love relationship. Thus, the LOVE IS A JOURNEY metaphor inherits its structure. There are certain special aspects in this particular metaphor. The metaphoric mappings relating to this metaphor is presented in Table 5-14.

Table 5-14 Metaphoric Mappings Between Source Domain and Target Domain

Source domain	Mapping	Target domain
Travelers	⟶	Lovers
Vehicle	⟶	Love relationship
Destination	⟶	Purpose of the relationship
Distance covered	⟶	Progress made in the relationship
Obstacles along the way	⟶	Difficulties encountered in the relationship

1) Image schema in LOVE IS A JOURNEY

An image schema is a "relatively abstract conceptual representation that arises directly from our everyday interaction with and observation of the world around us" (Evans, 2007). In other words, an image schema derives from embodied experience. One complex image schema is the Source-Path-Goal Schema which is used to present the steps or the stages exhibited in a love relationship. A relationship starts when two people agree to embark on a love journey which is the source. As the journey continues, they are bound to experience trials and the way they choose to tackle the trials is reminiscent of the path that they decide to take to help them reach their destination (goal). Anything that has an end also has a beginning (source). There are things that happen that dictate the direction (path) that a relationship takes and subsequently the end (goal) (Figure 5-7).

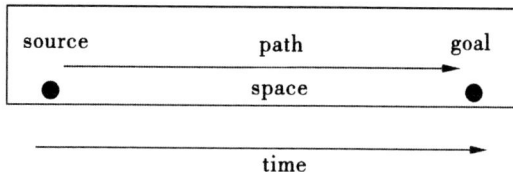

Figure 5-7 The Source-Path-Goal Schema

2) Categories generated in the pre-test and the post-test on LOVE IS A JOURNEY

Metaphors do not form a single image even though they are coherent with one another by virtue of being sub categories of a major category and therefore sharing a major common entailment. According to this, all the interpretations of this metaphor in the pre-test and the post-test can be grouped into six main categories, namely, movement, challenge, significance, mood, attribute and condition. And each main category also includes different entailments. Figure 5-8 shows the categories generated in the two tests.

The different metaphorical ways for thinking about love and journey result in varying entailments, appropriate for thinking and talking about different aspects of these experiences. According to the attributes of love and journey, the discussion of the four categories and their related entailments are as follows (Figure 5-8).

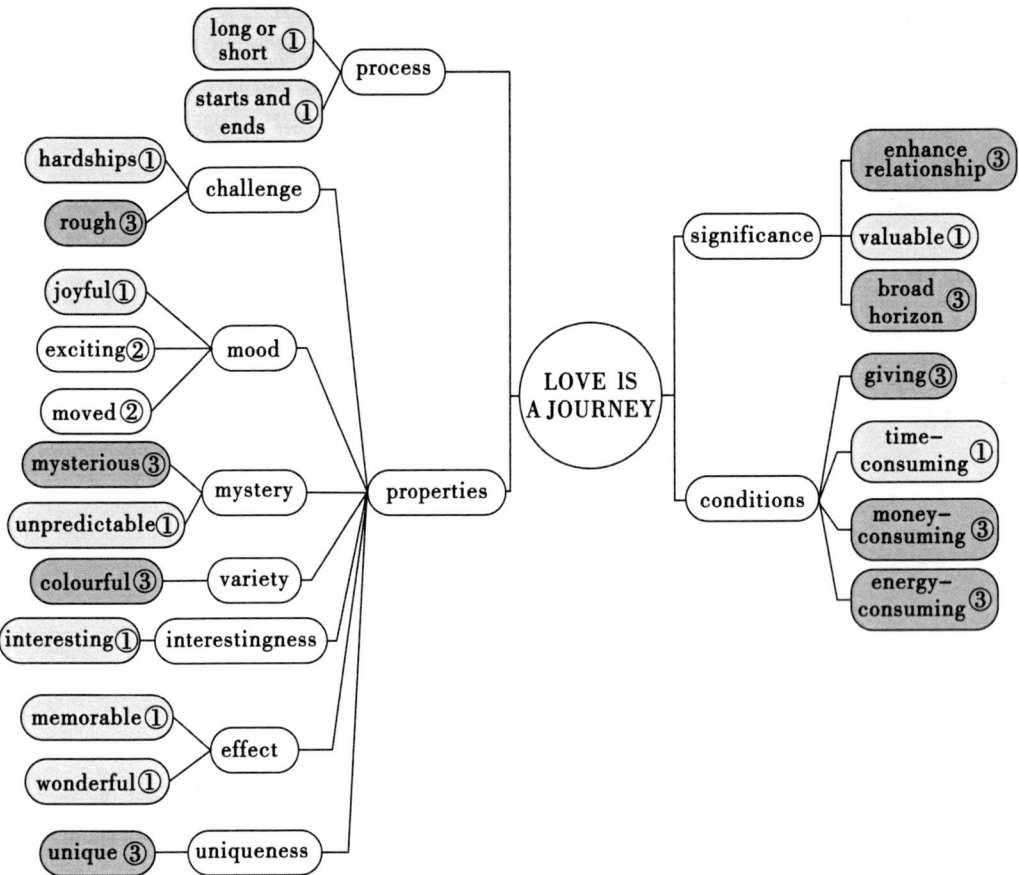

Figure 5-8 Categories Generated in the Pre-test and the Post-test on LOVE IS A JOURNEY (Ms Wang's Class)

Note. Words marked "①" are the categories generated in the pre-test and the post-test. Words marked "②" are the categories only generated in the pre-test. Words marked "③" are the categories only generated in the post-test.

The students' answers regarding the similarities were induced from different metaphorical highlighting and the corresponding entailed metaphors are presented as follows.

a. Metaphorical highlighting: Process

Most students hold the idea that both love and journey need a process, no matter how long or how short. As a process, both of them have starts and stops as a movement. These similarities coincide with the metaphor: ACTIONS ARE SELF-PROPELLED MOTIONS. There are no new similarities found in the post-test.

b. Metaphorical highlighting: Properties

For the properties of love and journey, the students' answers can be classified as seven sub-categories, namely, challenge, mood, mystery, variety, interest, effect and uniqueness. The mystery of love can be better conceptualized by the LOVE IS A NATURAL FORCE metaphor (Table 5-15).

Table 5-15 Similarities of Sub-category of LOVE IS A JOURNEY in the Pre-test and the Post-test (Ms Wang's Class)

Sub-categories of properties	Similarities		
	Pre-test and post-test	Pre-test only	Post-test only
Challenge	Hardship		
Mood	Joyful		
Mystery	Unpredictable		
Interest	Interesting		
Effect	Memorable/wonderful		
Variety			Colourful
Uniqueness			Unique

By explaining the seven sub-categories, the similarities between love and journey, challenge, mood, mystery and interest were mentioned in the two tests. Besides, variety (both are colourful) and uniqueness (both are unique) were new sub-categories in the post-test.

c. Metaphorical highlighting: Significance

For the significance of love and journey, the word "valuable" was mentioned in two tests, while the expressions "broaden horizon", and "enhance relationship" appeared only in the post-test.

d. Metaphorical highlighting: Conditions

For the conditions of love and journey, the word "time-consuming" was mentioned in two tests, while the words "giving", "money-consuming" and "energy-consuming" were mentioned only in the post-test.

(2) Analysis of IDEAS ARE FOOD

As a very popular and conventional metaphor in English, food is often used to conceptualize the English people's ideas, as both of them are essential to human survival and well-being. Ideas and food are both involved in the process of being taken in either by the mind or by the body, which is possibly the "experiential motivation" of this metaphor (Grady, 2007). A conceptual metaphor can be summarized: THINGKING IS EATING or ACQUIRING IDEAS IS EATING. There is a visual metaphor about ideas (Link 5-2).

Link 5-2 A Picture of IDEAS ARE FOOD

There are also many entailments which derived from IDEAS ARE FOOD.

INTEREST IN IDEAS IS APETITE FOR FOOD.
GOOD IDEAS ARE HEALTHY FOOD.
HEALTHY IDEAS ARE NUTRITIOUS FOOD.
DISTURBING IDEAS ARE DISGUSTING FOOD.
INTERESTING IDEAS ARE APPETIZING FOOD.
UNDERSTANDING IS DIGESTING.
ACCEPTING IS SWALLOWING.
THE NEED FOR INFORMATION IS HUNGER.
PROVIDING INFORMATION IS FEEDING.
FORMING AN IDEA IS COOKING AND PREPARING FOOD.
THINKING IS CHEWING OVER THE FOOD.
LEARNING IS EATING.

The systematic entailments mentioned above show that the IDEAS ARE FOOD metaphor is conventional in English. It is part of our daily conceptions of ideas and is a metaphor we live by in the English culture.

1) Image schema in IDEAS ARE FOOD

Conceptual metaphor refers to generic-level or specific-level ones. IDEAS ARE FOOD is a specific-level metaphor since ideas and food are specific-level concepts.

2) Categories generated in the pre-test and the post-test on IDEAS ARE FOOD

According to the answers of the students, all the interpretations of this metaphor in two tests can be grouped into three main categories, namely, significance, attribute, and condition, and each category also includes different entailments. Categories generated on IDEAS ARE FOOD can been seen as follows (Figure 5-9).

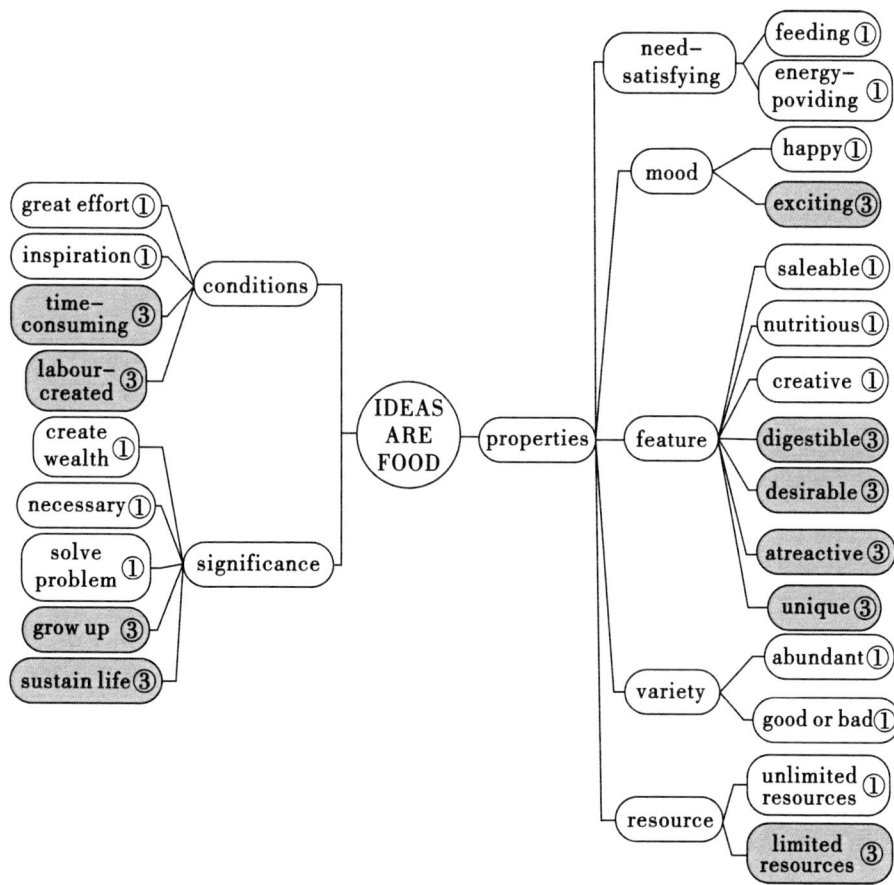

Figure 5-9　Categories Generated in the Pre-test and the Post-test on IDEAS ARE FOOD (Ms Wang's Class)

Note. Words marked "①" are the categories generated in the pre-test and the post-test. Words marked "②" are the categories only generated in the pre-test. Words marked "③" are the categories only generated in the post-test.

The students' answers of similarities were summarized from different metaphorical highlighting and their corresponding entailed metaphors are presented as follows:

a. Metaphorical highlighting: Properties

For the properties of ideas and food, there are five sub categories, namely, needs-satisfying, mood, feature, resource and variety. Table 5-16 shows the details of each sub-category.

Table 5-16 Similarities of Sub-category of IDEAS ARE FOOD in the Pre-test and the Post-test (Ms Wang's Class)

Sub-categories of properties	Similarities		
	Pre-test and post-test	Pre-test only	Post-test only
Needs-satisfying	Feeding		
	Energy-providing		
Mood	Happy	Exciting	
Feature	Nutritious	Desirable	
	Creative	Attractive	
	Saleable	Unique	
	Digestible		
Resource	Unlimited	Limited	
Variety	Abundant	Good or bad	

For the property of needs-satisfying function, the students mentioned "feeding" and "energy-providing" both in the pre-test and the post-test which coincided with the entailment: PROVIDING INFORMATION IS FEEDING.

For the property of mood, the students had positive attitudes towards ideas and food which showed that both of them could make people happy or excited.

For the good features, "nutritious" "creative" and "saleable" are the words used both in the pre-test and the post-test. The word nutritious coincides with the entailment: HELPFUL IDEAS ARE NUTRITIOUS FOOD. The words "desirable" "attractive" "unique" and "digestible" appeared only in the post-test, which coincided with the entailment: UNDERSTANDING IS DIGESTION, INTERESTING IDEAS ARE APPETIZING FOOD.

For the property of resources, the students viewed both of them as "unlimited resource" in the pre-test and the post-test, while some students regarded them as "limited resource" in the post-test.

For the property of variety, the word "abundant" was mentioned in two tests, while in the post-test, students believed both ideas and food could be divided into good or bad ones which coincided with the entailments: GOOD IDEAS ARE HEALTHY FOOD, UNINTERESTING IDEAS ARE FLAVORLESS FOOD.

b. Metaphorical highlighting: Significance

Many students emphasized the significance of ideas and food. "Necessary" "problem-solving" and "wealth-creating" are the three similarities mentioned in the pre-test and the post-test. Besides, "growth-enhancing" and "life-sustaining" were two new words that appeared in the post-test which focused on their roles in individual growth and life duration. There is an entailment: THE NEED FOR INFORMATION IS HUNGER.

c. Metaphorical highlighting: Conditions

For the conditions of these two domains, "inspiration" and "effort-taking" were mentioned in two tests, "labour-created" and "time-consuming" were two new similarities in the post-test which focused on the labour cost and time cost.

(3) Analysis of DEPRESSION IS FALLING INTO AN ABYSS

Depression is a condition that is almost unimaginable to anyone who has not experienced it. Words like tree, cliff and abyss can be used to talk about this experience. Solomon holds the idea that it is not an easy diagnosis since it relies on metaphor and the metaphors one patient uses are different from another (2001). The most common metaphors Solomon (2001) found being used to describe depression in English involved "falling into an abyss" or being "over the edge", though most people had never the experience of either falling into an abyss or off an edge. This metaphor can be seen as conveying the following conceptual structures.

DEPRESSION IS FALLING DOWN.
DEPRESSION IS DARKNESS.
DEPRESSION IS LACK OF CONTROL.

The concepts of falling down, darkness and lack of control are sub metaphors of DEPRESSION IS DOWN. DEPRESSION IS DOWN relates directly to the widely observed SADNESS IS DOWN metaphors. This conceptual metaphor is the opposite of HAPPINESS IS UP (Gibbs, 1994; Yu, 1998). Yu (1998) take the view that it comes from the fact humans have upright bodies. "The erect posture typically goes with positive emotional as well as physical states, whereas the opposite is true with a drooping posture" (Yu). Link 5-3 shows the process of falling into a hole.

Link 5 - 3 Photo Bank Gallery: Man Falling into A Hole

1) Image schema in DEPRESSION IS FALLING INTO AN ABYSS.

The verticality schema can be used to illustrate this kind of metaphor. It is an imageschema that involves "up" and "down" relations. The verticality schema is often used to explain the emotional scale between "happiness/sadness" as well as the social status. For instance, consider the expressions, "to be high in spirit" "to feel down" and "to climb the career ladder". The most frequently used one is UP-DOWN schema which can be used either in a static fashion (placing interface elements above or below another) or in a dynamic fashion (moving objects vertically, for example, with the mouse). Physical UP-DOWN placement and movements of objects may lead to analogous placement and movements in virtual space. Like DEPRESSION IS FALLING INTO AN ABYSS, it implies HEALTH IS UP, SICKNESS IS DOWN. Depression is a kind of sickness; therefore, the feeling of being depressed is like falling into an abyss.

2) Categories generated in the pre-test and the post-test on DEPRESSION IS FALLING

INTO AN ABYSS.

According to the students' answers, all the interpretations of this metaphor can be grouped into three main categories, properties, result, and mood. Each category also includes a different entailment. Figure 5-10 shows the categories generated in two tests.

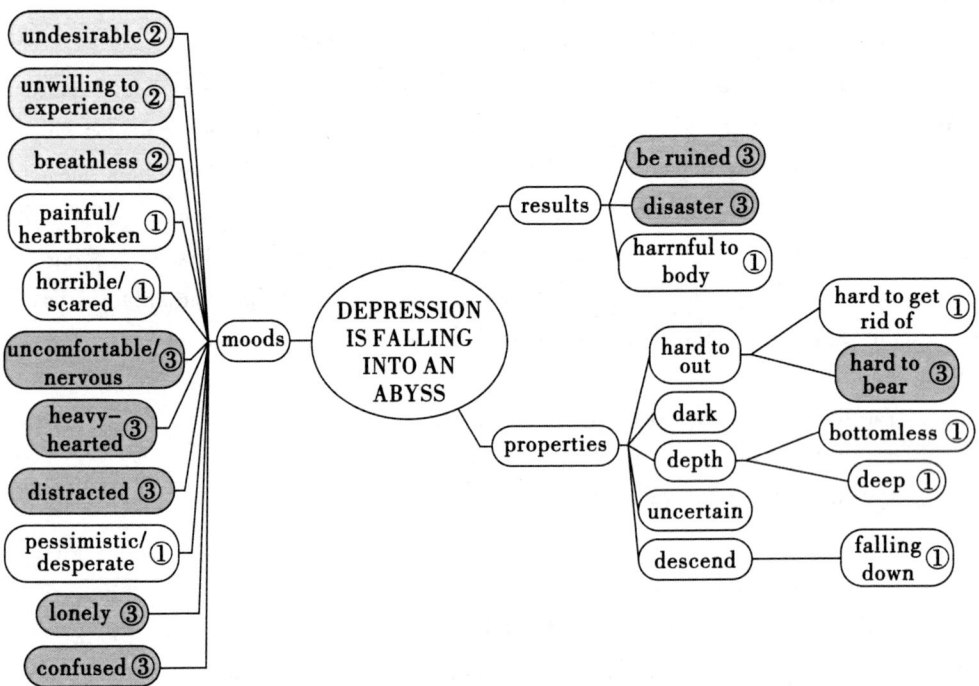

Figure 5-10   Categories in the Pre-test and the Post-test on DEPRESSION IS FALLING INTO AN ABYSS (Ms Wang's Class)

Note. Words marked "①" are the categories generated in the pre-test and the post-test. Words marked "②" are the categories only generated in the pre-test. Words marked "③" are the categories only generated in the post-test.

The students' answers of similarities can be discussed from different metaphorical highlighting and its corresponding entailed metaphors are presented as follows.

a. Metaphorical highlighting: Properties

For the properties of depression and falling into an abyss, there are five sub categories, namely, "descending" "dark" "deep/bottomless" "uncertain" "hard to get out". Table 5-17 shows the details of each sub-category.

Table 5-17 Similarities of Sub-category of DEPRESSION IS FALLING INTO AN ABYSS in the Pre-test and the Post-test (Ms Wang's Class)

Sub-categories of properties	Similarities		
	Pre-test and post-test	Pre-test only	Post-test only
Descending	Falling down		
Dark	Dark		
Depth	Deep		
	Bottomless		
Uncertainty			Uncertain
Hard to out	Hard to get rid of		Hard to bear

For the property of descending, most of the students mentioned the phrase "falling down" as one of the similarities which coincided with the entailment: DEPRESSION IS DOWN.

For the property of darkness, many students imagined the situation of the abyss, and used the words "dark" and "bottomless" to describe the inside which also coincided with the entailment: DEPRESSION IS DARK.

For the property of depth, two noticeable words are "deep" and "bottomless", which also implied people's fear of depression.

For the property of uncertainty, the word "uncertain" was mentioned frequently.

For the property of hard to get out, the expression "both are hard to get rid of" was used in the pre-test and the post-test, while the expression "both are hard to bear" appeared only in the post-test. These expressions coincided with the entailment: DEPRESSION IS LACK OF CONTROL, which means the person, will lose his control if he falls into an abyss.

b. Metaphorical highlighting: Moods

This category took the largest part in the students' answers. Many adjectives were used to describe the same feeling of depression and falling into an abyss like "painful" "horrible" "desperate" "undesirable" "unwilling" "breathless" "nervous" "distracted" "lonely" "confused", and so on. Among them, painful, horrible, desperate were mentioned in two tests; undesirable, unwilling, breathless were mentioned only in the pre-test; nervous, distracted, lonely and confused were mentioned only in the post-test. All these adjectives fell in the entailment: DEPRESSION IS HEAVY.

c. Metaphorical highlighting: Results

For the result of depression and falling into an abyss, "harmful (to body)" was mentioned in the pre-test and the post-test; while the words "disastrous" and "destructive" were mentioned only in the post-test which take the result as more serious one.

(4) Analysis of HUMAN BODY IS A BATTLEGROUND

This metaphor belongs to the structural metaphor. The idea that the human body is a battleground where good and evil clash, is as old as the story of Adam and Eve and as contemporary as the image of a micro-devil on one shoulder and an angel on the other. In the Odyssey, Odysseus makes a battleground of his own body. He has himself tied to the mast of his ship so he can experience the thrill of the Sirens' song without being drawn to his death, like a moth to flame. Odysseus-minded people nowadays go bungee jumping. There is a picture of Ferdinand-Philipped' Orléans which used the man, Gulliver as a metaphor for France in his 1830 cartoon, and it helps us understand the metaphor HUMAN BODY IS A BATTLEGROUND better(Link 5-4).

Link 5 – 4
Your Body is a Battleground
Note. Gulliver is a metaphor for France (a great nation tied down by petty factions) in this 1830 cartoon.

In this metaphor, the body has become a battleground between clean and dirty, health and illness, good and evil. It belongs to the military metaphor, such as armies of invading and defending cells, emphasizing the vulnerability of the body to the outside influences and suggested that the maintenance of health was a never-ending exercise. The metaphoric mappings between "body" and "battleground" are presented in Table 5-18.

Table 5-18　Metaphoric Mappings Between Source Domain and Target Domain

Source domain (HUMAN BODY)	Mapping	Target domain (BATTLEGROUND)
Invader	→	Virus or bacteria
Medicine	→	A rain of bullets
Immune system	→	Army
Health	→	Victory
Illness	→	Defeat

1) Image schema in HUMAN BODY IS A BATTLEGROUND

The image schema in this metaphor is COUNTERFORCE schema which is a sub category of FORCE schema. A force schema is an image schema that involves physical or metaphorical causal interaction. Johnson (1987) classifies the different types of forces into COMPULSION, BLOCKAGE, COUNTERFORCE, REMOVAL OF RESTRAINT, ENABLEMENT, DIVERSION, ATTRACTION, and REPULSION. Many aspects of HUMAN BODY IS A BATTLEGROUND involve counterparts, for example, attack and defense, victory and failure, competition and cooperation. It emphasizes the relationship between the two parts.

2) Categories generated in the pre-test and the post-test on HUMAN BODY IS A BATTLEGROUND

The interpretations of similarities between body and battleground in the pre-test and the post-test can be grouped into four main categories, properties, functions, results, and wars.

Figure 5-11 shows the categories generated in two tests.

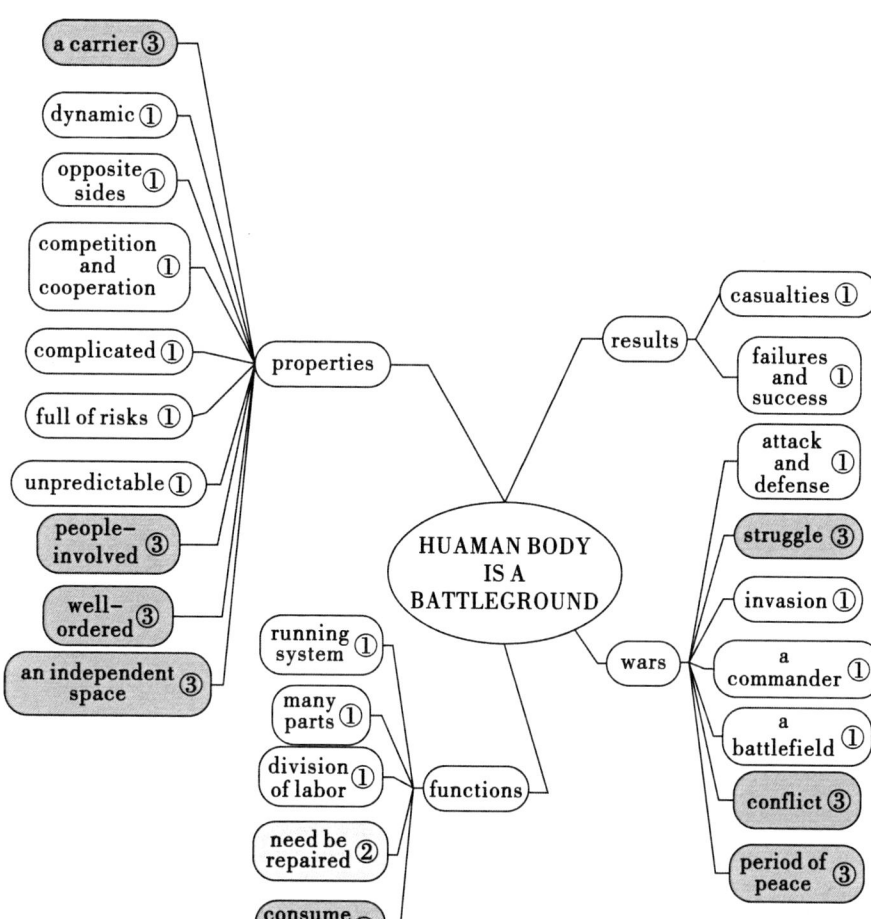

Figure 5-11 Categories Generated in the Pre-test and the Post-test on HUMAN BODY IS A BATTLEGROUND (Ms Wang's Class)

Note. Words marked "①" are the categories generated in the pre-test and the post-test. Words marked "②" are the categories only generated in the pre-test. Words marked "③" are the categories only generated in the post-test.

The students' answers which generated from different metaphorical levels and the corresponding entailed metaphors are presented as follows.

a. Metaphorical highlighting: Properties

Most students hold the view that both the human body and the battles are in a tense situation which means there are battles all the time. Another property is "complex", which means the two domains own a complex structure due to their large members and functions. "Updating" was a new item which appeared only in the pre-test which emphasized the feature of replacement. "Survival of the fittest" "many components" "unpredictability" are three new expressions that appeared only in the post-test.

b. Metaphorical highlighting: Wars

The war metaphor is a primary metaphor which can be used to explain many source domains like BODY or DISEASE. The students' answers showed some properties of warfare. For example, "both of them have attack and defense" "both of them have soldiers and enemies" and "both of them have the defense system" were mentioned in two tests. "Struggles" and "leader" are the two new words that appeared only in the post-test.

c. Metaphorical highlighting: Functions

As regards the functions of the human body and the battleground, "division of labour" was the only expression which appeared in the two tests, while there were four other words or expressions found in the post-test, namely, "running system" "many components" "entity" "eliminate harm substance".

d. Metaphorical highlighting: Results

As for the similarities in the result, "casualty" and "victory" were mentioned in both the pre-test and the post-test. "Casualty" implies the bad effect, while "victory" implies the good effect of the battle.

(5) Analysis of BRAIN IS A MACHINE

Probably, the first mechanical metaphor for the brain is attributed to Descartes. Heproposed that "animals, as distinct from men, were pure automata" (Daugman, 2001). Due to the fact that Descartes was a deist and religion played a major political and social role at that time, he limited this mechanical brain metaphor in its application only to animals. The enlightenment opened the door for even more progressive ideas; one of them is certainly La Mettrie's L'Homme machine (1748) in which the human body and the human brain are explicitly described as machines. Link 5-5 shows a visual metaphor which is very vivid.

Link 5-5 A Picture of BRAIN IS A MACHINE

There are some similarities between the human brain and a machine. Each has parts or components that work in unison, each has volume and mass, each can compute, each can be understood in part by understanding the parts that comprise it.

1) Categories generated in the pre-test and the post-test on BRAIN IS A MACHINE

The categories generated in the pre-test and the post-test aresummarized as follows.

The interpretations of similarities between the source domain and target domain in the pre-test and the post-test were summearized into three main categories, properties, functions and significance. Each main category includes different entailments. Figure 5-12 shows the categories generated in two tests.

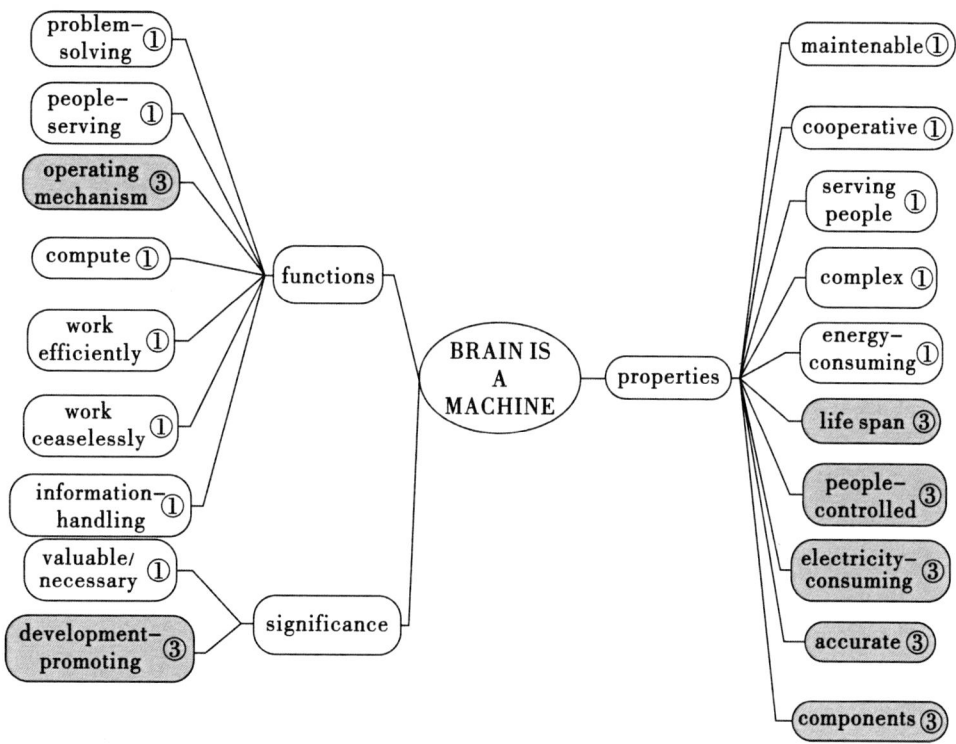

Figure 5-12 Categories Generated in the Pre-test and the Post-test on BRAIN IS A MACHINE (Ms Wang's Class)

Note. Words marked "①" are the categories generated in the pre-test and the post-test. Words marked "②" are the categories only generated in the pre-test. Words marked "③" are the categories only generated in the post-test.

The students' answers regarding the similarities can be discussed from different metaphorical highlighting and its corresponding entailed metaphors. They are presented as follows.

a. Metaphorical highlighting: Properties

For the properties of brain and machine, there are ten sub categories, namely, "maintainable" "cooperative" "complex" "energy-consuming" "life span" "people-controlled" "electricity-consuming" "accuracte" "components". Table 5-19 shows the details of each sub-category.

Table 5-19 Similarities of Sub-category of BRAIN IS A MACHINE in the Pre-test and the Post-test (Ms Wang's Class)

Sub-categories of properties	Similarities		
	Pre-test and post-test	Pre-test only	Post-test only
Maintainable	Both need maintenance and rest		
Cooperative	Both need coordination		
Serving people	Both can provide service		
Complex	Both have complex structures		

Continue to Table 5-19

Sub-categories of properties	Similarities		
	Pre-test and post-test	Pre-test only	Post-test only
Energy-consuming	Both need/consume energy		
Life span			Both have a life span
People-controlled			Both are controlled by people
Electricity-consuming			Both need charging
Accurate			Both are accurate
Components			Both are made up of many components

b. Metaphorical highlighting: Functions

For the six sub categories generated in the two tests, a noticeable function of the brain and the machine is that they work efficiently and ceaselessly. Besides, "problem-solving" "people-serving" "information-handling" "compute" were the other four words that surfaced in these two tests. The "operating mechanism" was a new word which appeared in the post-test which emphasized the systematic running of the two domains.

c. Metaphorical highlighting: Significance

There are only two sub categories relating to the significance; "valuable" was the most frequent word in both the pre-test and the post-test. While "development-promoting" is a new word which was mentioned in the post-test.

2) Implication of BRAIN IS A MACHINE

BRAIN IS A MACHINE belongs to the ontological metaphor. Ontological metaphoris so common in our life that most people are unaware that they are metaphors and are often considered to be self-evident, direct descriptions of psychological phenomena. For example, He has broken down, which contains a metaphor: BRAIN IS A MACHINE which people usually do not realize. Besides, by considering the brain as a machine, a lot of expressions about the connection between the brain and the machine can be got. For example, my mind just is not operating, or my mind is a little rusty.

The machine metaphor allows us to think of the brain as having a switch, an efficient level, a productive capacity, an internal mechanism, a source of energy, and a thing with operating conditions.

5.2.2.4 Part C in MCT of Ms Wang's class

(1) Types of metaphors generated by students on "Learning English is…"

Students were required to complete the sentence "Learning English is…" by using their imagination. According to the superordinate categories of the metaphors given by students, eight types of metaphors were generalized (Table 5-20). Through these types, students showed their perceptions of English learning.

(2) Types of metaphors generated by students on "Treating illness is…"

Students were required to complete the sentence "Treating illness is…" by using their imagination. According to their answers, nine types of metaphors were generalized (Table 5-21). Through these types, students showed their perceptions of treatment of disease.

Table 5-20 Metaphors Generated on "Learning English is…" (Ms Wang's Class)

Classification	Same source domain in the pre-test and the post-test	Source domain in the pre-test	Source domain in the post-test
Journey/Movement	A travel A journey A long distance running A marathon	Planting flowers	Solving a problem
Playing/Leisure	Listening to music Singing a song Playing a (computer) game Dancing Swimming in the sea Hiking	Climbing stairs	Surfing Playing football Walking in a beautiful garden Reading a beautiful story Watching a movie Drinking tea Sowing a seed
Exploration	Climbing a mountain Looking fortreasure		Walking in the stormy night Finding a new island
Experience	Making a friend Flying in the sky Opening a door/window (to a new world) Talking to a foreign friend Falling into an abyss Harvesting fruits/wheat Falling in love with someone Walking through the forest	Drawing a picture Enjoying the beautiful scenes Exploring new world Swimming in the knowledge of ocean	Mining stone Exploring in the forest Walking through the desert Planting flowers Collecting seashells on the beach Crossing the river Making an embroider Learning to drive a car well Breathing air

Continue to Table 5-20

Classification	Same source domain in the pre-test and the post-test	Source domain in the pre-test	Source domain in the post-test
Building	Building a house		
Farming/Planting	Planting a tree		Planting crops
Food and drinking	Eating (delicious) food/candy	Eating dark chocolate	Eating hotpot/a cake
	Taking pills	A glass of water when you are thirsty	Drinking coffee
		A cup of tea	
Things	A battle(with memory)		A tag of war
	An interesting game		A match
	An adventure		A campaign
			A pair of wings
			A bridge to foreign countries

Note. The first column is the categories generated from students' answers. The second column refers to the same expressions appeared both in the pre-test and the post-test. The third column is the unique expressions appeared in the pre-test. The fourth column is the unique expressions appeared in the post-test.

Table 5-21 Metaphors Generated on "Treating illness is…" (Ms Wang's Class)

Classification	Same source domain in the pre-test and the post-test	Source domain in the pre-test	Source domain in the post-test
Journey/Movement	A long/endless/lonely journey Climbing a mountain A marathon	Guarding our homeland	Crossing the desert Against death Putting out a fire
Playing/Leisure		Riding a roller coaster	Playing a game
Experience	Taking an exam	Working out a math problem Fixing bugs See the sunlight again Taking care of a plant Losing way home Updating system Nirvana of phoenix Climbing from the abyss	Struggling in the swamp Remodeling one's lifestyle Walking on the rainy day Waiting for spring Seeking the sun Jumping out of the dark Living with a tiger Falling into darkness Spreading love to the world Falling into the abyss Planting trees in the desert Beating a bad man
War/Battle/Gamble	Fighting a war/battle A fight with monster/devil	Gambling A fight with evil forces/ghost	A fight with invader
Enemy/Invader		Fighting with enemy Resisting the invasion	Defeating enemy Defensing Protecting the body

Continue to Table 5-21

Classification	Same source domain in the pre-test and the post-test	Source domain in the pre-test	Source domain in the post-test
Repair	Repairing/fixing/mending a machine		Mending clothes
Match/Race	A race against death		Racing with time
	A boxing match		Rowing
			A competition
Things	A long distance running		An abyss
			An exploration
			A nightmare
			A storm
			A smokeless war
Cleaning	Killing/catching pests (on the tree)	Cleaning dust	Cleaning trash
			Cleaning the blackboard
			Cleaning the house/room
			Cleaning the battlefield
			Treating the waste water
			Protecting our home

Note. The first column is the categories generated from students' answers. The second column refers to the same expressions appeared in two tests. The third column is the unique expressions appeared in the pre-test. The fourth column is the unique expressions appeared in the post-test.

5.2.3 Data analysis on metaphoric competence test (Ms Liu's class)

138 students of Ms Wang's class participated in the pre-test and the post-test. 128 of them completed and returned the questionnaires. For the results of the pre-test and the post-test, a statistic descriptive analysis was conducted.

5.2.3.1 Descriptive analysis of results of MCT and NCEE (Ms Liu's class)

Table 5-22 shows a statistic description of the participants' scores in the Metaphoric Competence Test (MCT) and the National College Entrance Examination (NCEE). The Table 5-22 shows the descriptive statistics of these two scores.

Table 5-22 Descriptive Statistics of MCT and NCEE (Ms Liu's Class)

	NCEE	MCT	
		Pre-test	Post-test
Num of valid cases	128	128	128
Mean	77.20	39.45	50.45
Std. Deviation	7.077	10.154	11.078
Range	41	46	59
Skewness	-0.827	-0.221	-0.623
Kurtosis	1.371	-0.249	0.708
Minimum	53	14	16
Maximum	94	60	75

Note. $N = 128$.

As is shown in Table 5-22, the arithmetical mark of NCEE is 77.20, of the pre-test is 39.45 and of the post-test is 50.45. It indicated student participants did not perform well in the pre-test and the post-test compared with their NCEE scores. Surely, their post-test marks had increased compared to their pre-test marks. In the 128 candidates, the highest mark of the NCEE is 94, and the lowest is 53. The range or the spread of different marks from the maximum 94 to the minimum 53 is 41. The highest mark of the pre-test (MCT) is 60 and the lowest is 14. The range or the spread of the different marks is 46. The highest mark of the post-test (MCT) is 75 and the lowest is 16. The range or the spread of different marks is 59. The standard deviation of NCEE is 7.077, of the pre-test (MCT) is 10.154 and of the post-test is 11.078.

Based on this histogram and the negative skewness -0.221 (pre-test) and -0.623 (post-test) reported in Table 5-22, we can find that it is negatively skewed. The kurtosis of the two curves was -0.249 (pre-test) and 0.708 (post-test) which means the curve of the pre-test was platykurtic and the curve of the post-test was leptokurtic. We can see that most of the two MCT marks centered in the middle and the lower part which is quite different from the scores of the NCEE. Figure 5-13 is the frequency of the NCEE scores.

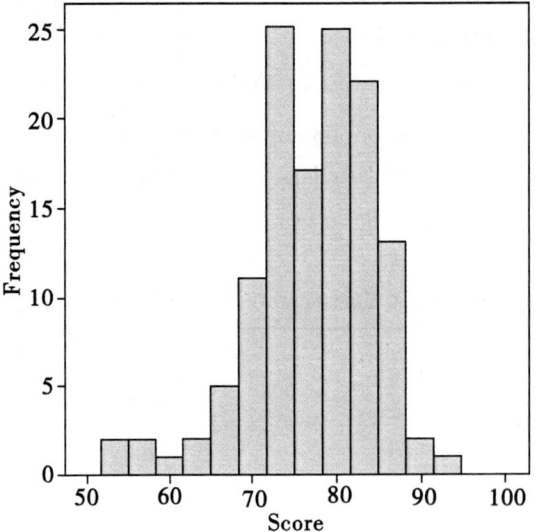

Figure 5-13 The National College Entrance Examination (Ms Liu's Class)

Note. N=128.

Figure 5-13 shows a vast majority of students have scored over 60 and more than a half of the students' scored over 75 which means they did well in the NCEE examination. Figure 5-14 shows the students' two MCT test marks.

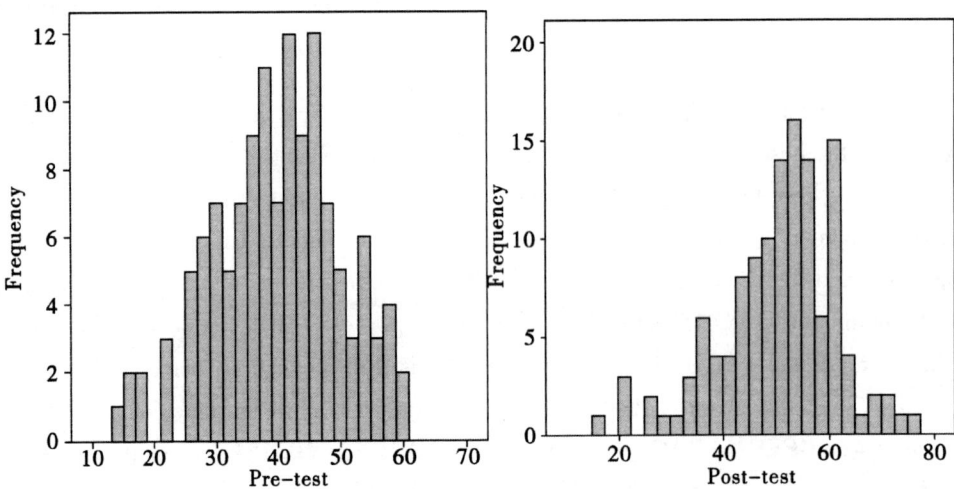

Figure 5-14 Pre-test and Post-test Metaphoric Competence Test Marks (Ms Liu's Class)

Note. N=128.

Figure 5-14 shows the average score of the vast majority in the pre-test is around 40 which is far from the passing mark of 60. Though there is an increase in their marks in the post-test, the mean score of most of the students in the post-test is around 50 which is still not satisfactory. Comparing Figure 5-13 and Figure 5-14, the students' metaphoric competence is poor even though they did well in the NCEE. The case is quite different with the native English speakers.

5.2.3.2 Part A in MCT of Ms Liu's class

The researcher did the analysis of each part between the pre-test and the post-test of the MCT to compare whether there is any increase in the two scores. The details can be seen in Table 5-23.

Table 5-23 Average Score of Each Part in the Pre-test and the Post-test (Ms Liu's Class)

	Average score of the pre-test	Average score of the post-test
Part A	21.70	21.55
Part B	11.73	16.36
Part C	6.02	12.54
Total score	39.45	50.45

From the Table 5-23, it is evident that there was an increase for Part B and Part C comparing the pre-test average score with the post-test one. There was a little decrease for Part A which means that the students may not have been familiar with the metaphor theories even after the implementation. Then a paired-samples t-test was conducted to compare the average score of the pre-test and the post-test (Table 5-24).

Table 5-24 Paired Samples Correlations Between the Pre-test and the Post-test (Ms Liu's Class)

N	Correlation	Sig.
128	0.429	0.000

There was a significant difference in the mean score of the pre-test and the post-test with $P=0.000$ ($P<0.05$). These results suggest that the Metaphor Enriched English Language Instruction Supplement really does increase the students' metaphoric competence.

5.2.3.3 Part B in MCT of Ms Liu's class

The metaphor LOVE IS A JOURNEY has been explained in the analysis of Ms Wang's MCT test, the explanation and comparison of categories generated in Ms Liu's class are the focus points of this part.

(1) Analysis of LOVE IS A JOURNEY

Categories generated in the pre-test and the post-test on LOVE IS A JOURNEY.

After analyzing the statistics, the interpretations of this metaphor in the pre-test and the post-test can be grouped into four main categories, process, properties, significance and conditions. Each main category includes different entailments. Figure 5-15 shows the categories generated in two tests.

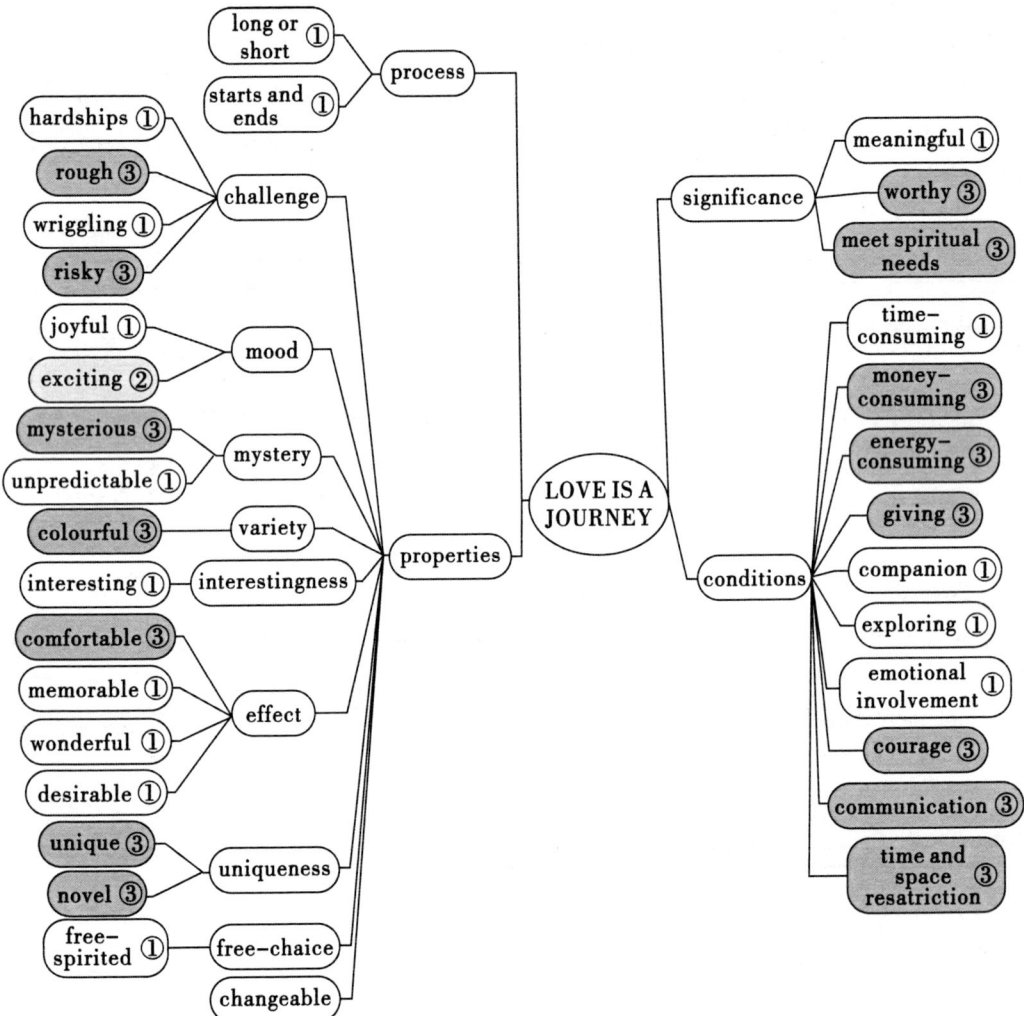

Figure 5-15 Categories Generated in the Pre-test and the Post-test on LOVE IS A JOURNEY (Ms Liu's Class)

Note. Words marked "①" are the categories generated in the pre-test and the post-test. Words marked "②" are the categories only generated in the pre-test. Words marked "③" are the categories only generated in the post-test.

Students' answers of similarities were concluded from different metaphorical highlighting and its corresponding entailed metaphors are presented as follows.

a. Metaphorical highlighting: Process

In the pre-test and the post-test, both love and journey are viewed as a process which can be long or short and both have a starting point and a terminal point. "Both are endless" appeared only in the per-test, "both can meet a wonderful person" and "both have departure" appeared only in the post-test.

b. Metaphorical highlighting: Properties

This category contained many sub-categories like challenge, mood, mystery, variety, interestingness, effect, uniqueness, free choice and changeable. For the property of challenge, the characteristics including full of "hardships" "wriggling" and "ups and downs" were mentioned by the students in the pre-test and the post-test. "Both are rough/bumpy" only appeared in the pre-test, "both need to experience trials" appeared only in the post-test. For the property of mood, "both are enjoyable (joyful/happy)" as well as "both have thorns and roses" were mentioned in the pre-test and the post-test. The expression "both can meet one's spiritual needs" appeared only in the pre-test. "Both are comfortable" only appeared in the post-test. For the property of mystery, "both are unpredictable" was mentioned in the pre-test and the post-test, "both are mysterious" was only appeared in the post-test. For the property of variety, "both are colourful" was only appeared in the post-test. For the property of interestingness, "both are interesting" was mentioned in the pre-test and the post-test.

For the property of effect, in the pre-test and the post-test, "both are beautiful/wonderful/fantastic/ interesting/unpredictable/ full of memories/desirable/free-spirited /expensive" and "both have companion (different views)/need management" were mentioned. For the property of uniqueness, "both are unique" and "both are novel" were only appeared in the post-test. For the property of free choice, "both are free-spirited" was only mentioned in the post-test. For the property of changeable, "both are changeable" was only mentioned in the post-test.

c. Metaphorical highlighting: Significance

The expressions "both are meaningful" were mentioned in the pre-test and the post-test. Besides, "both areworthy" and "both meet spiritual needs" appeared only in the post-test.

d. Metaphorical highlighting: Conditions

The characteristics of condition are also mentioned by the students. In two tests, "both need time/plans/giving/explore/feel with heart" were expressions written by the students. "Both need emotional involvement/earnest/learning" appeared only in the pre-test, "both need courage/energy/encouragement and support/chance/communication" appeared only in the post-test.

(2) Analysis of IDEAS ARE FOOD

According to students' answers, all the interpretations of this metaphor in the pre-test and the post-test were classified into three main categories, namely, significance, properties, and condition. Each main category also included different entailments. Figure 5-16 shows the categories generated in two tests.

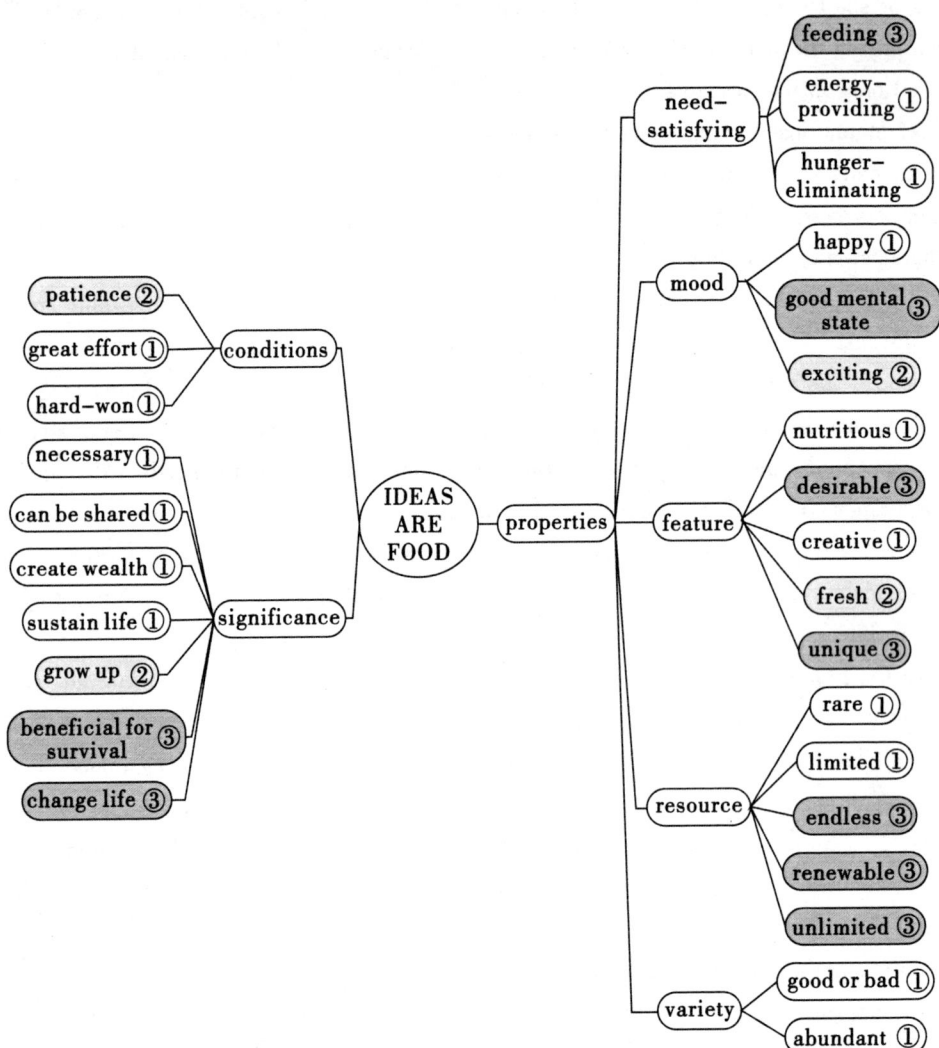

Figure 5-16   Categories Generated in the Pre-test and the Post-test on IDEAS ARE FOOD (Ms Liu's Class)

Note. Words marked "①" are the categories generated in the pre-test and the post-test. Words marked "②" are the categories only generated in the pre-test. Words marked "③" are the categories only generated in the post-test.

The metaphorical highlighting and its corresponding entailed metaphors are presented as follows.

a. Metaphorical highlighting: Properties

Five sub-categories of property, need-satisfying, mood, feature, resource and variety were mentioned in two tests. In terms of need-satisfying function, both idea and food were considered to provide energy and eliminate hunger in two tests. "Both can feed people" appeared only in the post-test. In terms of mood, "both are happy" was mentioned in two tests. "Both keep people in a good mental state" was mentioned only in the pre-test and "both are exciting" was mentioned only in the post-test. In terms of feature, "both are nutritious" and "both arecreative" were provided in two tests. "Both are fresh" appeared only in the pre-test. "Both are desirable" appeared only in the post-test. In terms of resource, "both are rare/limited" was mentioned in two tests. "Both are endless/ renewable/ unlimited" appeared only in the post-test. In terms of variety, "both are good or bad" and "both are abundant" were mentioned in two tests. There was no unique expressions neither in two tests.

b. Metaphorical highlighting: Conditions

The character of condition is also thought of by the students inthe pre-test. "Both need patience" was used only in the pre-test.

c. Metaphorical highlighting: Significance

"Both are necessary/important (for brain development)" and "both can create wealth/ be shared to others" were expressions mentioned in two tests. Besides, "both make people grow up" was used only in the pre-test. "Both are benefits to human progress and development" and "both can change life" were used only in the post-test.

(3) Analysis of DEPRESSION IS FALLING INTO AN ABYSS

All the interpretations of this metaphor in the pre-test and the post-test can be classified as three main categories, namely, properties, result, and moods. And each main category also included different entailments. Figure 5-17 shows the categories generated in two tests.

The students' answers regarding the similarities can be discussed from different metaphorical highlighting and its corresponding entailed metaphors are presented as follows.

a. Metaphorical highlighting: Moods

Negative mood, including misery, anxiety, danger and scare, is another category which was frequently mentioned about. "Both are negative for human survival/ unwilling to experience/inlows/painful/breathless/helpless/dangerous/frightening" were mentioned in the pre-test and the post-test. "Both make people feel heavy/ tormented/at a loss" were used only in the pre-test. "Both are heartbroken/confused/ shocked" appeared only in the post-test.

b. Metaphorical highlighting: Properties

There were eight sub-categories of property, hard to get out, depth, uncertain, descend, dark, want to escape, unknown and setbacks. In terms of "hard to get out" feature, "both are hard to get rid of/ hard to bear" were the expressions used both in two tests. In terms of "depth", "both are deep/ bottomless" were mentioned in two tests. "Both have the process of falling" was the most frequent similarity between depression and falling into an abyss found in two tests. The expression "both are dark" and "both make people want to escape" were presented both in two tests. In addition, there were three new properties which only appeared in the post-test. "Both are uncertain/unknown/setbacks" appeared only in the post-test.

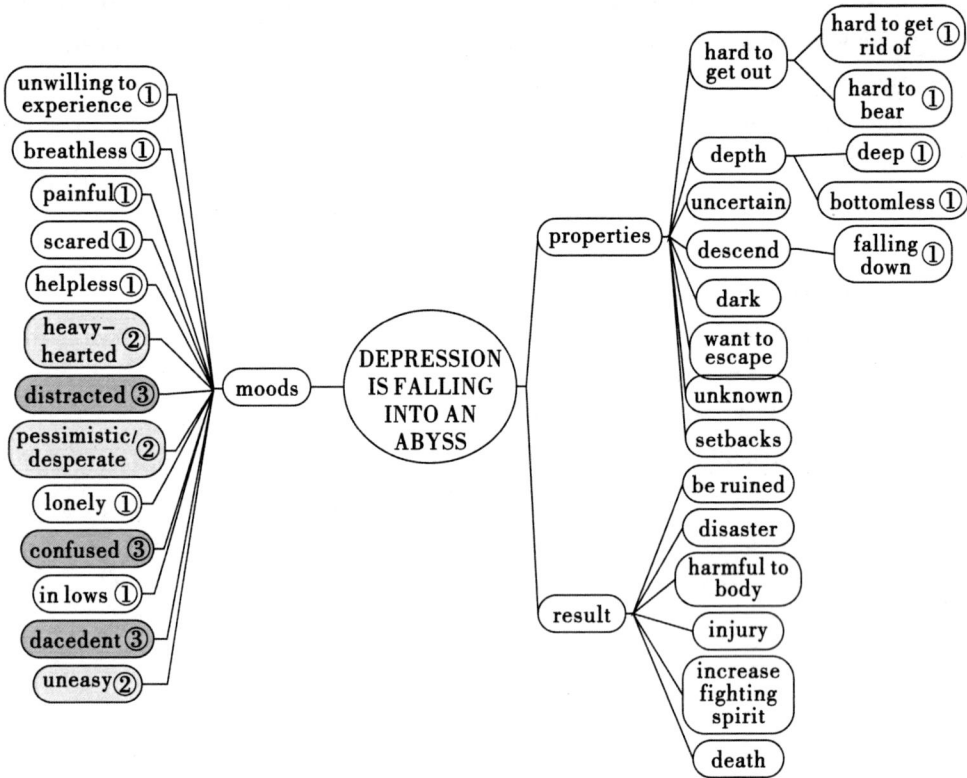

Figure 5-17 Categories Generated in the Pre-test and the Post-test on DEPRESSION IS FALLING INTO AN ABYSS (Ms Liu's Class)

Note. Words marked "①" are the categories generated in the pre-test and the post-test. Words marked "②" are the categories only generated in the pre-test. Words marked "③" are the categories only generated in the post-test.

c. Metaphorical highlighting: Result

"Both will result in death" and "both are harmful to body" were expressions mentioned in the pre-test and the post-test. "Both make people injured" was used only in the pre-test. "Both increase the fighting spirit" was used only in the post-test.

(4) Analysis of HUMAN BODY IS A BATTLEGROUND

The interpretations of similarities between source domain and target domain in the pre-test and the post-test can be grouped into four main categories, namely, properties, functions, results and wars. And each main categories also included different entailments (Figure 5-18).

The students' answers regarding the similarities can be discussed from a different metaphorical highlighting and its corresponding entailed metaphors, the details are listed as follows.

a. Metaphorical highlighting: Properties

Attribute is the main category found in the students' answers with regards to the similarity between the human body and the battleground. It has become a conventional metaphor. When mentioning of the different kinds of attribute, "war" was frequently mentioned. In the pre-test

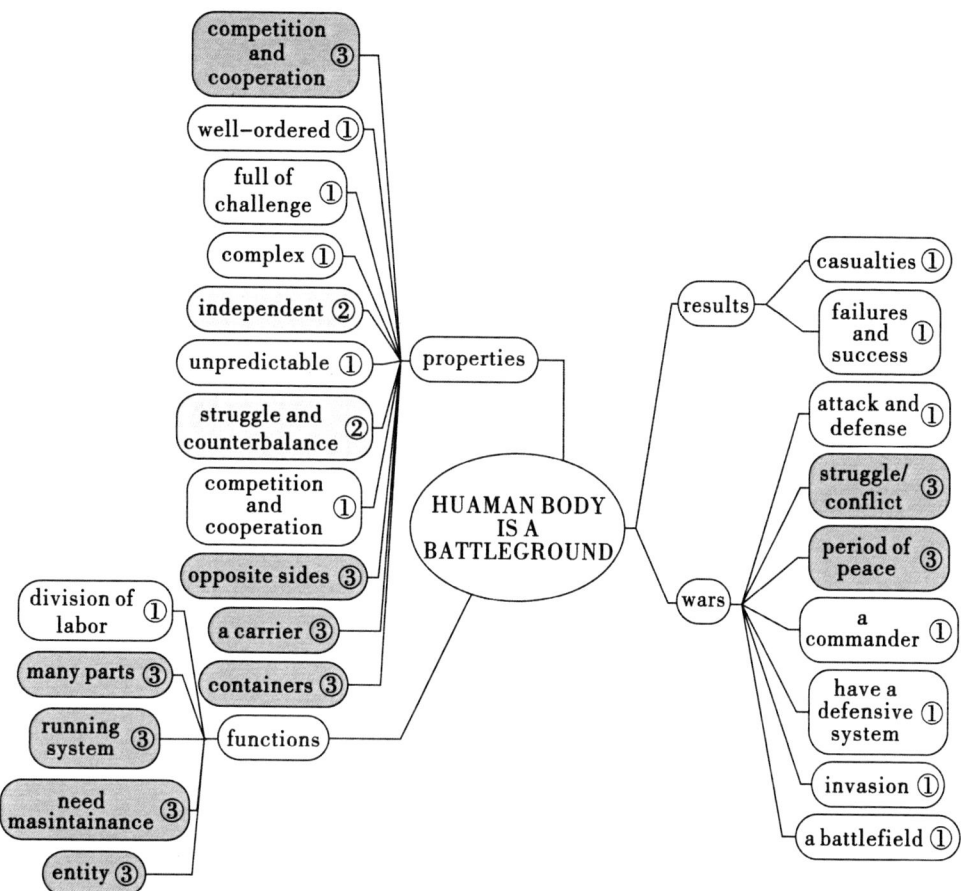

Figure 5-18 Categories Generated in the Pre-test and the Post-test on HUAMAN BODY IS A BATTLEGROUND (Ms Liu's Class)

Note. Words marked "①" are the categories generated in the pre-test and the post-test. Words marked "②" are the categories only generated in the pre-test. Words marked "③" are the categories only generated in the post-test.

and the post-test, "both can wage a battle/ have attack and defense/ suffer foreign invasion/ have confrontation/ have a commander/ have a (battle) field/ have a defensive line/ have defense systems" were the expressions used. "Both have enemies and weapons/ guardians/ period of peace and war/ a command center" were used only in the post-test.

b. Metaphorical highlighting: Functions

Some similarities regarding the functions of the human body and the battleground were mentioned. "Both are huge/ can protect itself/ need balance/ consist many parts/ have divisions of labour" were the expressions used in the pre-test and the post-test. "Both have protection systems/ running systems/ repair function" appeared only in the post-test.

c. Metaphorical highlighting: Results

The similarity as regards to effect was also mentioned. "Both have casualties/ injuries" was mentioned about in the pre-test and the post-test.

d. Metaphorical highlighting: Wars

War metaphor is another aspect of similarity that came from the students. "Both have a commander/a defensive system/invasion/a battlefield" was written in two tests.

(5) Analysis of BRAIN IS A MACHINE

The interpretations of similarities between brain and machine in the pre-test and the post-test can be summarized in three main categories, namely, properties, functions and significance. Figure 5-19 shows the categories generated in two tests.

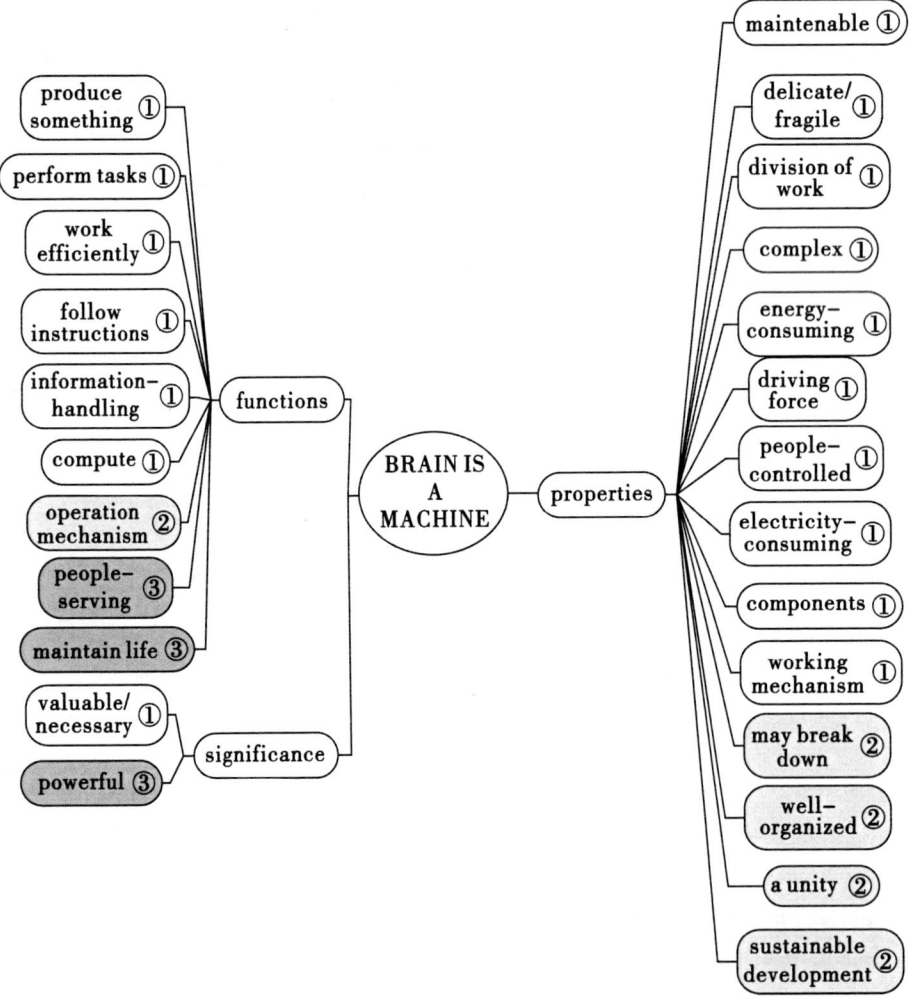

Figure 5-19 Categories Generated in the Pre-test and the Post-test on BRAIN IS A MACHINE (Ms Liu's Class)

Note. Words marked "①" are the categories generated in the pre-test and the post-test. Words marked "②" are the categories only generated in the pre-test. Words marked "③" are the categories only generated in the post-test.

The students' answers regarding the similarities can be discussed from different metaphorical aspects and are presented as follows.

a. Metaphorical highlighting: Properties

Eight sub-categories belong to the proprties of brain and machine, namely, break and maintain, division, composition, complexity, elaboration, creativity, mechanism, and importance. In the pre-test and the post-test, "both need charging/maintenance/are controlled by people/have a clear division of work/have many components are complicated/are delicate/need energy/consume energy/can produce something/have working principles" "both are valuable/necessary" "both canreceive/store/send/process information" were expressions listed by the students. "Both may be rusted" and "both are powerful" were used only in the post-test.

b. Metaphorical highlighting: Functions

Referring to similar functions between the brain and the machine, the expressions "both can perform a series of tasks/ work under instruction/ work efficiently or precisely" were mentioned in the pre-test and the post-test. "Both have an operating mechanism" was found in the pre-test, "both can store something/serve people" "both are systematic/one unity" and "both are intelligent/can be developed continually/need to be updated" were the answers found only in the post-test.

c. Metaphorical highlighting: Significance

"Both arevaluable/necessary" was the expression mentioned in the pre-test and the post-test. "Both are powerful" was used only in the post-test.

5.2.3.4 Part C in MCT of Ms Liu's class

(1) Metaphors generated on "Learning English is…"

According to Littlewood (2012), if a metaphor is creative and unique, it can reflect the active thought process of the user, including thoughts which cannot be expressed explicitly by speakers. When using metaphors, people's thoughts and perceptions will become more vivid. That is the reason why some studies use metaphors as a research tool (Kesen, 2013), such as in teacher education and in second language acquisition (as for example in Guerrero and Villamil, 2002).

According to the superordinate categories of the metaphors given by students, ninetypes of metaphors were mentioned both in the pre-test and the post-test. Besides, there were new sentences which only appeared in the pre-test or the post-test. The details can be seen in Table 5-25. Through these types, students showed their perceptions of English learning.

(2) Metaphors generated on "Treating illness is…" (Ms Liu's class)

The Table 5-26 shows metaphors generated on "Treating illness is…" There are seven types of metaphors which were mentioned both in two tests. Afterwards, there are new sentences which only appeared in the pre-test or the post-test.

Table 5-25 Metaphors Generated on "Learning English is…" (Ms Liu's Class)

Classification	Same source domain in the pre-test and the post-test	Source domain in the pre-test	Source domain in the post-test
Journey/Movement	A (long/interesting/wonderful) journey/travel/trip A running/jogging/marathon	Finishing a race	Going hiking (in the rainforest) Driving a ship on the sea/rowing Playing soccer
Playing/Leisure	Enjoying life Watching a movie Singing a (new) song Reading a (an interesting) book Cooking Playing a game	Listening to music Wearing a beautiful clothes Swimming in a rapid river/ across the Yangtze river	Watching an interesting play Going to a prairie Playing piano Playing with my best friend Enjoying the scenery Playing a (computer/exciting/ Level or cooperation) game Appreciating a beautiful poem Bathing in the sunshine Dancing with the foreign culture Playing basketball
Exploration	An adventure Climbing mountain/stairs Mining		Seeking treasures Removing a big mountain Walking on a new road
Love	Falling in love with someone		Pursuing a lady who is beyond reach A date
Experience	Planting a tree Flying in the sky Learning walk as a baby		Growing/watering flowers Flying in a language world/ Flying my own soul

Continue to Table 5-25

Classification	Same source domain in the pre-test and the post-test	Source domain in the pre-test	Source domain in the post-test
Building	Building a house/bridge		Building a skyscraper/a road/ blocks/ tower/a beautiful garden
Food and drinking	Eating (delicious) food/meal Drinking water/a cup of tea/coffee	Eating dessert/breakfast/sugar/chocolate	Eating apple/durian/candy/bitter medicine/nuts Food for thought
Things	The road to the world/an endless road		
Communication	Making new friends	Learning a person	Contacting a stranger/talking with foreigner/a master/a wise man
Unique expressions in the pre-test or the post-test			
Gains		Harvesting in autumn	Reaping crops Taking the fruit of wisdom Lying in the honey pot
Playing		Guessing a maze	Playing the jigsaw Going through the checkpoint
Thing		An investment/ a feast/ a sponge A storm/ gold/ a bridge/ a ticket Ladder to heaven Path to foreign country War/battle	A treasure/getting a fortune A golden brick to halls of knowledge

Continue to Table 5-25

Classification	Same source domain in the pre-test and the post-test	Source domain in the pre-test	Source domain in the post-test
Challenge			Getting over yourself
			Cracking a hard nut
			A persistent competition/match
			Dispelling the clouds and see the sun
			Walking on an endless road
			Reading Oracle
			Conquering
Experience			Seeing the words dancing in the paper
			Entering a new world/a key to the world
			Opening a door/window to the future
			Grinding the pearl
Farming/Planting			Making the desert to forest
Movement			Removing a big stone
Eating/Drinking			Eating coptis (Chinese medicine)
			Eating a traditional Chinese medicine
			Drinking a bitter soup

Note. Coptis refers to small genus of low.

Table 5-26 Metaphors Generated on "Treating illness is…" (Ms Liu's Class)

Classification	Same source domain in the pre-test and the post-test	Source domain in the pre-test	Source domain in the post-test
Journey/Movement	A journey/a long running/a marathon Climbing the mountain		A long road/travel/walking/tour (to patient) Going hiking crossing the endless road
Playing/Leisure	Riding a roller coaster	Taking a pirate ship	Passing a narrow bridge
War/Battle/Gamble	Fighting/defeating with evil/ enemies/ monster/difficulties Awar/battle/campaign/match/combat/ struggle/ gamble	Fighting with tiger	Fighting with bad guy/foe/disease/ invaders A race/competition with illness/ virus confronting enemies in the battleground Resisting the enemy along the boarder A live-fire drill A breath-taking rescue operation Having a successful weapon Winning the war
Repair	Repairing/fixing/mending a machine	Being repaired by God	Mending a house/a car Replacing machine parts Sewing your own clothes
Thing	An adventure		
Removing	Moving a (big) mountain	Getting rid of trouble Climbing up an abyss	Reeling off raw silk from cocoons Spraying pesticides for crops Getting rid of dark Escaping the devil's claws

Continue to Table 5-26

Classification	Same source domain in the pre-test and the post-test	Source domain in the pre-test	Source domain in the post-test
Solution	Working out a difficult problem Putting out the fire		Finding the exit of the maze Pulling back to the cliff Providing support to the soldiers Watering the withered plants/flowers Correcting some errors Investing and solving a crime Arresting a bad guy Killing the computer virus
Thrilling	Taking a roller-coaster	Taking a pirate ship	Passing a narrow bridge
Unique expressions in the pre-test or the post-test			
Experience			Breaking through a stormy sea Swimming in the flood Getting through the tides in better days Walking in the cold wind Opening a heavy door Building up a barrier to prevent virus
Cleaning			Cleaning the floor/rubbish/the bedroom Sweeping Building a house Standing up from the ground

Continue to Table 5-26

Classification	Same source domain in the pre-test and the post-test	Source domain in the pre-test	Source domain in the post-test
Thing		Hurdle race	A stumbling block in travel
		A choice between heaven and hell	A form of update
		An angel spreading love to human	A revolution of human body
			A sauce bottle which has many tastes
Uncertain			Closing the Pandora's box
			Crossing the river
			Pressing spring
Solution		Fixing plumbing	Checking circuit
Challenge			Walking in the desert
			Walking on mountain road
			Crossing a swamp
			Walking a thorny path
			Living in winter
			Playing a (level) game
			Running against time
Hope			The warm sun melts the winter snow
			drawing a picture of the dark world
			Seeking hope in the sea
			Grass growing through the soil
			Rainbow after the storm
			Waiting for spring in winter

5.3 Research Question 3: What are the Teachers' Performance and Reflection on the Metaphor Enriched Language Instruction?

The classroom observation is the instrument for assessing the teachers' performance and reflection. During the implementation process, the researcher did the classroom observation on Ms Wang's and Ms Liu's metaphor enriched English language teaching and Ms Liu was invited to observe the researcher's class. They completed the checklist after each lecture, and wrote down comments on it (Appendix D).

The classroom observation checklist was adapted from The Sheltered Instruction Observation Protocol (2008). It consists of demography, five main topics and other comments. For each question under the topics, there are five rating scales which represent outstanding, good, fair, poor, and not observed. The five topics are metaphor enriched class structure, teaching strategies, teacher's use of materials, teacher's use of language and students' performance. The explanations of each part are listed. The feedback of each participant teacher is to be listed with regards to each unit.

5.3.1 Classroom observation checklist for Unit 2

For this part, five topics were discussed and the observer's observation and reflection are given in comments.

5.3.1.1 Metaphor enriched class structure for Unit 2

Metaphor enriched class structure includes whether the teaching goals or objectives was achieved, the theories and methods used in the instruction, the input of supplement and the assignment design and analyses (Table 5-27).

Table 5-27 Metaphor Enriched Class Structure for Unit 2

Metaphor enriched class structure	Outstanding 5	Good 4	Fair 3	Poor 2	Not observed 1
	Ms Wang			Ms Liu	
1. Clearly states goals or objectives for the metaphor-related content		4		4	
2. Clearly explains metaphor theories		4		5	
3. Interprets metaphors in General English or Medical English	5			5	

Continue to Table 5-27

Metaphor enriched class structure	Outstanding 5	Good 4	Fair 3	Poor 2	Not observed 1
		Ms Wang		Ms Liu	
4. Links General English with Medical English in terms of metaphor		4		3	
5. Assigns and analyzes the metaphor enriched homework		4		5	

Table 5-27 shows the five aspects towards the metaphor enriched class structure, namely, objectives of metaphor instruction, metaphor theories, metaphor interpretation, combination of General English (GE) with Medical English (ME), and metaphor enriched homework. As a whole, all of the three teacher participants did well except the merging of GE with ME. From the post-class feedback, we can find that although they have taught GE for more than ten years, they seldom mentioned ME in their class and they still need to learn more about the medical aspect. All the teachers had assigned and analyzed the metaphor enriched homework which means they have a positive approach to it.

(1) Comments on Ms Wang's metaphor enriched class structure

At the beginning of Unit 2, Ms Wang mentioned the objectives of Metaphor Enriched English Language Instruction (MEELI) which made the students realize that they were supposed to acquire the medical knowledge as medical students (Item 1). She also had interpreted the metaphors in the video (Item 3). What impressed the researcher is her explanation of the Chinese word "shen jing bing". It is normally used to describe a person with a mental disorder, while it refers to the disease of the nervous system in Medicine. In effect, this had transferred the topic to the nervous system (Item 4). In dealing with the assignment of identifying metaphors in the given pictures, Ms Wang had analyzed the three given pictures (Booklet) and explained the metaphor theories in detail (Item 5).

(2) Comments on Ms Liu's metaphor enriched class structure

After summarizing the metaphors in the text of Unit 2, Ms Liu had analyzed the characteristics of the metaphor and how it differs from the similes. She cited a metaphor in the animation *Crayon Shin-chan* to tell the importance of using a metaphor. The objectives of MEELI were emphasized afterwards. Here is an extract from her work.

Ms Liu

While traditionally, the so-called metaphor, also known as comparison, makes analogy between two objects without the use of "like" or "as". Metaphor is different from simile in the basic aspects, but they are the same. There are a lot of metaphors in the conversations between doctors and patients. For example, *cancer is a monster. It wants to eat me.* Or, *cancer is a wildfire. It is burning and cannot be extinguished.* These are very visual, very infectious, metaphorical descriptions. I still remember that when I watched Crayon Shin-chan, there was a plot that impressed me. He had a stomachache; the teacher asked him what kind of ache? He described it for a long time, didn't know how to describe the extent of pain, after all, he was a kindergarten child. He said: "*the pain is like a hundred elephants stepping on me*". Sometimes, doctors need to have some imagination to understand the patients' description of his pain or disease. So, in order to explain your ongoing treatment to your patient in the future, or in order to better understand some symptoms that your patient is describing, I think everyone should learn how to use metaphors to learn Medical English.

When talking about the function of the sympathetic nervous system, Ms Liu explained the similarities between the sympathetic nervous system and boxing. Once you see a fist coming, the sympathetic nerves will give instructions to protect yourself. She cited another example, a movie *Never Say Die* which was a hit comedy movie about boxing. Here is an extract from her.

Ms Liu

How do you protect yourself when you punch? The most important thing is to protect your head with your arms, so it makes you to react. It helps you to react quickly to threats and dangers from the outside world. And it can protect you; the sympathetic nerve tells you: protect your head. Right? Sometimes, the sympathetic nerve will tell you something is very hot and free your hand. This is your sympathetic nervous system.

(3) Comments on Ms Zhang's metaphor enriched class structure

After introducing the anxiety of Emma Ston in the set induction part, the researcher provided more similes on anxiety to help the students understand the functions of metaphor (simile is a kind of metaphor). These similes enhanced the students' understanding of metaphor theories (Item 2).

Similes of ANXIETY

Anxiety is like walking down a dark and scary alley without knowing what is awaiting you.

Anxiety is like swimming in the ocean with no land in sight.

Anxiety is like trying to memorize all of the conversations within a crowded restaurant.

Anxiety is like being the only person that knows the world is ending but everyone calls you crazy.

Anxiety is like being brutally beaten at different points throughout the day but you do not know when the beating will occur again.

When interpreting the video assignment *The Nervous System* in period 2 of week 7, the researcher supplemented the knowledge of amygdala which are important structures in the neural mechanism of emotional cognition (Item 5). Here is an extract from her interaction.

Ms Zhang

Suppose you take a walk in the forest, and in the corner of your eye, you see a long bar on your left, rustling, and when you have no time to think of the word snake, your body is already stiff, your heartbeat speeds up and your palms sweat. Which part of your brain caused this response? It's amygdala, an important structure for emotional learning and memory. Because fearful memories are blurred images, many objects similar to a certain fearful memory will cause you fear. A tube in the grass in the backyard could immediately take you back several steps. Therefore, you will produce the above response when you see a long bar if you once were bitten by snakes.

5.3.1.2 Teaching strategies for Unit 2

Table 5-28 shows the five aspects towards the teaching strategies, namely, employs non-lecture learning activities, employs other tools, provides students opportunities to use, times activities appropriately and supports high-level thinking. The two teachers did well in employing videos in class and assigning homework while they did not employ non-lecture learning activities due to the students' lack of theoretical basis and class size.

Table 5-28 Teaching Strategies for Unit 2

Teaching strategies	Outstanding 5	Good 4	Fair 3	Poor 2	Not observed 1
	Ms Wang			Ms Liu	
6. Employs non-lecture learning activities (small group discussion, student-led activities)			1		1
7. Employs other tools/instructional aids (technology, video)		4			5
8. Provides students opportunities to use metaphors				2	2
9. Times the activities appropriately			1		1
10. Supports high-level thinking		4			4

(1) Comments on Ms Wang's teaching strategies

As the first unit to apply Metaphor Enriched English Language Instruction (MEELI), metaphor theories and cognitive mechanism were given priority rather than group discussion and activities in implementing Unit 2. In addition, the class size (about 240 students) was another factor to consider. Since the class time was limited, the video *The Nervous System* was assigned as homework (Booklet) and was explained during period 3 to the students. When interpreting the answers to the exercise, the three teachers played the video again in the class in order to enhance the students' understanding of the materials. The second assignment for students was to watch a video *Structure of a Neuron* and complete the related exercise (Booklet). Ms Wang played the video at the end of period 4 and briefly introduced it which aroused the interest of the students. The two assignments targeted the improvement of the students' metaphoric comprehension ability. The first one was to come up with a metaphor according to the pictures and the second one was to match the metaphorical descriptions with the correct terms. Both of them required the students to write down the similarities between the source domain and target domain which did provoke the students' high-level thinking.

(2) Comments on Ms Liu's teaching strategies

Like Ms Wang, Ms Liu did not employ non-lecture learning activities in class and did not arrange time for student activities, and two homework exercises were assigned to students to encourage their use of metaphors and their high-level thinking.

What impressed the researcher was her own supplement video before the video *The Nervous System*. In order to make the students acquire the medical knowledge easily, she played another short video (1 minute) as a transition. After the short video, three questions were asked to review the main idea and she interpreted them one by one. After introducing the metaphor theories, Ms Liu asked what were the cognitive functions of metaphor by offering them a picture. In fact, in our daily life, people often use metaphors to describe objects, for example, naming the mountain parts in terms of body parts (Figure 5-20).

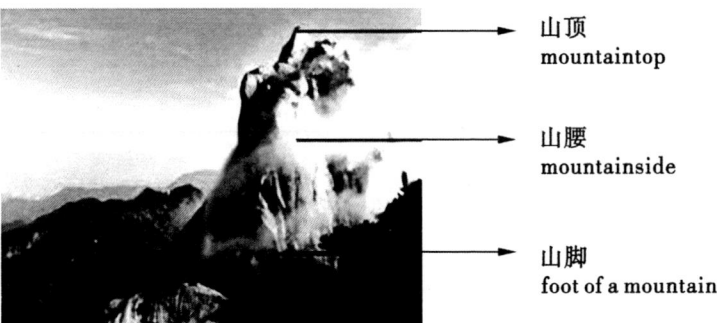

Figure 5-20 Metaphors between Mountain and Human Body

Note. "顶" means "the top of the head" in Chinese, 腰 means "waist" in Chinese, 脚 means "foot" in Chinese.

Figure 5-20 inspired the students' understanding of the functions of a metaphor (Item 10). The researcher summarized other functions and gradually transgressed to the objective of metaphor enriched supplement. First, they could generate or understand concepts by giving the concepts a terminological framework, like the picture above. Second, they could give new meanings to words already in common use, like the word "virus" which is used in the computer field. Third, they could reduce the overload in the mental storage of knowledge, thereby facilitating word memory, like medical vocabulary learning. Fourth, they could relate our experiences in a rich and vivid language which are usually found in poems. Fifth, they could enhance the listeners' or readers' ability to grasp an abstract or unfamiliar concept by using a more concrete or familiar concept. Sixth, they could generate new metaphors, which could generate additional expressions in speaking or writing processes.

5.3.1.3 Teacher's use of materials for Unit 2

Table 5-29 shows the five aspects towards teacher's use of materials, namely, provides well-designed metaphor-related materials in an organized manner to meet the objectives, uses high reliable metaphor-related materials, uses moderately difficult metaphor-related materials, adopts various metaphor-related resources as supplement and relates metaphor concepts to teachers' or students' experience. The metaphor-related materials were adapted from reliable sources and were viewed by Professor Wen who is an experienced teacher in the field of Anatomy. Therefore, the supplemented materials are well-designed and reliable. However, analyzing the students' homework, some of them did not understand the requirement and some thought the video assignment about the nervous system was quite difficult. The two teachers did relate metaphor concepts to their experience which increased the students' interest.

Table 5-29 Teacher's Use of Materials for Unit 2

Teacher's use of materials	Outstanding 5	Good 4	Fair 3	Poor 2	Not observed 1
	Ms Wang		Ms Liu		
11. Provides well-designed metaphor-related materials in an organized manner to meet the objectives	5		5		
12. Uses high reliable metaphor-related materials	5		5		
13. Uses moderately difficult metaphor-related materials	3		4		
14. Adopts various metaphor-related resources (pictures, video) as supplement	4		5		
15. Relates metaphor concepts to teachers' or students' experience	5		5		

(1) Comments on Ms Wang's use of materials

What impressed the researcher was that Ms Wang related her yoga experience to the explanation of the metaphor THE FUNCTION OF NERVOUS SYSTEM IS DOING YOGA. As an experienced yoga fan, she had been practicing yoga for many years. Therefore, her explanation was very professional and enhanced the students' understanding of this metaphor. Here is an extract from her work.

Ms Wang

Make balance is often mentioned in yoga because there are many postures in yoga requiring balance. There are some dance postures in yoga, everyone should have seen it, for example, stretch back with the legs, with arms straight forward. The famous vertical posture in yoga is just like posing as a pheasant standing on one foot (金鸡独立). The second function: coordinate all the activities of the body, which is a function of the nervous system, some students will ask; can yoga coordinate all the activities of the body? Yes, it can. Because when you are doing yoga, if you can not coordinate, the consequences are very serious. Do you know why Xie Na(compere) was absent from Happy Camp (TV series) in the past period? She broke her ribs when she practiced yoga at home. Once when she came out, she was knocked down by a wheelchair. If the yoga movements are not coordinated, it is easy to strain, but our nervous system can regulate the whole body. Third, regulate heart rates, yoga emphasizes breathing, inhale and exhale. Breathing can make your heart rate stable; these are their similarities. Next there is an example: The nervous system is a coordinator because it can coordinate all the activities of the body.

(2) Comments on Ms Liu's use of materials

Ms Liu did well in item 14 and she supplemented her own materials on the basis of the common materials (*The Nervous System* and *Structure of a Neuron*). She supplemented an example of the nervous system analogy, using Prezi. Prezi is a presentation software that makes ideas more interesting by zooming in and out. It breaks the traditional slides' single-line timing, using systemic and structural integration to demonstrate, in the way of route presentation, from one object suddenly to another, with rotation and other actions for more visual impact. It creates and edits documents through multi-terminals (web page, Windows and Mac desktop, ipad and iphone) to help people develop ideas and make the connection between ideas clearer. Figure 5-21 is a picture of the nervous system metaphors.

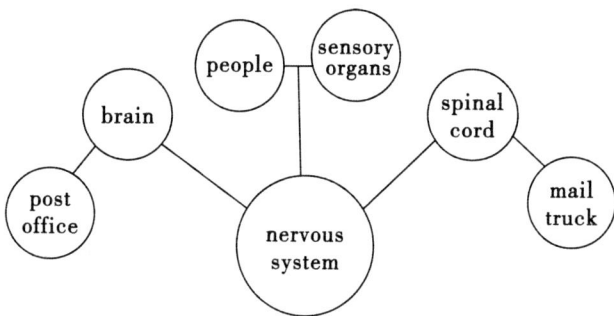

Figure 5-21 Metaphors of the Nervous System in Prezi

This metaphor scenario contains five conceptual metaphors and their similarities are listas follows (Table 5-30).

Table 5-30 Nervous System Metaphors in Prezi

Target domain	Source domain	Similarities
Brain	Post office	Both are center of its system
		Both can and receives information
Sensory organs	People	Both can pick up the information
Spinal cord	Mail truck	Both are carriers of message or mails
CNS	Central postal system	Both are control centers
PNS	Peripheral postal system	Both are made up of nerves/mails

Note. CNS means central nervous system, PNS means peripheral nervous system.

The five metaphors are as follows.

1) The brain is a post office

The brain is the control center of all of the body systems which can send messages to the body and receive the messages from the body. Similarly, a post office is the center of the mail service which can send and receive mail from around the world.

2) Sensory organs are people in the post office

Sensory organs pick up information from your environment and send it to the brain. Similarly, people also write letters and send them to the post office.

3) Spinal cord is a mail truck

The spinal cord is a bundle of nerves that runs down your back which carries messages to and from the brain. Similarly, the mail truck carries the messages to and from the post office.

4) Central nervous system is the central postal system

The central nervous system which consists of the brain and the spinal cord is the control center of the body. Similarly, the central postal system which consists of the post office and the mail trucks is the control center of all mails.

5) Peripheral nervous system is the peripheral postal system

The peripheral nervous system is made up of all of the neurons in the body except of the spinal cord and the brain. Similarly, the peripheral postal system is made up of all the people and mails in the world.

(3) Comments on Ms Zhang's use of materials

The researcher also supplemented metaphors of the brain in Unit 3. After viewing the assigned video, *The Cardiovascular System*, students had already known about the structure of brain. The researcher mentioned about the comparison of the brain and the computer which is a frequently used metaphor. She cited the former American president Obama's words: As humans, we can identify galaxies light years away, we can study particles smaller than an atom, but we still haven't unlocked the mystery of the three pounds of matter that sits between our ears. It shows how complex the human brain is. Then the students asked as to what were the similarities and differences between the brain and the computer. After listening to the students' answers, the researcher analyzed the conceptual metaphor and gave some more examples of brain metaphors. The details are as follows.

e. g. , THE BRAIN IS LIKE A COMPUTER.

Similarities: The sensory organs in brain are like the input devices of a computer, because both of them can receive signals of vision, touch, hearing, smell, and taste.

The brain is the host like a computer because both of them can complete the task switching and message processing.

Difference: The computer is made up of a central processor while the brain is made up of many modules.

The researcher listed more metaphors of the brain which was aimed at enhancing the creative thinking of the students.

Brain is a one and a half-kilo mushroom shaped matter of gray and white tissue of gelatinous consistency.

Brain is an old attic containing the mementos of a lifetime.

Brain is a black box.

Brain is like a vast, unexplored continent.

5.3.1.4 Teacher's use of language for Unit 2

Table 5-31 shows the five aspects of the teacher's use of language, namely, uses metaphorical expressions in the process of instruction, uses clear questioning or coaching, engages the students actively, explains important ideas simply and clearly, makes evaluation and gives feedback according to the students' performance. All the teachers did well in using clear questioning and coaching as well as explaining important ideas simply and clearly. However, except the feedback of the assignment, they did not give feedback of the students' performance due to the fact that there was no arrangement for the students' activities in the class.

Table 5-31 Teacher's Use of Language for Unit 2

Teacher's use of language	Outstanding 5	Good 4	Fair 3	Poor 2	Not observed 1
	Ms Wang			Ms Liu	
16. Uses metaphorical expressions in the process of instruction		3		5	
17. Uses clear questioning or coaching		4		5	
18. Engages the students actively	5			4	
19. Explains important ideas simply and clearly		4		5	
20. Makes evaluation and gives feedback according to the students' performance					1 (Ms Wang), 1 (Ms Liu)

(1) Comments on Ms Wang's use of language

Unit 2 is the first supplemented unit which is quite unfamiliar to the students, Ms Wang explained as to what was to be done with the assignment very clearly. The first exercise was to come up with a metaphor, taking a clue from the picture of doing yoga. She told the students, "It is difficult to find out as to which body part is involved in yoga." Some students said, "What did the teacher ask me to write?" Here "body part" refers to the nervous system, and "sport" refers to yoga. In fact, the key is to find their similarities. Why does the speaker compare the nervous system to yoga? Why does the speaker think the function of the nervous system is like doing yoga? Ms Wang used clear questioning and coaching in her explanation of the assignment.

(2) Comments on Ms Liu's use of language

Ms Liu used metaphors when talking about the function of the nervous system (Item 16). The following extract explains how she and her husband understand the function of the nervous system.

Ms Liu

We can say the nervous system is like a CEO, or a manager, a chief executive, a commander. I remember that I asked my husband who is a doctor in the army that if he were to create a metaphor, what will he compare the nervous system to? Since he is a soldier, his first reaction was to metaphorize the brain into a commander. Then he compared a variety of the nerve cells to a telephone line which is the channel to send instructions. He compared the organs of the body, which are controlled by the nervous system, to the soldiers. The nervous system is controlling our body.

What impressed the researcher is that Ms Liu explained metaphors in the text clearly (Item 19). For example, when talking about the metaphoric meaning of "bug", she interpreted very clearly. Here is an extract from her work.

> Ms Liu: *Stop bugging me. What does bug mean?*
> Students: *Disturb.*
> Ms Liu: *Bug is a small insect.*
> Students: *Ah?*
> Ms Liu: *Its original meaning is an insect. Its metaphorical meaning in this sentence is annoying, right? Annoy means making someone a little angry. How can these two meanings be connected?*
> Students: *There are a lot of people who hate bugs.*
> Ms Liu: *Because this is a kind of empathy. When you see bugs, few people will like it. Except a few weird people, others don't like bugs, we want to kill it when we see them. So, the word has the meaning of annoying.*

Another example refers to the explanation of the metaphoric sentence: My stomach is full of knots. Here is an extract from Ms Liu.

> *Knot means a fastening of a rope, when I say my stomach is knotted, what does it mean? It makes you feel the uneasy, uncomfortable, nervous and other similar emotions. For example, the phrase "make my blood boil", which some students may translate into "burning blood", generally expressed during an excitement, but in English, it means "make someone very angry".*
>
> *What are they? They are metaphors which use one thing to describe various actions, states, and properties. A common thing is used to describe a thing or action that is difficult to describe, so that everyone can understand it better. For example, my stomach is full of knots, if I tell you, I am worried or I am concerned. To what extent? The reader cannot understand your feelings, right? But if you tell him that my stomach is knotted and he will generate empathy immediately. There is a feeling that his stomach is also knotted. Such metaphors are actually very vivid. There are similes and metaphors. However, I personally feel that in many language environments, simile is a kind of metaphor.*

5.3.2 Classroom observation checklist for Unit 3

For this part, five topics involving the metaphor enriched class structure were discussed and the observer's observation and reflection were written in the comments. The details of each item can be seen in detail.

5.3.2.1 Metaphor enriched class structure for Unit 3

Since the objectives for the metaphor-related content was explained at the beginning of Unit 2, the teachers did not mention it again in this unit. For the metaphor theories, the three teachers explained it when teaching the supplemented materials about heart. They supplemented the discussed materials *Metaphorical meanings of heart* as well as *Metaphorical Expressions of Heart that are Unique to Chinese*. Therefore, they did well in Item 3 and Item 5 (Table 5-32). A video of the cardiovascular system also was provided to students as self-study material as well as its transcript. Because of the difficulty, no submission was required.

Table 5-32 Metaphor Enriched Class Structure for Unit 3

Metaphor enriched class structure	Outstanding 5	Good 4	Fair 3	Poor 2	Not observed 1
	Ms Wang			Ms Liu	
1. Clearly states goals or objectives for the metaphor-related content	1			1	
2. Clearly explains metaphor theories	5			3	
3. Interprets metaphors in General English or Medical English	5			5	
4. Links General English with Medical English in terms of metaphor	4			3	
5. Assigns and analyzes the metaphor enriched homework	5			4	

(1) Comments on Ms Wang's metaphor enriched class structure

What impressed the researcher is Ms Wang's clear explanation of the death metaphor. There is a sentence "His father has been gone for many years now" (line 45) in the text. When discussing this sentence, she mentioned euphemism and metaphor of death. Here is an extract from Ms Wang.

Ms Wang

The sentence His father has been gone for many years now is a euphemism for death. There are many euphemisms of death, like pass away, demise, depart, rest in peace, eternal rest, asleep, lost, kick the bucket, did not make it, breathe one's last, go to heaven, go to be with the Lord, in a better place. Some of them also are metaphors. For example, this sentence implies a conceptual metaphor: DEATH IS DEPARTURE. If we take LIFE IS A JOURNEY, then death is the end of the journey. There are many entailments of it and their euphemisms are in brackets:

> *Death is the end of the journey(pass away).*
> *Death is departure(depart).*
> *Death is going to the final destination(go to heaven, go to be with the Lord, in a better place).*

There are many other metaphors which talk of death as the withering of plants, the night, sleep, loss of the fluid, final scene, deliverance, release from the burden, loss of one's possession, loss of contest and the process of falling. The details are listed as follows.

> People are plants, human death is the death of plants.
> A life is a day, death is the night.
> Death is sleep.
> Life is fluid in the body, death is loss of the fluid.
> Life is a play, death is the final scene.
> Life is bondage, death is deliverance.
> Life is a burden, to die is to get released from the burden.
> Life is a precious possession, death is the loss of the possession.
> Life is a contest, to die is to lose the contest.
> Death is falling.

(2) Comments on Ms Liu's metaphor enriched class structure

There is a phrasal verb *take a dive* in paragraph 10 of the text which is metaphoric. Ms Liu interpreted all the metaphoric meanings of it and had analyzed it in detail (Item 3). The following are the meanings and examples she had expressed in the class.

Ms Liu

> *The phrase take a dive has three metaphoric meanings. Its original meaning is a headlong plunge into water. It can be used to other fields.*
>
> *In boxing, it means to pretend to be knocked out by one's opponent (Generally done as a means of rigging the outcome of the match, so as to exploit betting odds and trends).*
>
> *In soccer (football), it means to fall to the ground and make a very ostentatious display that one is in pain and anguish after making contact with an opposing player. For example: It is so obvious that the player from England took a dive!*
>
> *In the stock market, it means to very suddenly become lower in value, as of the shares in a company or in the market as a whole which emphasizes a sharp downward movement.*

5.3.2.2 Teaching strategies for Unit 3

All the teachers organized a role-play, depicting a heart problem in the class. The transcript of the dialogues was provided to the students before the commencement of the lecture and the students were required to modify it according to their needs. This student-led activity enhanced their interest in medical conversation as well as added to their medical knowledge. Video watching was also included in this unit to widen the horizon of their medical vocabulary (Table 5-33).

Table 5-33 Teaching Strategies for Unit 3

Teaching strategies	Outstanding 5	Good 4	Fair 3	Poor 2	Not observed 1
	Ms Wang			Ms Liu	
6. Employs non-lecture learning activities (small group discussion, student-led activities)	5			5	
7. Employs other tools/instructional aids (technology, video)		4		5	
8. Provides students opportunities to use metaphors		4		4	
9. Times the activities appropriately		4		4	
10. Supports high-level thinking		4		4	

Regarding Item 10, Ms Liu's showed the capacity of transforming the students' interest into a high-level thinking. Different from Ms Wang's set induction, Ms Liu did it from the angle of cultural similarity. Here is an extract from her work.

> Ms Liu
>
> *A Good Heart to Lean On.* What does this title mean? What is a good heart? Kindness, right? One's conscience or good qualities. Followed by an infinitive verb to lean on which is a post-positioned attributive. Depends on someone's good heart, right? So, heart here doesn't mean the organ heart, right? Heart here means some good qualities, right? Good is used to describe the heart, its antonym is evil, evil heart means one's heart is relatively bad, both good and evil refer to one's qualities, right?

5.3.2.3 Teacher's use of materials for Unit 3

The topic of Unit 3 is a good heart, the three teachers taught metaphors of heart in the class. This supplementary material included the metaphoric meanings of heart and the metaphorical expressions of heart which are unique to Chinese. Students mastered it well and they began to think about these words and expressions from the perspective of metaphor. These supplementary materials are adapted from *A Usage Dictionary of English and Chinese Conceptual Metaphors* and *Cambridge Dictionary* which are highly reliable and moderately difficult. Further, in describing the characteristics of a father, the teachers and the students used metaphors to describe their father (Table 5-34).

Table 5-34 Teacher's Use of Materials for Unit 3

Teacher's use of materials	Outstanding 5	Good 4	Fair 3	Poor 2	Not observed 1
		Ms Wang		Ms Liu	
11. Provides well-designed metaphor-related materials in an organized manner to meet the objectives		5		5	
12. Uses high reliable metaphor-related materials		5		5	
13. Uses moderately difficult metaphor-related materials		3		4	
14. Adopts various metaphor-related resources (pictures, video) as supplement		4		5	
15. Relates metaphor concepts to teachers' or students' experience		5		4	

(1) Comments on Ms Liu's use of materials

Along with the supplementary metaphors of heart, Ms Liu also provided some hot expressions relating to the heart. On October 18, 2017, the Chinese president Xi Jinping pointed out in the report of the 19th National Congress of the Communist Party of China that the theme education should "remain true to our original aspiration" and to be carried out in the whole party. There are several different translations as regards the title of this theme, education. In order to enlarge the students' vocabulary and translation skills, the researcher supplied a very hot Chinese idiom of heart, and compared its English translation in different contexts. Here are the examples.

1) (Chinese) 不忘初心,牢记使命。

(English) *Remain true to our original aspiration* and keep our mission firmly in mind.

2) (Chinese) 不忘初心,方得始终。

(English) *Never forget why you started*, and you can accomplish your mission.

3) (Chinese) 无论是弱小还是强大,无论是顺境还是逆境,我们党都初心不改、矢志不渝……

(English) Whether in times of weakness or strength, whether in times of adversity or smooth sailing, our Party has *never forgotten its founding mission*, nor wavered in its pursuit...

4)(Chinese)在全党开展"不忘初心、牢记使命"主题教育。

(English) We will launch a campaign on the theme of *staying true to our founding mission*.

Note. Different translations of metaphoric phrases regarding to heart are in italics.

Students were very interested in the different translations and learned more about the metaphoric meanings of heart.

(2)Comments on Ms Wang's use of materials

Apart from the supplementary metaphors of heart, Ms Wang provided a video *The Cardiovascular System* to students for self-study. Considering the difficulty of this material, she provided also the transcript and summarized metaphoric words of the video to students. The details can be seen in Booklet. What's more, she also recommended an article *Your blood type can seriously affect your health* from Daily Mail to students as further reading material which might help them widen the horizon of their knowledge. They could learn more about the relation between blood type and health. The details can be seen in Booklet.

5.3.2.4 Teacher's use of language for Unit 3

Ms Liu used metaphors in her process of instruction and it can be seen in the following part. When interpreting the assignment of reading an excerpt from *I am Joe's body*, the three teachers did a commendable job in analyzing the metaphors within the text. Further, they interpreted the supplementary metaphors about heart in detail. After the students' role-play in the class, the two teachers made an evaluation and gave feedback in accordance with their performance(Table 5-35).

Table 5-35　Teacher's Use of Language for Unit 3

Teacher's use of language	Outstanding 5	Good 4	Fair 3	Poor 2	Not observed 1
	Ms Wang		Ms Liu		
16. Uses metaphorical expressions in the process of instruction	3		5		
17. Uses clear questioning or coaching	4		5		
18. Engages the students actively	5		4		
19. Explains important ideas simply and clearly	4		4		
20. Makes evaluation and gives feedback according to the students' performance	1		1		

(1) Comments on Ms Wang's use of language

Ms Wang cited a theme song of *Titanic* as the set induction and continued to interpret several metaphoric meanings of heart which engaged the students actively. Here is an extract from her work.

> Ms Wang: *Today, we are going to talk about metaphors about heart, because the title is "A Good Heart to Lean on". Let's have a look. First, Heart is a very important organ, right?*
> Students: *Yes.*
> Ms Wang: *Which is the most important organ in our body? It is heart, isn't it? And we know that it is heart which pumps blood to all parts of our body. Heart also refers to your feelings, your emotions, and so on. What do you understand when someone tells you, "Please follow your heart"? Do you know the theme song of Titanic? Have you seen the movie Titanic?*
> Students: *Yeah.*
> Ms Wang: *Do you know the theme song?*
> Students: *Wo Xin Yong Heng (Chinese).*
> Ms Wang: Yes, *my heart will go on.* It means my feelings, my emotions will go on and on.

(2) Comments on Ms Liu's use of language

The main idea of Unit 3 is that the author recalls as to what kind of person his father is and what his father has done for him. Before reading the text, Ms Wang first asked the students to think about their fathers. The students were asked to use some words to describe their own father and 18 students raised their hands to talk about their fathers. This approach engaged the students actively and Ms Liu used a metaphor to summarize the characteristics of a father. Here is an extract from her work.

> Ms Liu: *OK, our time is limited. In fact, I don't know what your fathers often say, maybe some advices about your life, your studies, or his opinions on something, and so on. Here are three examples, some of them are very typical. For example, he always says: Go and ask your mother. Right? The father is like a person who wears the white makeup in the Beijing opera (play the villain), he always says: you're grounded. This is usually said by most of the fathers.*

5.3.3 Classroom observation checklist for Unit 5

For this part, five topics were discussed and the observer's observation and reflection were written in comments.

5.3.3.1 Metaphor enriched class structure for Unit 5

All the teachers talked about war metaphors in Unit 5, and the researcher supplemented its usage in other fields. Since the topic of Unit 5 is AIDS, all the teacher participants discussed the metaphors of the immune system and assigned different types of homework, including watching and recording videos which enthused the students greatly. The two teachers interpreted the metaphorical expressions of health and medicine that are unique to Chinese which also widened the students' horizon and the understanding of cultural difference. A video, Inner world discovery: *The Immune System* was assigned as another homework for metaphor recognition (Table 5-36).

Table 5-36 Metaphor Enriched Class Structure for Unit 5

Metaphor enriched class structure	Outstanding 5	Good 4	Fair 3	Poor 2	Not observed 1
		Ms Wang		Ms Liu	
1. Clearly states goals or objectives for the metaphor-related content		4		4	
2. Clearly explains metaphor theories		4		5	
3. Interprets metaphors in General English or Medical English	5			5	
4. Links General English with Medical English in terms of metaphor		4	3		
5. Assigns and analyzes the metaphor enriched homework		4		5	

(1) Comments on Ms Wang's metaphor enriched class structure

During the third period of unit 5, at the beginning of the class, Ms Wang replayed the video and then explained the exercises in it. She used war metaphors to describe how AIDS affected one's health. Here is an extract from her work (item 2).

Ms Wang

The HIV virus enters Helper T cell. What is Helper T cell? When our bodies encounter attack from the invaders, pay attention to the word invader, it is a metaphor. It compares the human body to a country which is a private area. You are not allowed to come in, but if someone comes in, he is called an invader. Here invader is a metaphor for bacteria or viruses. When entering the human body, our Helper T cell is equivalent to our PLA (People's Liberation Army), Right? It will make a quick response, as they are front-line forces. The front-line troops feel that they can't beat their enemies. They will call immediately: Taishan (code), Taishan, we are the Yellow River (code). We are in danger here. Please support us quickly. So many white blood cells will come quickly. When they come, they find that there are still a few soldiers. A simple way is to make these white cells multiply. Due to lack of soldiers and time to mobilize forces from a distance, they will start to publish advertisements: everyone is welcome to join PLA and let's fight the enemy out. So, the Helper T cell is equivalent to the front-line of PLA. This metaphor is used to explain the role of HIV which uses the Helper T cell to disintegrate these cells. So, we can imagine, would you feel safe if we have no one on the front-line? Our defense system is destroyed.

(2) Comments on Ms Liu's metaphor enriched class structure

After supplementing the medical metaphors, Ms Liu analyzed the characteristics of war metaphor basing on the conceptual metaphor theories. Here is an extract from her.

Ms Liu

There is a kind of common metaphors in medicine, war metaphor. Disease is metaphorized to a war. Then the source domain can be a series of things, such as war, field, enemy, arm; the target domain is disease. What is the target domain, that is, use war as a metaphor for disease, the battlefield is your body; the enemy is bacteria or viruses; your weapon is medicine, right? The medicine you eat. When you are fighting, both sides must have their own defense system. When fighting against the disease, your defense system is your immune system. If you win the war, your body will recover; if you fail, you may die. War metaphor is the most common metaphor in medicine. Now let's look at some examples of the metaphors of illnesses, the most commonly used source domains are war, physical conflict, or intruders. Look at this sentence, viruses and bacteria are described as external agents that attack the body, the immune system defends the body by attempting to eliminate any harmful invasion from outside. Pay attention to the word attack, in fact, external agents can not attack the body, so attack is used metaphorically, right? Defence itself is also made by living things. This is also a metaphor.

5.3.3.2 Teaching strategies for Unit 5

A student-led activity was assigned to students for this unit. The requirement was to create a video about AIDS. Three topics were suggested, AIDS education, diagnosis of AIDS and encouragement for AIDS patients. This team work achieved a good result that many students completed successfully. As the *World AIDS Day* was approaching during the study of this unit, the three teachers supplemented MV and movie clips of public-interest on AIDS. Thus videos are the main instructional aid for Unit 5 (Table 5-37).

Table 5-37 Teaching Strategies for Unit 5

Teaching strategies	Outstanding 5	Good 4	Fair 3	Poor 2	Not observed 1
	Ms Wang			Ms Liu	
6. Employs non-lecture learning activities (small group discussion, student-led activities)	5			5	
7. Employs other tools/instructional aids (technology, video)	4			5	
8. Provides students opportunities to use metaphors	2			2	
9. Times the activities appropriately	3			3	
10. Supports high-level thinking	4			4	

(1) Comments on Ms Wang's teaching strategies

For the Item 7, Ms Wang played two videos as the set induction. Ten minutes before the lecture of Unit 5, Ms Wang played a MV, *Together Forever*, which was an AIDS public service announcement to students. She had introduced a leading singer and a HIV positive kid in the MV. Here is an extract from her work.

> Ms Wang: *Madam Peng, who is the leading singer of this MV, also we should know Madam Peng is the AIDS ambassador of the United Nations in China. I think she has been the ambassador for a long time even before she became the first lady. That's why she has been known both in the domestic (in this country) and in the international arena. She used to be much more famous than her husband. Right?*
>
> Students: *Yes.*
>
> Ms Wang: *All the children in this MV are HIV positive kids. I did not use the words "AIDS patients" because they are just HIV carriers. These children are infected through mother-to-child transmission. Mothers of many of them had passed away. The little boy we just saw, Gao Jun, is an AIDS orphan. Why did he say that the person who took care of him was his grandma, because his parents died of AIDS.*

Students were very interested in this MV and were moved by the innocent smiles of those HIV positive kids which made them realize the importance of fighting against AIDS and being kind to AIDS patients.

When talking about the people's fear of AIDS, Ms Wang played in the class another movie clip, *Together* which is a movie about AIDS. The movie was starred by Aaron Kwok and Zhang

Ziyi as well as other famous actors such as Pu Cunxin, Jiang Wenli and Cai Guoqing. As Hu Zetao's mother had died of AIDS, he had become HIV positive. When having meals, his father and stepmother did not allow him to pick up the vegetables with his chopsticks. They told the boy that they would pick for him what he wanted. He had his own separate bowl and chopsticks. There is a follow-up to the movie, which mentioned that after the filming, Hu Zetao could finally take his food from the pot with his father and stepmother. Then Ms Wang commented on this movie clip: Anyone with a basic medical knowledge should know that AIDS will not be transmitted through saliva, respiratory or digestive tract. In fact, this method is for preventing hepatitis patients. If there is a hepatitis patient at home, a set of disinfected tableware will be prepared for him. But this child is HIV positive. After the filming, the experts gave his parents a lecture on AIDS, and they could learn more about AIDS. So, they allowed the child himself to pick vegetables from the plate.

Then Ms Wang assumed a situation to test whether students felt scared when they knew that they were HIV positive. This made the students laugh several times. Here is an extract from her work.

Ms Wang: *You can imagine, I am standing here, And I tell you all:" I am so sorry, babies, I am so sorry to tell you that, you know this morning, I just did my blood test, and it said that I am HIV positive." As soon as I finish my words, I think the guys in the first row will try their best to move back. Right? As far as possible. I dare say that the first row of students is thinking," What is the excuse I can find?" Boys may raise their hands and say that they want to go to the toilet.*

Students *laugh*.

Ms Wang: *Then enter through the back door and sit in the last row. They do not want to embarrass me, yet very scared to sit close to me. They must be paranoid as to what if the current science is wrong and maybe later what if it is said that this disease spreads through air. So, I was wondering, in that case, when I get into the classroom…*

Students *laugh*.

Ms Wang: *What would our classroom look like? whoever I go to, he or she will cover his nose. (make the action of covering her nose)*

Students *laugh*.

Ms Wang: *That's what we can say for AIDS. Most people feel scared about this disease, because we are not actually familiar with it.*

According to the observation of the researcher, the students had a better understanding of the AIDS transmission routes and gave up their fear and discrimination towards AIDS patients. This was evident in their laughter.

(2) Comments on Ms Liu's teaching strategies

In order to inspire the students' high-level thinking, Ms Liu showed students a picture which contained three items and asked them to find out the similarities between them (Figure 5-22).

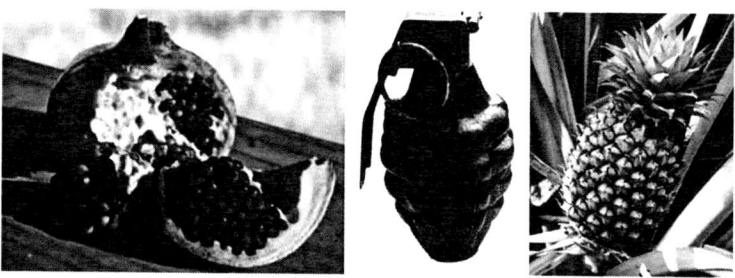

Figure 5-22   A Picture of Grenade and Its Origin

Students were asked why grenade was designed like a fruit. Then she explained its etymology and metaphoric functions. The word "grenade" is derived from the Middle French word "pomegranate", while pomegranate comes from the Anglo-French "pome garnette" meaning, literally, "seedy fruit". The grenade was called a pineapple grenade due to its similarity in appearance. Phrases like "seeds of destruction" "fruits of war" and "bitter harvest" are other examples of metaphors that relate war to food or farming. Perhaps metaphor is the only way to make the insanity of war seem comprehensible to us. Students agreed with the researcher's point of view and showed a great interest in the similarities between the grenade and the pomegranate as well as the pineapple.

5.3.3.3   Teacher's use of materials for Unit 5

The three teachers used the story of Greg Louganis as well as video materials as the set induction for Unit 5. All these materials were not only reliable and metaphor-related, but also were moving and interesting and they produced a good effect. During the instruction, the teachers related the metaphor concepts to their experience and emphasized the importance of preventing AIDS as well as adopting the correct attitudes towards AIDS patients (Table 5-38).

Table 5-38   Teacher's Use of Materials for Unit 5

Teacher's use of materials	Outstanding 5	Good 4	Fair 3	Poor 2	Not observed 1
		Ms Wang		Ms Liu	
11. Provides well-designed metaphor-related materials in an organized manner to meet the objectives		5		5	

Continue to Table 5-38

Teacher's use of materials	Outstanding 5	Good 4	Fair 3	Poor 2	Not observed 1
	Ms Wang			Ms Liu	
12. Uses high reliable metaphor-related materials	5			5	
13. Uses moderately difficult metaphor-related materials	3			4	
14. Adopts various metaphor-related resources (pictures, video) as supplement	4			5	
15. Relates metaphor concepts to teachers' or students' experience	5			4	

(1) Comments on Ms Wang's use of materials

What impressed the researcher was that Ms Wang related the supplementary content to movies she had watched (Item 15). In the supplementary video *HIV and AIDS* there was a picture of an arm affected with Kaposi's sarcoma which is an opportunistic infection of AIDS. It reminded Ms Wang of a film she watched before and she recommended it to students and made a brief introduction of the film. Here is an extract from her work.

> Ms Wang: ... *The name of the movie is Philadelphia. You will watch this movie clip later. He had acted in it as a gay with AIDS. I didn't say he is HIV positive which means he had already developed AIDS. There is a scene in the court in which he removes his shirt and shows his chest, and his decayed skin. It looks terrible; it is Kaposi's sarcoma. I have seen documentaries showing people with advanced AIDS. They had ended up in this way. Their situations were so bad that the nurses who took care of them were overworked. Nurses changed their sheets every half hour because they were festering and constantly oozing out body fluids. I recommend you to watch this film.*

During the process of talking about some metaphorical expressions of heart that are unique to Chinese, Ms Wang related one expression "empty nest syndrome" to her experience (Item 20). Here is an extract from her work.

> Ms Wang: *For example, many parents face the "empty nest syndrome" when their children leave home. You can imagine, if you are an only child, when you come to college, your parents may get the empty nest syndrome. Another name is "empty nest elderly" or "empty nest*

signs". Just like the couple on the 11th floor of my home. When her daughter studied in the high school, she was very busy. I heard her staying around the house all day long. Her daughter studied hard until midnight. Then around 12 o'clock, when her daughter felt hungry, I always heard the sounds of her cooking. We had been neighbors for 8 or 9 years. When you get used to it, suddenly one day, the upstairs is quiet, very quiet, you will wonder where have the people upstairs gone? Later, in the elevator, I met the neighbour and asked her why her family was so quiet. She said her daughter had gone to college. She stayed at home all alone as her husband was often on business tours. I often met her outside and asked why she didn't stay home; she said that she couldn't stand the feeling of missing her daughter at home. Therefore, the empty nest syndrome is a very common social phenomenon.

(2) Comments on Ms Liu's use of materials

In order to enable the students' knowledge of treatment of AIDS grow, Ms Liu provided the students a metaphor-related material, HAART, which was usually called the cocktail therapy (Item 11). She explained in detail why it was called cocktail therapy. Here is an extract from her work.

Ms Liu: *We know that there is a treatment named HAART which can inhibit the continued development of HIV. What does the word HAART represent? Highly active antiretroviral therapy. UNAIDS (The Joint United Nations Programme on HIV and AIDS) has put forward a goal to the world, that by the year 2020, hoping about 90% of patients diagnosed with HIV will receive HAART, an antiretroviral therapy. Why 90% patients want to receive this treatment? Have you ever thought about it?*

Students *silence*.

Ms Liu: *Because it is a very effective therapy. Of course, we can refer to it as cocktail therapy. Do you know cocktail?*

Students: *A kind of wine.*

Ms Liu: *It is a combination of three or more antiretroviral drugs. This combination is like blending cocktails. Cocktail is a mix of wines. Therefore, cocktail therapy is a very effective drug that can inhibit the continued development of HIV.*

5.3.3.4 Teacher's use of language for Unit 5

Ms Liu did well in questioning and coaching on videos *HIV and AIDS* as well as *Inner World Discovery: The Immune System*. She paused after several sentences, questioned the students and interpreted the answers in detail which resulted in an increased participation. For the students' self-recorded videos, the three teachers chose some excellent ones and displayed in the class, then gave their feedback immediately after playing the videos (Table 5-39).

Table 5-39 Teacher's Use of Language for Unit 5

Teacher's use of language	Outstanding 5	Good 4	Fair 3	Poor 2	Not observed 1
	Ms Wang			Ms Liu	
16. Uses metaphorical expressions in the process of instruction	5			5	
17. Uses clear questioning or coaching	4			5	
18. Engages the students actively	5			4	
19. Explains important ideas simply and clearly	5			5	
20. Makes evaluation and gives feedback according to the students' performance	2			2	

(1) Comments on Ms Wang's use of language

After playing an AIDS public service MV, she went on to talk about the AIDS village in the Henan province. Since Xinxiang Medical University is located in the Henan province and most of the students are from this province, they have heard of the location of the AIDS village. This supplementary material engaged students actively (Item 18). Here is an extract from Ms Wang's speech.

Ms Wang: *There is a "Wenlou" village in Shangcai county, Zhumadian city. When AIDS first appeared in China, the main spreading route was blood transmission. In some poor areas, the land was barren, some places only grew potatoes, and all the farmers could harvest potatoes. We all know potatoes are very cheap. We have only heard of "Brutal Garlic", have you heard of Brutal Potatoes?*

Students laugh.

Ms Wang: *So the price of potatoes is too cheap. So, people who live in these places have no idea how to make a living. What should they do? They sell their blood. Maybe it is their only choice to make money. So, they often sell blood, but the place where they sell blood is not a regular hospital, but someone who was previously called "blood heads". These people go to the villages to collect blood, the only test they do is for the blood type. Because they have at least the basic medical knowledge, type A blood and type B blood cannot be put together. That's fatal. So, the only test is about blood types. They even do not distinguish RH negative from RH positive. RH negative blood is very rare and is called "panda blood", right? What's even worse is that only one needle was shared by the whole village for saving costs. A needle is used many times until it bent.*

Students laugh.

Ms Wang: *And only young adults can sell blood, if an old lady of more than 80, taking a cane, ask people to take her blood, people would not. Right, if drawing blood hurt the old lady's health, they had to compensate. Children will not be chosen, so young adults are the best choice. Therefore, in that village, most infected people are strong labors. And most infected people are males, who then spread AIDS to their wives through sexual transmission. Their wives don't know about it and give birth to babies. Then, after the latency stage, both the parents get sick. In the latency stage, they can use drugs to control, just like rabies, if the vaccine was given early, and the problem would not have been serious. However, if you don't get a vaccine, you may have no problem for the first month or two, because the latency stage of rabies virus can last up to 10 years. So does the HIV.*

(2) Comments on Ms Liu's use of language

When introducing the reason as to why AIDS is difficult to cure, Ms Liu came up with a metaphor: HIV IS A SPY and related it to an actor in a famous Chinese television LURK which helped in the students' understanding (Item 16). Here is an extract from her speech.

Ms Liu: *The first reason why AIDS is difficult to cure lies in its hiding in your T cells. But if you kill all the HIV, you are killing human T cells at the same time. Then you are also destroying the immune system. Then in the end, the human body will lose the protection of the immune system, HIV lurks inside, how to say, like a…*

Students: *Spy.*

Ms Liu: *Like Yu Zecheng (the character in television LURK) in the revolutionary team, a spy, there is no way to screen it. No matter how effective the drugs are, they cannot attack it. This is the problem.*

After playing the video *HIV and AIDS*, Ms Liu questioned the students what was the metaphor related to the immune system and encouraged them to come up with more metaphors (Item 17). Then she explained the main idea of the video in brief. Here is an extract from Ms Liu's lecture.

Ms Liu: *After watching this video, who can make a metaphor of the immune system? Soldier? Army? They are soldiers or guards of our body. It acts like a guard and protects us like a soldier. What is the role of helper T cells? The explanation in the video is very clear. Is it for fighting?*

Students: *No.*

Ms Liu: *It helps you to identify infections, viruses, other antigenic cells. What kind of soldier does it look like?*

Students: *Scout.*

> Ms Liu: *Scouts, it is not the kind of special army, the Flying Tigers, the soldiers who are responsible for the fighting, it is responsible for identifying. Once HIV enters the human body, the main attacking target is the scout, your CD 4+ cells. What does HIV treat CD 4+ cells, namely, helper T cells as? A hotbed, right? It can breed on it, and after the breeding is completed, it will destroy the hotbed, and all the small babies that have been born in it will come outside, like entering into a new society, then they will look for their CD 4+ cells or Helper T cells to infect continually. I think this process is quite interesting. Medical students should study more about the pathogenesis mechanism of AIDS and then try to find a cure.*

What impressed the researcher is Ms Liu explained what AIDS is in simple and clear terms (Item 19). She first introduced the full name of AIDS and three main stages in the development for HIV into AIDS. Here is an extract from her speech.

> Ms Liu: *The full name of AIDS is acquired immune deficiency syndrome, or acquired immunodeficiency syndrome. In Chinese, huo de xing mian yi que xian zhong he zheng. Syndrome means a group of symptoms, know what the symptoms of syndrome. Next, we all know that HIV, human immunodeficiency virus, right? Of course, its full name in Chinese is ren lei mian yi que xian bing du. Everyone knows that AIDS and HIV are different, right? Virus is the cause of AIDS, while HIV may not develop to AIDS which means HIV actually has a period of latency in the human body.*
> Students: *There is an incubation period.*
> Ms Liu: *In the incubation period, it actually has no signs, but once it enters the AIDS period, nothing can be done but waiting for death, right? AIDS usually causes death while HIV may lead to AIDS. This virus will develop in the human body. Let's learn about the three main stages. This is the supplementary material which does not figure in the slides.*
> Miss Liu wrote some words on the blackboard.
> Ms Liu: *The first stage is acute HIV infection. The second stage is clinical latency, and the third period is AIDS.*

5.3.4 The implications of implementing metaphor enriched English language instruction supplement

Suggestions for the MEELI supplement were discussed before the class discussion by the three teacher participants. The discussions mainly focused on teaching objectives, supplementary materials, student-led activities, and the teacher's professional development (TPD). Each aspect is elaborated in the following sections.

5.3.4.1 Implications of teaching objectives

At the discussion stage, teaching objectives were analyzed by the three teachers. They felt that the medical students, should not only study the General English well, but also learn about Medical English as much as possible. Compared to the previous first-year college students, the students in 2017 got higher NCEE (National College Entrance Examination) scores and they were more eager to learn the Medical English. Although there is a Medical English course in the third year, they have already learned the anatomy course in this semester which is lectured in Chinese. So the three teachers confirmed the objective of implementing the supplement and tried their best to widen the students' medical knowledge. Ms Liu thought that teachers could broaden the medical vocabulary via lecturing. The three teachers searched for some metaphoric words with reference to the three selected units. Ms Wang suggested that they should combine the learning interest with the implementation. More videos and pictures should be provided to the students. The researcher emphasised on taking metaphor as the bridge to connect GE and ME which could achieve the two objectives mentioned by the other two teachers.

5.3.4.2 Implications of supplementary materials

For the supplementary video *The Nervous System* for Unit 2, Ms Wang thought that teachers should consider whether students could understand the medical words in the video and the supplementary materials should match the students' English proficiency. After implementing Unit 2, the three teachers discussed to lower the difficulty level of the supplementary materials for unit 3 which meant that the video of *The Cardiovascular System* was not assigned as homework but as self-study material. An easier article *Heart* was chosen as the homework. Ms Liu also tried to search for some interesting materials, including the metaphors of brain in Prezi and a short video of HIV and AIDS which received the desired effect from the students. The researcher did a lot of search for related materials and tried to find reliable and interesting passages and videos from different resources in order to improve the experiment.

5.3.4.3 Implications of student-led activities

In order to enhance the classroom fun and provide the students more opportunities to use metaphors in class, more student-led activities were designed in Unit 3 and Unit 5. Since students were not familiar with metaphors before the implementation, more time was spent on interpreting the metaphor theories for Unit 2. After lecturing on this unit, the teachers discussed and decided to conduct more student-led activities in the next two units. For Unit 3, students were encouraged to do a role play about heart problem voluntarily. Considering that their Medical English vocabulary was poor, the transcripts of example conversations were provided to them. They were required to use metaphors in their performance. For Unit 5, as the World AIDS Day was approaching, in order to raise the students' awareness of AIDS and reduce the discrimination against AIDS patients, the students were encouraged to record a video, relating to AIDS as a team work. All the students participated in these activities. There were some excellent ones which were selected and played in the class. All these activities were beneficial to the students in their learning.

5.3.4.4 Implications of teacher professional development

Professional development of teachers is widely accepted as a way to foster improvement in teaching. The reflections of the three teachers were discussed in order to understand how the participants carried out their teaching practices. The most effective professional development occurs when there are meaningful interactions (Clement and Vanderberghe, 2000). The collaborative preparation of class and after class discussion did accumulate the teachers' reflection on their teaching practices and raised their awareness of life-long learning.

The researcher found the other teachers' English teaching style via classroom observation and reflected on her own teaching. As an experienced teacher with 12 years of teaching experience, Ms Liu's lecture was informative and well-prepared. In order to interpret the supplementary materials well, she had searched extensively for information regarding the nervous system, the cardiovascular system and the immune system. Besides, when uncertain about some information, she would discuss with her husband who is an army doctor and ensure the accuracy. Her explanation of supplemented videos was specific. Her rich and wide knowledge can be observed through her lecture on AIDS therapy (HAART). Ms Wang's lecture was humorous and interesting, just like her character. She always related the supplementary materials to her experience which actively engaged the students. For example, during the lecture of Unit 5, she talked about her experience in Australia, especially her mental make-up when she knew that her teacher was a faggot. She also compared the situation of AIDS in Australia with the one in China which left a deep impression on her students as well as the researcher. Another example was her talking about her neighbour's disappointment when her daughter was studying outside the hometown while interpreting the expression "empty nest syndrome". It aroused the students' empathy and deep concern for those people. From these two colleagues, the researcher had learned a lot and tried to adopt some good approaches learned from them in her own class. The researcher extensively prepared for her supplementary materials, including consulting the anatomy professor Wen and discussed some points with the doctors she knew. Further, she downloaded many reliable video materials and discussed with the other two colleagues to decide on which was suitable to be played in the class. Then she made the supplementary materials into slides and shared with the other teachers. Afterwards, she combined all the collected materials into a bookletand provided it to the students for their review and further reading. The researcher found that the other teachers had evinced interest in Medical English and metaphor theories and was informed by them that they would continue to learn it in the future.

5.4 Research Question 4: What are the Students' Feedback on the Metaphor Enriched Language Instruction Supplementary Materials?

For the student feedback questionnaire (Appendix E), the data of items were analyzed in terms of percentage, while the open-ended comments were analyzed with NVivo 11.

5.4.1 Ms Wang's student feedback questionnaire

5.4.1.1 Data analysis of items of part I

The first part of the questionnaire is about opinions formed regarding the learning experience of Metaphor Enriched English Language Instruction (MEELI). There are six items relating to metaphor theories, metaphoric competence, medical knowledge, and the effect of MEELI. The students' opinions for each unit are puttogether to study about their overall opinions. Table 5-40 shows the opinions of the students about the learning experience from Ms Wang's class.

Table 5-40 Percentage of Part I : Your Learning Experience of the MEELI (Ms Wang's Class)

Questionnaire items	Unit	SA/%	A/%	N/%	D/%	SD/%
1. I fully understand the metaphor theories	U2	20.0	56.7	16.7	3.3	3.3
	U3	50.0	36.7	10.0	3.3	0.0
	U5	20.0	46.7	33.3	0.0	0.0
2. I can identity and understand the metaphors of this unit	U2	3.3	73.3	16.7	6.7	0.0
	U3	26.7	53.3	16.7	3.3	0.0
	U5	16.7	53.3	30.0	0.0	0.0
3. I have a basic understanding of the nervous system via MEELI	U2	23.3	66.7	6.7	0.0	3.3
	U3	30.0	50.0	20.0	0.0	0.0
	U5	26.7	46.7	16.7	0.0	0.0
4. The learning activities (e.g., lectures, discussions, presentations) have helped me to understand the supplementary nervous system knowledge	U2	30.0	53.3	16.7	0.0	0.0
	U3	30.0	53.3	16.7	0.0	0.0
	U5	50.0	33.3	16.7	0.0	0.0
5. I better understand medical metaphor concepts and try to understand new knowledge via it	U2	26.7	50.0	16.7	6.7	0.0
	U3	26.7	66.6	6.7	0.0	0.0
	U5	26.7	66.6	6.7	0.0	0.0
6. I think MEELI is a good way to combine General English with Medical English	U2	50.0	43.3	3.3	0.0	3.3
	U3	33.3	53.3	10.0	3.3	0.0
	U5	50.0	36.7	13.3	0.0	0.0

Note. SA = Strongly agree, A = agree, N = No strong view, D = Disagree, SD = Strongly disagree. $N = 30$.

Item 1 relates to the comprehension of metaphor theories, the percentages of strongly agree and agree for each unit were 76.7% of Unit 2, 86.7% of Unit 3, and 66.7% of Unit 5. It showed more than a half of the students can understand it. The percentages of disagree and strongly disagree were reduced from 6.6% of Unit 2, to 3.3% of Unit 3, and to 0 of Unit 5. Item 2 concerns the metaphoric competence. The percentages of strongly agree and agree for each unit were 76.6% of Unit 2, 80.0% of Unit 3, and 70.0% of Unit 5. The students who had the positive opinions formed the majority. The percentages of disagree and strongly disagree were reduced from 6.7% of Unit 2, to 3.3% of Unit 3, and to 0 of Unit 5. Item 3 is about supplement medical knowledge, the percentages of strongly agree and agree for each unit were 90.0% of Unit 2, 80.0% of Unit 3, and 73.4% of Unit 5. The percentages of disagree and strongly disagree reduced from 3.3% of Unit 2, to 0 of Unit 3 and Unit 5. Item 4 involves in the learning activities relating to the supplement, the percentages of strongly agree and agree for each unit was 83.3%. The percentages of disagree and strongly disagree for each unit was 0. Item 5 relates to the understanding of medical metaphors, the percentages of strongly agree and agree for each unit were 76.7% of Unit 2, 93.4% of Unit 3, and 93.4% of Unit 5. The percentages of disagree and strongly disagree for each unit were 6.7% of Unit 2, 6.7% of Unit 3, and 0 of Unit 5. Item 6 concerns the opinion about MEELI, the percentages of strongly agree and agree for each unit were 73.3% of Unit 2, 86.6% of Unit 3, and 86.7% of Unit 5. The percentage of disagree and strongly disagree for each unit were 3.3% of Unit 2, 3.3% of unit 3, and 0 of Unit 5.

5.4.1.2 Data analysis of comments on subject

There are two open-ended questions in part Ⅰ. The first one is "What aspects of MEELI are most useful to your learning?" The second one is "How could the MEELI be improved for your better learning?" The answers of the students were fed into NVivo and a project map was drawn to show the related themes (Figure 5-23).

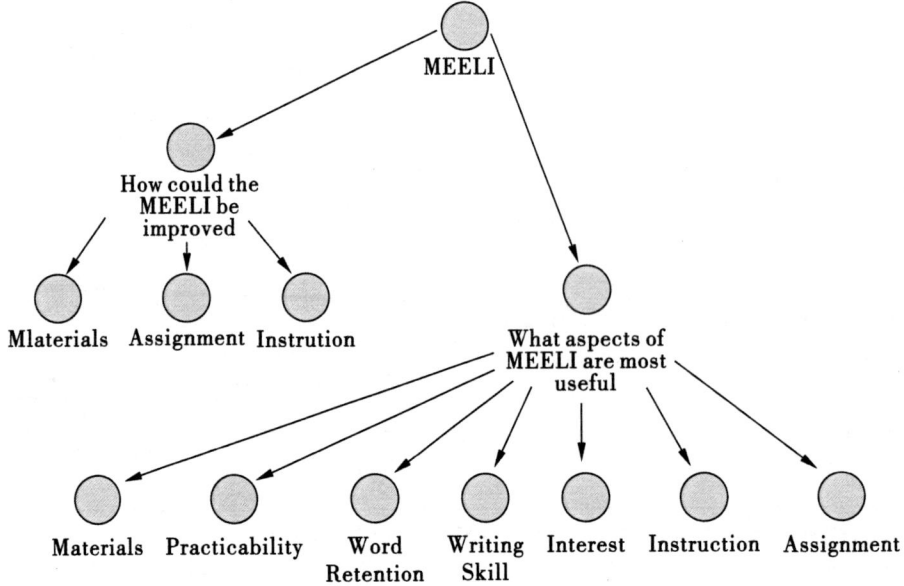

Figure 5-23 Project Map of Comments on MEELI (Ms Wang's Class)

For the most useful aspect of MEELI, seven themes were mentioned by the students and they were materials, practicability, word retention, writing skill, interest, instruction and assignment. As for the materials, the students hold the view that it has made them better understand metaphors and the text via combining General English with Medical English, especially the theoretical anatomy concepts. As to the practicability, they better understood the multiple meanings of some nouns, comprehended things by association and analogy, and it is helpful for their future Medical English study. In addition, it enabled them to better remember English words as well as improving their writing skills. The vivid metaphors have kindled their interest in learning English. The teacher's explanation was vivid and intuitive they felt. The assignment helped them learn Medical English with ease.

As for how to improve MEELI, the students' suggestions mainly focus on materials, assignment and instruction. For materials, they have suggested to the teachers to add subtitles to the video, send one Medical English articles regularly, and recommend some interesting articles to students.

5.4.1.3 Data analysis of items of part II

The second part of the questionnaire deals with opinions about the teachers providing Metaphor Enriched English Language Instruction (MEELI). There were six items related to the materials, language, questioning and coaching, and the effect of instruction. The Table 5-41 shows the students' opinion about Ms Wang's instruction.

Table 5-41　Percentage of Part II: Teacher's Instruction of the MEELI (Ms Wang's Class)

Questionnaire items	Unit	SA/%	A/%	N/%	D/%	SD/%
1. Provided well-designed metaphor-related materials in an organized manner to meet the objectives	U2	43.3	40.0	16.7	0.0	0.0
	U3	46.7	46.7	6.7	0.0	0.0
	U5	43.3	50.0	6.7	0.0	0.0
2. Adopted various metaphor-related resources (pictures, videos) as supplement	U2	56.7	36.7	6.7	0.0	0.0
	U3	46.7	43.3	10.0	0.0	0.0
	U5	36.7	60.0	3.3	0.0	0.0
3. Explained important ideas or concepts simply and clearly	U2	50.0	40.0	10.0	0.0	0.0
	U3	50.0	43.3	6.7	0.0	0.0
	U5	50.0	43.3	6.7	0.0	0.0
4. Encouraged students to ask questions and discuss ideas in class	U2	43.3	40.0	13.3	3.3	0.0
	U3	40.0	40.0	20.0	0.0	0.0
	U5	43.3	43.3	13.3	0.0	0.0

Continue to Table 5-41

Questions	Unit	SA/%	A/%	N/%	D/%	SD/%
5. Teacher's instruction stimulated my interest in metaphor and Medical English	U2	36.7	30.0	20.0	13.3	0.0
	U3	53.3	33.3	13.3	0.0	0.0
	U5	40.0	50.0	6.7	3.3	0.0
6. Provided students with a valuable learning experience	U2	40.0	56.7	3.3	0.0	0.0
	U3	63.3	26.7	10.0	0.0	0.0
	U5	46.7	46.7	6.7	0.0	0.0

Note. SA = Strongly agree, A = Agree, N = No strong view, D = Disagree, SD = Strongly disagree.

Item 1 involves the quality of the supplement, to ascertain if well-designed metaphor-related materials were provided. The percentages of strongly agree and agree were 83.3% for Unit 2, 93.4% for Unit 3, and 96.7% for Unit 5. The percentage of disagree and strongly disagree for each unit was 0. Item 2 refers to the resources of the supplement to ascertain if various metaphor-related resources were adopted. The percentages of strongly agree and agree for each unit were 93.4% for Unit 2, 90.0% for Unit 3, and 70.0% of Unit 5. Majority of the students gave a positive opinion. The percentage of disagree and strongly disagree was 0. Item 3 is about the teacher's language, to ascertain if important ideas or concepts were explained simply and clearly. The percentages of strongly agree and agree for each unit were 90.0% for Unit 2, 93.3% for Unit 3, and 93.3% of Unit 5. The percentage of disagree and strongly disagree for each unit was 0. Item 4 is to as certain if the students were encouraged to ask questions and discuss ideas in the class. The percentages of SA and A were 83.3% for Unit 2, 80.0% for Unit 3, and 86.6% for Unit 5. The percentages of disagree and strongly disagree reduced from 3.3% of Unit 2, to 0 of Unit 3 and Unit 5. Item 5 is about the interest of the students in teacher's instruction. The percentages of strongly agree and agree were 66.7% for Unit 2, 86.6% for Unit 3, and 90.0% for Unit 5. The percentages of disagree and strongly disagree were 13.3% for Unit 2, 0% for Unit 3, and 3.3% for Unit 5. Item 6 relates to the effect of teacher's instruction. The percentages of strongly agree and agree for each unit were 96.7% for Unit 2, 90.0% for Unit 3, and 93.4% for Unit 5. The percentage for disagree and strongly disagree was 0.

5.4.1.4 Analysis of comments on the teacher

There are two open-ended questions in part II. The first one is "What aspects of teacher's instruction are most useful to your learning?" The second one is "How would you like the teaching be changed (if at all), for your better learning?" There is a project map to show the related themes (Figure 5-24).

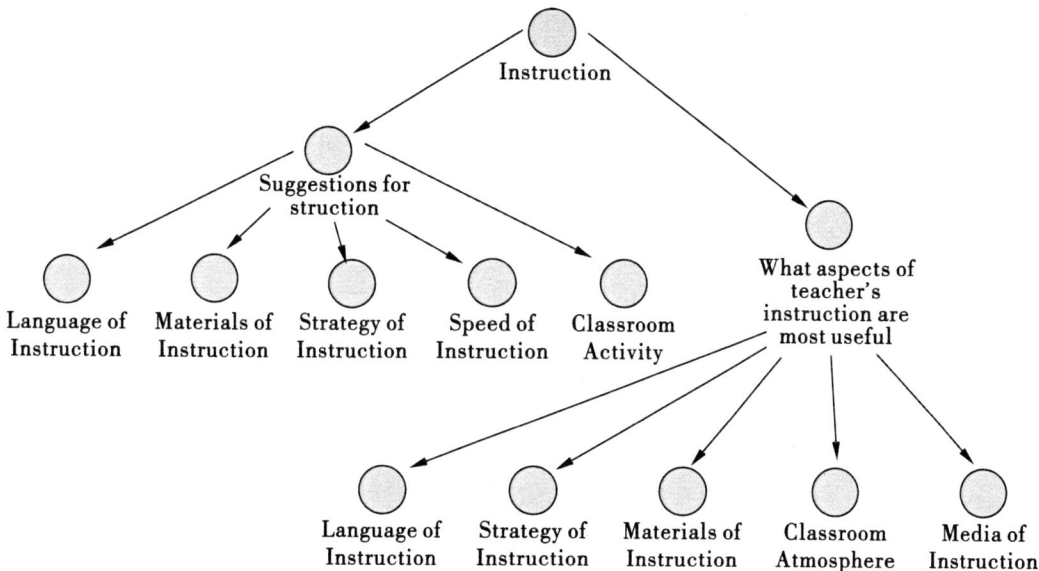

Figure 5-24   Project Map of Comments on Instruction (Ms Wang's Class)

For the most useful aspect of the teacher's instruction, five themes were mentioned and they are language, strategy, materials, classroom atmosphere and media. For the language, the students hold the view that the teacher's explanations were interesting and humorous which aroused their interest in learning. As for the strategy, they were encouraged to ask questions and rewarded with marks. The teacher was suggested to simplify the questions and make them easy to understand. The strategy of interpreting some words and telling stories were very helpful to memorize words and more detailed explanations through pictures and videos were preferred to gain a deeper understanding. Concerning materials, the students stated that the supplementary materials enriched their knowledge, widened their horizon and taught them more about the cultural background. For the media, supplementary animations made them more engaged, examples and pictures inside helped them understand the content visually.

As for suggestions regarding instruction, materials, language, strategy, speed and instruction were mentioned. Concerning the materials, more interesting short videos as well as metaphors were suggested to supplement. The Chinese translation to the terms could be added. As for strategies, the teacher was advised to give more oral English practice and recommend some interesting English articles to them. A slow speed was preferred. As for the instruction, the teacher was suggested to provide more analysis of metaphor structures and more guidance for reading medical articles.

5.4.2 Ms Liu's student feedback questionnaire

5.4.2.1 Data analysis of items of part I

For the opinions of students about the learning experience of Metaphor Enriched English Language Instruction (MEELI). There are six items relating to the metaphor theories, metaphoric competence, medical knowledge, and the effect of MEELI. The students' opinions for each unit are put together to learn about their overall opinions. Table 5-42 shows the opinions of students learning experience from Ms Liu's class.

Table 5-42 Percentage of Part I: Your Learning Experience of the MEELI (Ms Liu's Class)

Items	Unit	SA/%	A/%	N/%	D/%	SD/%
1. I fully understand the metaphor theories	U2	13.3	60.0	23.3	3.3	3.3
	U3	13.3	60.0	26.7	0.0	0.0
	U5	23.3	40.0	36.7	0.0	0.0
2. I can identity and understand the metaphors of this unit	U2	20.0	63.3	13.3	3.3	0.0
	U3	3.3	73.3	20.0	0.0	0.0
	U5	30.0	40.0	30.0	0.0	0.0
3. I have a basic understanding of the nervous system via MEELI	U2	23.3	50.0	23.3	3.3	0.0
	U3	16.7	70.0	13.3	0.0	0.0
	U5	30.0	53.3	16.7	0.0	0.0
4. The learning activities (e.g., lectures, discussions, presentations) have helped me to understand the supplementary nervous system knowledge	U2	13.3	63.3	23.3	0.0	0.0
	U3	13.3	60.0	26.7	0.0	0.0
	U5	23.3	60.0	26.7	0.0	0.0
5. I better understand medical metaphor concepts and try to understand new knowledge via it	U2	13.3	46.7	40.0	0.0	0.0
	U3	26.7	50.0	20.0	3.3	0.0
	U5	13.3	63.3	23.3	0.0	0.0
6. I think MEELI is a good way to combine General English with Medical English	U2	53.3	43.3	3.3	0.0	0.0
	U3	30.0	63.3	6.7	0.0	0.0
	U5	33.3	53.3	13.3	0.0	0.0

Note. SA=Strongly agree, A=Agree, N=No strong view, D=Disagree, SD=Strongly disagree.

Item 1 refers to the comprehension of metaphor theories, the percentages of strongly agree and agree for each unit were 73.3% for Unit 2, 73.3% for Unit 3, and 63.3% for Unit 5. The percentage of disagree and strongly disagree were reduced from 6.6% for Unit 2, to 0 for Unit 3 and Unit 5. Item 2 involves to the metaphoric competence. The percentages of strongly agree and agree for each unit were 83.3% for Unit 2, 76.6% for Unit 3, and 70.0% for Unit 5. Majority of the students gave a positive opinion. The percentages of disagree and strongly disagree were reduced from 3.3% for Unit 2, to 0 for Unit 3 and Unit 5. Item 3 concerns the supplementary medical knowledge, the percentage of strongly agree and agree for each unit was 73.3% for Unit 2, 76.7% for Unit 3, and 83.3% for Unit 5. The percentages of disagree and strongly disagree were reduced from 3.3% for Unit 2, to 0 for Unit 3 and Unit 5. Item 4 involves the learning activities related to the supplement. The percentages of strongly agree and agree for each unit were 76.6% for Unit 2, 73.3% for Unit 3, and 83.3% for Unit 5. The percentage of disagree and strongly disagree for each unit is 0. Item 5 refers to the understanding of the medical metaphors, where the percentages of strongly agree and agree for each unit were 60.0% for Unit 2, 76.7% for Unit 3, and 76.6% for Unit 5. The percentages of disagree and strongly disagree for each unit were 0 for Unit 2, 3.3% for Unit 3, and 0 for Unit 5. Item 6 refers to the opinion about MEELI, where the percentages of strongly agree and agree for each unit were 96.6% for Unit 2, 93.3% for Unit 3, and 86.6% for Unit 5. The percentage of disagree and strongly disagree for each unit was 0.

5.4.2.2 Data analysis of comments on subject

There are two open-ended questions in part I. The first one is "What aspects of MEELI are most useful to your learning?" The second one is "How could the MEELI be improved for your better learning?" The answers of the students were fed into Nvivo and a project map was drawn to show the related themes (Figure 5-25).

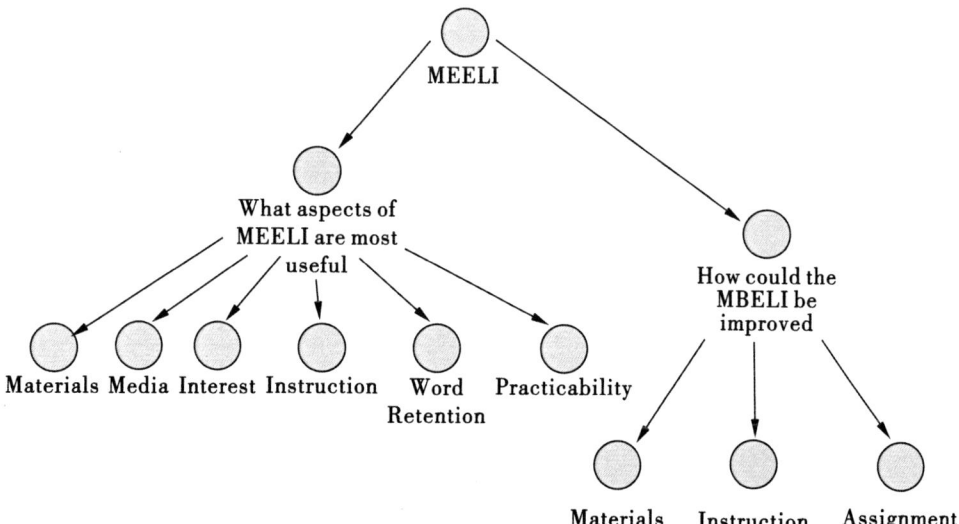

Figure 5-25 Project Map of Comments on MEELI (Ms Liu's Class)

As for the most useful aspect of MEELI, six themes were mentioned and they are materials, media, interest, instruction, word retention, and practicability. As for the materials, the students held the view that it helped them better in understanding General English, Medical English and English culture. It also helped them to better understand the text and the function of various organs of the human body. As for media, the videos and articles were good according to the students. It kindled their interest and they soon felt that English learning was not monotonous. As for the instruction, the teacher's explanations were vivid and enlarged their thinking capacity by using metaphors. The MEELI enabled them to better remember medical terms. As for the practicability, the professional knowledge could be learned thoroughly and metaphors would enable them to communicate better with their patients in the future.

As for how to improve the MEELI, the students' suggestions mainly focused on materials, assignment and instruction. Concerning the materials, they suggested that the teachers should supplement the lessons with more animation and music and make the learning process more fun. They advised the teachers to provide more metaphors about medicine as mentioned in the previous lecture. As for assignment, providing some useful materials and some relevant hints on some particularly difficult points were required. As for instruction, the teachers could give more guidance after class, provide more medical information, give more explanations and encourage more discussions. In addition, other suggestions were made which including explaining the mechanism of metaphors, making the class more interesting, playing more games, simplifying the content and slowing down the speed.

5.4.2.3 Data analysis of items of part II

The second part of the questionnaire deals with the opinions of the students about the teacher's instruction. There are six items relating to materials, language, questioning and coaching, and the effect of instruction (Table 5-43).

Table 5-43 Percentage of Part II: Teacher's Instruction of the MEELI (Ms Liu's Class)

Questionnaire items	Unit	SA/%	A/%	N/%	D/%	SD/%
1. Provided well-designed metaphor-related materials in an organized manner to meet the objectives	U2	33.3	50.0	16.7	0.0	0.0
	U3	26.7	60.0	13.3	0.0	0.0
	U5	30.0	53.3	16.7	0.0	0.0
2. Adopted various metaphor-related resources (pictures, videos) as supplement	U2	56.7	40.0	3.3	0.0	0.0
	U3	16.7	66.7	16.7	0.0	0.0
	U5	46.7	46.7	6.7	0.0	0.0
3. Explained important ideas or concepts simply and clearly	U2	46.7	46.7	6.7	0.0	0.0
	U3	16.7	70.0	13.3	0.0	0.0
	U5	40.0	40.0	20.0	0.0	0.0

Continue to Table 5-48

Questionnaire items	Unit	SA/%	A/%	N/%	D/%	SD/%
4. Encouraged students to ask questions and discuss ideas in class	U2	46.7	40.0	13.3	0.0	0.0
	U3	30.0	36.7	33.3	0.0	0.0
	U5	50.0	36.7	33.3	0.0	0.0
5. Teacher's instruction stimulated my interest in metaphor and Medical English	U2	46.7	40.0	13.3	0.0	0.0
	U3	20.0	60.0	20.0	0.0	0.0
	U5	50.0	20.0	30.0	0.0	0.0
6. Provided students with a valuable learning experience	U2	50.0	43.3	6.3	0.0	0.0
	U3	36.7	53.3	10.0	0.0	0.0
	U5	26.7	46.7	26.7	0.0	0.0

Note. SA = Strongly agree, A = Agree, N = No strong view, D = Disagree, SD = Strongly disagree.

Item 1 refers to the quality of the supplement. It is regarding whether a well-designed and metaphor-related materials were provided. The percentages of strongly agree and agree for each unit were 83.3% for Unit 2, 86.7% for Unit 3, and 83.3% for Unit 5. The percentage of disagree and strongly disagree for each unit was 0. Item 2 involves the resources of the supplement, to ascertain whether various metaphor-related resources were adapted. The percentages of strongly agree and agree for each unit were 96.7% for Unit 2, 83.4% for Unit 3, and 93.4% for Unit 5. Students with the positive opinion formed the majority. The percentage of disagree and strongly disagree for each unit was 0. Item 3 concerns the teacher's language, ascertaining whether important ideas or concepts were explained simply and clearly. The percentages of strongly agree and agree for each unit were 93.4% for Unit 2, 86.7% for Unit 3, and 80.0% for Unit 5. The percentage of disagree and strongly disagree for each unit was 0. Item 4 pertains to the teacher's coaching, to ascertain whether the students were encouraged to ask questions and discuss ideas in the class. The percentages of strongly agree and agree for each unit were 86.7% for Unit 2, 66.7% for Unit 3, and 86.7% for Unit 5. The percentage of disagree and strongly disagree for each unit was 0. Item 5 refers to the interest in the instruction. The percentages of strongly agree and agree for each unit were 86.7% for Unit 2, 80.0% for Unit 3, and 70.0% for Unit 5. The percentage of disagree and strongly disagree for each unit was 0. Item 6 refers to the effect of the instruction. The percentages of strongly agree and agree for each unit were 73.3% for Unit 2, 90.0% for Unit 3, and 73.4% for Unit 5. The percentage of disagree and strongly disagree for each unit was 0.

5.4.2.4 Analysis of comments on teacher

There are two open-ended questions in part Ⅱ. They are "What aspects of the teacher's instructions were most useful to your learning?" "How would you like the teaching be changed (if at all), for your better learning?" There is a project map to show the related themes (Figure 5-26).

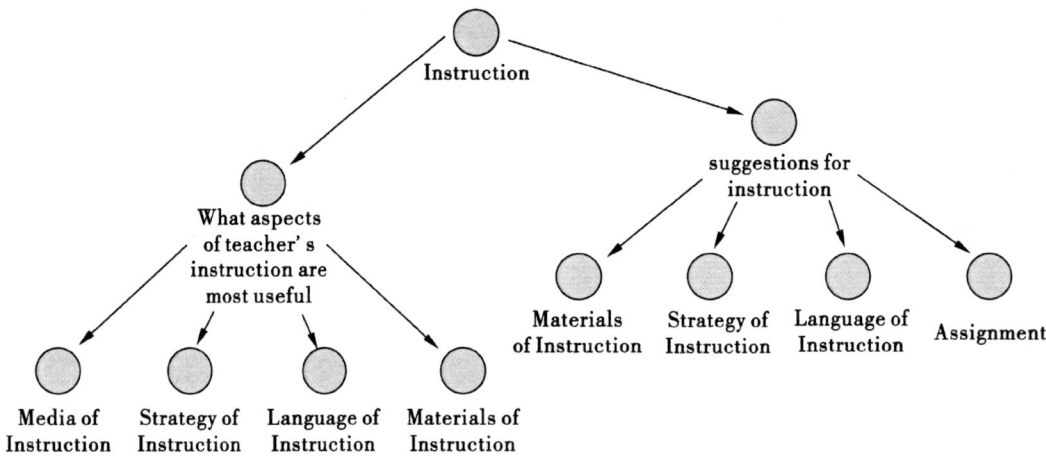

Figure 5-26　Project Map of Comments on Instruction (Ms Liu's Class)

As for the most useful aspect of the teacher's instruction, four themes were mentioned by the students and they are language, strategy, materials and media. As for the language, the students hold the view that the teacher's explanations were interesting. As for the strategy, they thought that the derivatives and usages of vocabulary were good. In addition, the teacher's explanation of the origin of metaphor was good, which was easy to understand and remember. An in-depth analysis of the answers was conducted. It has shown that their ability of interaction has increased and their confidence in speaking English in public is hugely assuaged. The students also believed that the comparison between the Chinese metaphors and English ones were very helpful. What's more, interpreting some words and telling some small stories were very helpful to memorize new words. As for materials, they could get a better understanding and sharp memory about the functions and forms of the nervous system with the help of metaphors and the materials made the understanding of medical terms more easily. As for media, they confirmed videos and pictures have enriched their imagination.

As for suggestions regarding instruction, the students' suggestions mainly have focused on materials, language, strategy and assignment. As for materials, they have suggested that the teacher can share the materials after the class, add subtitles to the video and provide more English proverbs and proverbs related to metaphors. In addition, more humorous videos as homework and more examples of metaphors were preferred to arouse a greater interest in learning metaphors. They opined that the teachers should use less difficult materials. As for strategy, they have opined that the teacher should make lists of words and idioms to make it easier for students to learn and remember. The teacher was advised to recommend some exercises and give some hints on some difficult questions. The teacher should design more questions and allow students to answer confidently in the class and interpret metaphors in the form of animations. Metaphors which kept up with the latest knowledge were preferred. Additionally, there should be more interaction in the class to let students be more active and make the classroom atmosphere more lively. As for the assignment, some relevant metaphorical words and simple short essays were preferred. More metaphors could be provided to enlighten the students and make them understand difficult words and sentences. In the process of instruction, more pictures and exercises were proposed to the teachers.

Chapter 6

Conclusions and Recommendations

This research used a convergent mixed method research as an inspection tool to find out the effective teaching methods of metaphor enriched supplement in the General English class in Xinxiang Medical University, China. The data were collected by the triangulation of data sources and research instruments and were analyzed by SPSS 22.0 and NVivo. The results showed that the Metaphor Enriched English Language Instruction (MEELI) supplement did improve students' metaphoric competence and medical language learning. This chapter states the conclusions of the research which involve in students' metaphoric cognitive ability, implementation of metaphor enriched English language instruction, students' metaphoric competence, supplementary materials development and teacher professional development. At the end of this chapter, recommendations for further study are provided for the researchers in this field.

6.1 Implications

This study has contributed to three areas in language education: theory, practice and product design.

For the theoretical research, Du Huiling (2019) reported that the theoretical research of Metaphor Enriched English Language Instruction is still relatively scarce. This is especially true in the Chinese context. Therefore, any intervention on the subject matter, namely, that relates to Metaphor Enriched English Language Instruction, would benefit the corpus of literature in the field. The significance of conceptual metaphors in foreign language teaching was further emphasized by teacher participants and student participants. Language is a part of the cognitive process which is based on human general knowledge of time, space and environment, and expressed in the form of a language symbol. This process embodies the inherent cognitive characteristics of human beings, with similarities and differences between languages. The similarities are the basis to learn another language, and the differences are the parts that have to be overcome in the process of learning another language. Students can learn the vocabulary easily with strong interest. Therefore, conceptual metaphor theory shows its application value in language teaching and was chosen to be the main metaphor theory. However, before the implementation, students were not clear about this theory, when reviewing the first metaphor-related assignment, it was obvious that quite a number of students could not come up with the corresponding metaphors. This implies that students are lack of linguistic knowledge and adequate exercises. They could understand metaphors as the figure of speech easily, but could not realize its cognitive functions and seldom used it in their speaking and writing, which also proved the gap in metaphorical thinking between English as a Foreign Language learners and English native learners. In order to arouse students' awareness of the difference in Chinese metaphorical expressions and English ones, some metaphorical expressions which are unique to Chinese were provided. Knowing the difference in metaphorical meanings enhanced their understanding and using of metaphors. Another issue with metaphor theories is teachers' master of metaphor theories. In this research, Ms Liu mentioned she had read the related articles and interpreted the theory in detail in the classroom. Ms Wang had not learned the theory, the researcher recommended her some theoretical books before the implementation. Although Ms Wang's use of language is vivid with some metaphors, her explanation of metaphor theories is not as clear as Ms Wang's. Therefore, the training of metaphor theories is very necessary before the implementation.

The implications of practical research consist of teachers' part and students' part. For English as a foreign language teachers, the applied research refers to using the existing conceptual metaphor theories to guide our foreign language teaching practice to improve students medical English learning was implemented in this study. The first step was to formulate the teaching objectives on language knowledge and student development. The curriculum reform (2014) emphasizes language competence which can be improved by increasing students' metaphoric competence. At the same time, English is a vital subject which lasts from basic education to higher education, masters and doctoral degrees. The current society is highly internationalized which makes English learning an essential part of students' study and future work. This also increases students' interest in medical English learning. In the process of Metaphor Enriched English Language Instruction, they felt the importance of metaphor in vocabulary and medical therapy which stimulated their potential and autonomic learning after class which was beneficial to their all-round development.

Another factor referring to the effectiveness of implementation is the teaching approach. Du Huiling (2019) states three fundamental aspects of mode of classroom instruction which included presentation, practice, and application. This mode was adopted in this study with students' interaction. Teacher participants first presented the language content, followed by the exercises, and finally the students are guided to use it flexibly. There are three phases in the classroom instruction: set induction, presentation and summary. The specific design include the following. First, they decided to supplement three body systems which can relate to the topics of the textbook and realized the transition from the unit topics to their related medical knowledge by the set induction. For example, talking about anxiety, metaphors of anxiety were added and brainstorming was conducted. "Which body part experiences the human's anxiety?" was the question asked by the teachers to ignite the process of thinking in the students. Second, time arrangement was another thing to consider. In this research, the metaphor enriched supplement took 30–40 minutes which took near a quarter of the whole unit hour. Besides, students were provided more opportunities to use metaphors. For example, they were required to complete the metaphor-related assignments and make more metaphorical sentences. The three teachers employed student-led activities. Two activities were implemented in Unit 3 and Unit 5 respectively. One is students' role play on heart problems which corresponds to the cardiovascular system. Students were encouraged to have a role play by using metaphors to explain the condition of patients' heart problems. This activity not only cultivated their metaphorical thinking, inspired them to communicate with patients effectively, but also enriched their medical knowledge about heart problems. The other activity was to make a self-recorded video on AIDS which corresponds to the immune system. Students were divided into groups of 6–8 people in terms of dormitories. The video themes include AIDS education, diagnosis of AIDS and encouragement for AIDS patients. This activities aroused great interest in students. They not only had a better understanding of transmission of AIDS and had empathy with AIDS patients, but also improved their metaphoric competence. Fourth, students' high-level thinking were supported. For example, the researcher used several pictures, the picture of a mountain and grenade to inspire students' understanding of the cognitive functions of metaphor and the origin of the word "grenade". Therefore, teachers can use pictures to inspire students' metaphorical thinking.

Student's feedback showed their comments on two open-ended questions. The first question referred to the most useful aspect of the Metaphor Enriched English Language Instruction and the suggestions for its improvement. As for the most useful aspect, students claimed the metaphor enriched supplement did help them in understanding and memorizing English words; the professional knowledge could be learned thoroughly and metaphor enabled them to communicate better with patients; the supplement materials helped them better understand the text, English culture and the functions of various organs of the human body; the vivid metaphors had kindled their interest in learning English and it improved their English proficiency. This findings confirmed the effectiveness of MEELI and were consistent with Lu Fengxiang's conclusion. She claimed that medical English vocabulary is a basic element in students' medical English learning. Metaphors play an important role in understanding, mastering and using vocabulary. Therefore, it should not only be taught as a kind of knowledge, but a way to understand the medical world (2015). As for the suggestions for the MEELI, the strategy, materials and classroom atmosphere were mentioned. More animations, as well as more metaphors in the medicine, were suggested to supplement to the lecture to increase the enjoyment. The students hoped teachers to give more guidance after class, provide more medical knowledge, give more explanations and encourage them to discuss in class. The medical supplement was suggested to be synchronized with the anatomy class which could deep their understanding of the professional knowledge. More student-led activities like playing games were proposed to make the class more interesting. The second open-ended question concerned about the most useful aspect of the teacher's instruction and the suggestions for the improvement. Students confirmed the three teachers' instruction from the aspects of language, strategy, classroom atmosphere. They hold the idea that the teacher's introduction and explanations of medical English was clear and the bilingual teaching was beneficial for understanding the content; the teacher could timely summarize the answers of the assignments and translate difficult points into Chinese. The teachers' interesting and humorous instruction made the classroom atmosphere more active. As for the suggestions for the improvement, more oral English practice was suggested as well as some interesting English articles. Besides, a slow speed was preferred. More analysis of metaphor structures were advised to provide. Leonardo (2017) emphasized the importance of explaining how prototypical meanings become realised in the literal uses of the concept. This approach was also applied in the present study to compare the prototypical meanings and metaphorical meanings of words used. According to several metaphor scholars (Evans and Green, 2006; Knowles and Moon, 2006; Lakoff and Johnson, 1980, 1999), metaphor is experientially motivated. That is, the ways in which we have experienced and interacted with the world have an important role in how we not only talk about the world but in how we think about it. The implication of this for the teaching of metaphor-related words is that language teachers must rely upon their understanding of how language, especially metaphorical words, are rooted in our primary bodily experiences with the world.

Furthermore, Leonardo (2017) suggested that teachers should notice and often use metaphors in the English classroom. They should also prepare to deal with metaphors in a way that allows students to see the underlying systematicities. Teacher education programs should be provided for teachers dealing with methodological and pedagogical tools to treat metaphors as a matter of language and thought rather than a poetic or literary devices. This aspect was also referred to by three teachers who tried to use more metaphorical expressions in the process of instruction and believed this experience did contribute to the teacher professional development. In Unit 2, which referring to the nervous system, Ms Wang used clear questioning and coaching in her explanation of the pictures of Yoga. Ms Liu used war metaphors to describe the functions of the nervous system and introduced metaphors when interpreting the sentence "My stomach is full of knots". In Unit 3, which referring to the cardiovascular system, Ms Wang used the song *Titanic* as the set induction and introduced the metaphors of heart. Ms Wang used a metaphor "The father is the white mask (who play the villain) in Beijing opera" to describe the characteristics of a father in a family. In Unit 5, which referring to the immune system, Ms Wang supplemented the background of an AIDS village in Henan province which is very close to the university. This supplement engaged the students actively and she also clearly explained the difference between HIV positive and AIDS. Ms Liu introduced the reason why AIDS is difficult to cure by a metaphor HIV IS A SPY and encouraged the students to come up with more metaphors. These creative applications of language were helpful to visualize the teacher's intended meaning as well as articulate more abstract and complex concepts in an easy way. In addition, a teacher's metaphoric competence is important in creating a good learning platform during medical students' learning experience. It is useful in the teacher-student communication by facilitating better understanding in the transfer of knowledge. In this process, mutually understanding can be achieved with resonant metaphors.

The implications of practical research on students relate to students' improvement in the results of the metaphor cognition questionnaire and the metaphoric competence test. The result of metaphor cognition questionnaire showed that, first, although the first-year college students acknowledged the importance of metaphor in General English and Medical English, they still did not know how to apply metaphors in their English speaking and writing. Therefore, cultivating students' metaphoric cognitive ability is very important in General English and Medical English teaching. Since the metaphorical cognitive mechanism, understanding the unknown target domain through the already known source domain, is consistent with the process of English learning which is an interaction between the old language knowledge and the new one. Second, although students realized some metaphors in English were different from the ones in Chinese. They could not have an image of the compared object in their minds when finding a metaphor. This is in part because they did not know the metaphorical cognitive mechanism. This also explains why students could not consciously apply metaphors which they had learned in their writing and speaking, not to speak of expressing their ideas through new metaphors. Third, metaphor cognitive ability plays a vital role in learning Medical English. Many medical terms which originated from Greek and Latin are metaphorical. It is necessary to understand them by metaphoric thinking, that is, to perceive as many morphemes as possible from the existing Medical English terms, and remember these terms in relation to their forms. Students can also understand the characteristics of word formation. In vocabulary learning, the etymology of words, the root of medical vocabulary, as well as the compound words, can be analyzed to enhance students' understanding and memorizing of words. Students can relate the original meanings of these medical words to their metaphoric meanings by reasoning and associating. This cognitive style has showed its advantages in comparison with the traditional one. More importantly, new words relating to new diseases are created by using analogy, association in the creating process which also involves with the metaphor cognition. Therefore, metaphor cognitive ability should be emphasized in cultivating students language proficiency and be used to improve the the current test-oriented teaching approach. Metaphor Enriched English Language Instruction could be adopted to the curriculum and the metaphor cognitive ability should have its place in students' language proficiency. Littlemore and Low (2006) claimed that high proficient participants in their study were more aware of the need to enhance their English skills and especially learning metaphorical expressions that accordingly enhanced their metaphoric competence which is as important as communicative and grammatical competences to follow their future career. Compared the mean scores of the National College Entrance Examination (NCEE) with the score of the Metaphoric Competence Test, the mean score of the NCEE was above 70 and the mean score of MCT was under 60 which was the passing score for the test. It showed that they did well in the NCEE while their mean score of MCT was relatively low. The result of the paired-samples t-test showed that, for all three teacher participants, there was a significant difference in the mean score of the pre-test and the post-test with $P=0.000$ ($P<0.05$) which suggested that the Metaphor Enriched English Language Instruction Supplement did help to increase the students' metaphoric competence.

The result of Metaphoric Competence Test shows that, for the metaphor recognition part (Part A), students did best in recognizing metaphors which belong to "The Same or Nearly the Same Concepts or Conceptual System". It is easy for students who know both Chinese and English to understand this type of conceptual metaphors since these two languages share the same or nearly the same underlining concepts or conceptual systems. Then followed by "Non-corresponding Concepts or Conceptual Systems". Although this type of conceptual metaphors stem from a different social and cultural background, they have already been the conventional metaphors which can be understood. Students did bad in recognizing metaphors which belong to "Different Concepts or Conceptual Systems". This type of conceptual metaphors that are based on different concepts or conceptual systems results in much confusion, since the concepts in different languages are not the same and people tend to understand the concepts of their own. The data of the metaphor interpretation (Part B) and the metaphor production (Part C) showed that students came up with more similarities and generated more metaphors in the post-test compared to the pre-test, after completing the same kind of assignments and learning from the teachers' interpretation of the metaphorical mappings. Therefore, metaphor enriched supplement is an effective approach to improve students' metaphorical competence which has been proved to be correlated with the English proficiency. It can be used to solve the current test-oriented English teaching. This finding is in line with Cooper's (1999) statement that students with metaphoric competence could interpret idiomatic expressions in L2 successfully. Andreou and Galantomos (2008) also suggested that metaphoric competence could be included as part of communicative competence pedagogy because its various functions that can be connected to grammatical and lexical cues.

For the implication of supplementary metaphor-related materials, according to the students' feedback, there are several advantages. First, it clearly linked the curriculum of college English to the Medical English which helped students better understand the text and the medical terms. Second, it is authentic in terms of text and tasks which are productions of authoritative companies and publishers. Third, it stimulated interactions in students with various resources and activities. The supplementary videos are novel and informative and the stories are interesting, which aroused students' great interest in learning. The supplementary metaphorical words, which cited from the textbook of medical terminology, brought them a new approach to memorize medical vocabulary and improved their ability to read English papers. Fourth, the supplementary materials broadened their horizon on linguistics as well as improved their metaphoric competence. Zhao (2018) claims animation is extremely helpful, especially during the explanation of the underlying force dynamics for the semantic network of the word, since different force patterns can be well illustrated through the animated movement of the objects. These findings are also in line with Tomlinson's statement that second language acquisition is facilitated by a rich and meaningful exposure to language in use; affective and cognitive engagement; making use of mental resources used in communication in L1; noticing how L2 is used; being encouraged to interact and allowed to focus on meaning (2013). There are also some suggestions for improvement. First, the supplementary materials should be moderately difficult. During the implementation of Unit 2 which is the first selected unit, a video *The Nervous System* was assigned as the homework, while students could not fully understand the video due to the medical terms inside. Subtitles for this video was suggested to be added. The three teachers discussed the students' feedback and provided the transcript to students. Second, the speed of the supplementary videos should be lowered due to the lack of Medical English vocabulary. In a word, the supplementary materials did improve their metaphoric competence and paved the way for the future Medical English study.

6.2 Recommendations

Based on the findings of this research, the further recommendations have been made from the aspects of teachers' part and students' part.

For teachers who are going to conduct the metaphor enriched instruction, using of the collected materials is the first step which need to be considered. First, the supplement should link to the curriculum of college English. Second, it should be authentic in terms of text and tasks. Third, it should stimulate interactions in students with various resources and activities. Fourth, it should broaden students' horizon on linguistics as well as improved their metaphoric competence. Fifth, it should be moderately difficult. Before the implementation, the teachers could take the students' metaphoric competence into consideration and how to improve students' metaphoric competence should be regarded as one objective and more linguistic metaphor-related knowledge should be provided to enhance students' understanding and application of metaphors. Besides, it is very necessary to survey the teacher's understanding of the conceptual metaphor before the implementation of metaphor enriched supplement. During the implementation, the teacher can use set induction to realize the transition from the unit topics to the related medical knowledge. The time for the supplement could be considered on the premise of the syllabus.

Students could be provided with more opportunities to use metaphors. Pictures and videos can be used to increase the enjoyment and inspire students' metaphorical thinking. More guidance, medical knowledge, medical articles, explanations, discussion and student-led activities could be conducted in class. The medical supplement can be synchronized with the anatomy class which can deep students' understanding of the professional knowledge. More analysis of metaphor structures could be provided. In addition, teachers could try to use more metaphorical expressions in the process of instruction to increase mutually understanding.

For the cultivation of students' metaphoric competence, students can easily understand the Chinese and English conceptual metaphors which share the same or nearly the same underlining concepts or conceptual systems. Then followed by metaphors which share "Non-corresponding Concepts or Conceptual Systems". Students did bad in recognizing metaphors which belong to "Different Concepts or Conceptual Systems". For these metaphors, teachers could introduce more cultural background in the interpretation to reduce the negative influence of Chinese concepts on English ones. In addition, students could be encouraged to find out more similarities between the source domain and the target domain, and generate more metaphorical sentences in their writing. According to this research, scenarios writing could be adopted as an approach to put students in the position of the therapists and inspire them to make use of metaphors in their future treatment for clients.

6.3　Suggestions for Further Research

Metaphors in the text were identified by Metaphor Identification Procedure in this research. The numbers of metaphors in texts are limited. In further research, the computer-aided methods within Corpus linguistics can be used to conduct the automated metaphor retrieval. The development of software can help researchers identify metaphors in corpora. In addition, it could be applied to the study of lexis and grammar due to its collection of authentic texts. This is a relative new trend in the study of metaphors.

This research tried to investigate the students' application of metaphors in the form of scenario writing. This is an effective method to enhance students' production of metaphors and writing skills which could be conducted as further research.

Except metaphor, metonymy and analogy are two types of generating new meanings for existing expressions. A metaphor is considered a substitution of one concept in terms of another concept, while a metonymy is considered an association of one concept with another one. There are similarities between two concepts in metaphors, while there is an associated word in a metonymy. As for analogies, ametaphor is literally false, while an analogy is literally true. Therefore, future research could include all these literary devices to improve students' use of figurative language.

In the development of human life, language, as a tool for communication, can be achieved through diligent approach, continuous efforts and a conscious understanding. Like when learning an art, modern and novel tools are used to expedite the process of mastering it. Metaphorical language necessitates novel and modern techniques and methods so that the process of learning becomes easy and enjoyable. Just like the stories with the intended instructions and lessons do create indelible memories in both kids and adults. The metaphors in any language can stay in the minds of those who come across them and make their communication more effective. This approach especially will immensely benefit those who have selected a medical career. The researcher feels strongly that teaching and learning the English language through using metaphors will go a long way, creating an everlasting impression on the learners and benefit them enormously. Although there are still many issues waiting for research in the field of metaphor and English language teaching, the researcher will always keep her original aspiration in mind. Just like what George Bernard Shaw (1922) said: "You see things; and you say why? But I dream things that never were; and I say why not?" The following conversation which indicates the role of metaphors could be an appropriate end of this book.

Bateson: "*Logic won't quite do...because that whole fabric of living things is not put together by logic.*"
Capra: "*So what do they use instead?*"
Bateson: "*Metaphor.*"
Capra: "*Metaphor?*"
Bateson: "*Yes, metaphor. That's how the whole fabric of mental interconnections holds together. Metaphor is right at the bottom of being alive.*"

(as cited Capra, 1988)

References

[1] ANDREOU G, GALANTOMOS I. Designing a conceptual syllabus for teaching metaphors and idioms in a foreign language context [J]. Porta Linguarum, 2008, 9:69-77.

[2] ANDREOU G, GALANTOMOS I. Conceptual competence as a component of second language fluency [J]. Journal of Psycholinguistic Research, 2009, 38(6):587-91.

[3] ARISTOTLE. Rhetoric and poetics [M]. New York: The Modern Library, 1954.

[4] BERENDI. Metaphor in vocabulary teaching. A cognitive linguistic approach [M]. Pecs: JPTE, 2005.

[5] BERTHOFF A. Richards on rhetoric [M]. Oxford: Oxford University Press, 1991.

[6] BOGDAN R C, BIKLEN S K. Qualitative research for education: An introduction to theories and methods [M]. 5th ed. New York: Pearson Education, 2011.

[7] CALSAMIGLIA H, VAN DIJK T A. Popularization discourse and knowledge about the genome [J]. Discourse & Society, 2004, 14(4):369-389.

[8] CAMERON L. Identifying and describing metaphor in spoken data [M]. Cambridge: Cambridge University Press, 1999.

[9] CAMERON L. Metaphor ineducational discourse [M]. London: Continuum, 1999.

[10] CHENG A, WANG Q. English language teaching in higher education in China: ahistorial and social overview. In multilingual education [M]. Berlin, German: Springer, 2012.

[11] CLEMENT M, VANDERBERGHE R. Teachers' professional development: a solitary or collegial adventure? [J]. Teaching and Teacher Education, 2000, 16(1):81-101.

[12] COLLINS C E, DEPETRIS A. A Short course in medical terminology [M]. 2nd ed. Philadelphia: lippincott Williams & Wilkins, 2011.

[13] CORBETT E P J, CONNORS R J. Classical rhetoric for the modern student [M]. Oxford: Oxford University Press, 1971.

[14] COOPER T C. Processing of idioms by L2 learners of English [J]. TESOL Quarterly, 1999, 233-262.

[15] CRESWELL J W. Research design: qualitative, quantitative, and mixed methods approaches [M]. 3rd ed. London: SAGE Publications, 2009.

[16] CRESWELL J W, MILLER D L. Determining validity in qualitative inquiry [J]. Theory Into Practice, 39, 2000:124-130.

[17] CRESWELL J W. Research and evaluation in education and psychology: integrating diversity with quantitative, qualitative, and mixed methods [M]. 3rd ed. London: SAGE Publications, 2010.

[18] GUBA E G, LINCOLN Y S. Paradigmatic controversies, contradictions, and emerging con-

fluences. In the SAGE handbook of qualitative research[M]. 3rd ed. London:SAGE Publications,2005.

[19] CUDDON J A. A dictionary of literary terms and literary theory [M]. 5th ed. New York: John Wiley & Sons Publication,2013.

[20] DANESI M. The role of metaphor in second language pedagogy [J]. Rossegna ana diLinquistica Applicata,1986,18(3):1-10.

[21] DANESI M. The development of metaphorical competence:a neglected dimension in second language pedagogy[J]. Rosary College,1988:1-10.

[22] DANESIM. Metaphor and classroom second language learning[J]. Romance Languages, 1992,3:189-193.

[23] DANESI M. Metaphorical competence in second language acquisition and second language learning:the neglected dimension. In Language,communication,and social meaning[M]. Washington DC:Georgetown University Press,1993.

[24] DANESI M. Recent research on metaphor and the teaching of Italian[J]. Italica,1994,71 (4):453-464.

[25] DANESI M. Learning and teaching languages:The role of conceptual fluency[J]. International Journal of Applied Linguistics,1995,5:3-20.

[26] DANESI M. Conceptual errors in second-language learning. InCognitive approaches to pedagogical grammar:a volume inhonour of René Dirven [M]. Berlin: Mouton de Gruyter,2008.

[27] DAUGMAN J. Brain metaphor and brain theory. In philosophy and the neurosciences [M]. Oxford:Blackwell Publishers,2001.

[28] DENZIN N K,Lincoln Y S. The SAGE handbook of qualitative research[M]. 4th ed. London:SAGE Publications,2011.

[29] DUDLEY-EVANS T,ST JOHNS M J. Developments in English for specific purposes[M]. Cambridge:Cambridge University Press,1998.

[30] DUIT R. Students conceptual frameworks:Consequences for learning science. In the psychology of learning science[M]. Hillsdale:Lawrence Erlbaum Associates,1991.

[31] EVANS V,GREEN M. Cognitivelinguistics:an introduction[M]. Mahwah:Lawrence Erlbaum Associates Publishers,2006.

[32] FLICK U. The SAGE handbook of qualitative data analysis[M]. London:SAGE Publications,2014.

[33] FRIEDBERG R D,WILT L H. Metaphors and stories in cognitive behavioral therapy with children[J]. Journal of Rational-Emotive & Cognitive-Behavior Therapy,2010,28(2): 100-113.

[34] GARDNER H,WINNER E. The development of metaphoric competence:implications for the humanistic disciplines[J]. Critical Inquir,1978,5(1):123-141.

[35] GARDNER R C. Social psychological aspects of second language acquisition. In Language

and social psychology[M]. Oxford:Basil Blackwell,1979.

[36] GEARY J. I is an other:The secret life of metaphor and how it shapes the way we see the world[M]. NY:Harper Perennial,2011.

[37] GEORGE W B. Healing withstories:your casebook collection for using therapeutic metaphors[M]. NY:John Wiley & Sons,2007.

[38] GIBBS R W. The poetics of mind:figurative thought,language,and understanding[M]. Cambridge:Cambridge University Press,1994.

[39] GIBBS R W,FRANKS H. Embodied metaphor in women's narratives about experience [J]. Health Communication,2002,14(2):139-166.

[40] GRADY J E. The Oxford handbook of cognitive linguistics[M]. Oxford:Oxford University Press,2007.

[41] GUERRERO M C M D,VILLAMIL O. Metaphorical conceptualizations of ESL teaching and learning[J]. Language Teaching Research,2002,6(2):95-120.

[42] HERRON C. Foreign language learning approaches as metaphor[J]. Modern Language Journal,1982,66(3):235-242.

[43] HYMES D. On communicative competence. In sociolinguistics[M]. NY:Penguin Publishing Group,1972.

[44] JOHNSON M. The body in the mind:the bodily basis of meaning,imagination,and reason [M]. Chicago:University of Chicago Press,1987.

[45] JOHNSON B,ONWUEGBUZIE A. Mixed methods research:a research paradigm whose time has come[J]. Educational Researcher,2004,33(7):14-26.

[46] JOHNSON J,ROSANO T. Relation of cognitive style and second language proficiency [J]. Applied Psycholinguistics,1993,14(2):59-175.

[47] JORDAN R R. English for academic purposes:a guide and resources book for teachers [M]. Cambridge:Cambridge University Press,1997.

[48] KANTHAN R,SHERYL M. Using metaphors,analogies and similes as aids in teaching pathology to medical students[J]. Journal of the International Association of Medical and Science Education,2006,16(1):19-26.

[49] KACHRU B. Standards,codification and sociolinguistic realism:the English language in the outer circle[M]. Cambridge:Cambridge University Press,1985.

[50] KECSKES I. Conceptual fluency and the use of situation-bound utterances in L2[J]. Links & Letters,2000,7:143-158.

[51] KECSKES I. On my mind:thoughts about salience,context and figurative language from a second language perspective[J]. Second Language Research,2006,22(2):1-19.

[52] KESEN A. What lies beneath teacher beliefs? A study on metaphoric perceptions[J]. Journal of Human Sciences,2013,10(1):1491-1502.

[53] KNOWLES M,MOON R. Introducing Metaphor[M]. London:Routledge,2006.

[54] KNUDSEN S. Communicating novel and conventional scientific metaphors:a study of the

development of the metaphor genetic code[J]. Public Understanding of Science,2005,14(4):373-392.

[55] KOPP RR. Metaphor therapy: Using client-generated metaphors in psychotherapy [M]. London: Psychology Press,1995.

[56] KÖVECSES Z. Metaphor and emotion: language, culture, and body in human feeling[M]. Cambridge: Cambridge University Press,2002.

[57] KÖVECSES Z. Metaphor: a practical introduction[M]. Oxford: Oxford University Press, 2002.

[58] KÖVECSES Z. Studying American culture through its metaphors: dimensions of variation and frames of experience[J]. Journal of American Studies In Hungary,2007,3(1):1-17.

[59] KÖVECSES Z. Metaphor: a Practical Introduction[M]. Oxford: Oxford University Press, 2010.

[60] LAKOFF G. The contemporary theory of meataphor. In metaphor and thought[M]. 2nd ed. Cambridge: Cambridge University Press,1993.

[61] LAKOFF G, JOHNSON M. Philosophy in the flesh: the embodied mind and the challenge to western thought [M]. NY: Basic Books,1999.

[62] LAKOFF G, JOHNSON M. Metaphors we live by[M]. Chicago: The University of Chicago Press,2003.

[63] LANKTON S. The use of therapeutic metaphor in social work. In social workers' desk reference[M]. Oxford: Oxford University Press,2002.

[64] LATHER P. Critical frames in educational research: feminist and post-structural perspectives[J]. Theory and Practice,1992,31(2):1-13.

[65] LITTLEMORE J. The use of metaphor in university lectures and the problems that it cause for overseas students[J]. Teaching in Higher Education,2001,6(3):335-351.

[66] LITTLEMORE J. Metaphoric competence: a language learning strength of students with a holistic cognitivestyle? [J]. TESOL Quarterly,2001,35(3):459-491.

[67] LITTLEMORE J, LOW G. Figurative thinking and foreign language learning[M]. New York: Mcmillan,2006.

[68] LITTLEMORE J. Metaphoric competence in the first and second language: similarities and differences[M]. Amsterdam: John Benjamins Publishing Company,2010.

[69] LITTLEWOOD W. Learners' metaphors stimulate thinking and discussion[J]. Modern English Teacher,2012,21(4):33.

[70] LOW G D. On teaching metaphor[J]. Applied Linguistics,1988,9 (2):125-147.

[71] LOW G D. In researching and applying metaphor[M]. Cambridge: Cambridge University Press,2007.

[72] GWINYAI M, ZUMLA A. Analogies and metaphors in clinical medicine[J]. Clinical Medicine,2012,12(1):55-56.

[73] LEONARDO V. A route to the teaching of polysemous lexicon: benefits from cognitive lin-

guistics and conceptual metaphor theory[J]. International Journal of Applied Linguistics & English Literature,2017,7(1):215-216.

[74] MAXCY S J. Pragmatic threads in mixed methods research in the social sciences: the search for multiple modes of inquiry and the end of the philosophy of formalism. In Handbook of mixed methods in social & behavioral research[M]. London:SAGE Publications, 2003.

[75] MCLEOD J, COOPER M. Pluralistic counselling & psychotherapy[M]. London: SAGE Publications,2011.

[76] MERTENS D M. Research and evaluation in education and psychology: integrating diversity with quantitative,qualitative,and mixed methods[M]. 3rd ed. London:SAGE Publications,2010.

[77] MORGAN D. Paradigms lost and pragmatism regained: methodological implications of combining qualitative and quantitative methods[J]. Journal of Mixed Methods Research, 2007,1(1):48-76.

[78] MORRISON G R, ROSS S M, KEMP J E et, al. Designing effective instruction[M]. 6th ed. New York:John Wiley & Sons,2011.

[79] MUNGRA P. Metaphors among titles of medical publications:an observational study[J]. Iberica,2007,14(Fall 2007):99-122.

[80] NACEY S. Comparing linguistic metaphors in L1 and L2 English[M]. Norway:University of Oslo,2010.

[81] NIKITINA L, FURUOKA F. "A language teacher is like...": Examining malaysian students' perception of language teachers through metaphor analysis[J]. Electronic Journal of Foreign Language Teaching,2008,5(2):192-205.

[82] NING Y. The contemporary theory of metaphor: a perspective from Chinese[M]. Amsterdam:John Benjamins Publishing Company,1998.

[83] ORTONY A. Metaphor and thought[M]. Cambridge:Cambridge University Press,1979.

[84] PATTON M Q. Qualitative evaluation and research methods[M]. 2nd ed. London:SAGE Publications,1990.

[85] PATTON M Q. Qualitative research & evaluation methods[M]. London:SAGE Publications,2002.

[86] PENA, GIL P, ANDRADE-FILHO J D S. Analogies in medicine: valuable for learning, reasoning, remembering and naming[J]. Adv Health Sci Educ Theory Pract. ,2010,15(4):609-619.

[87] POPOVA Y. The fool sees with his nose: metaphoric mappings in the sense of smell in Patrick Suskind's Perfume[J]. Language and Literature,2003,12(2):139.

[88] Pragglejaz Group. MIP: a method for identifying metaphorically used words in discourse [J]. Metaphor and Symbol,2007,22(1):1-39.

[89] POLIT D, HUNGLER B. Nursing research:principles and methods[M]. 3rd ed. Pennsyl-

vania:Lippincott Williams & Wilkins,1993.

[90] GARDNER R C,SMYTHE P C,CLÉMENT R. Intensive second language study in a bicultural milieu:An investigation of attitudes, motivation and language proficiency[J]. Language Learning,1979,29(2):305-320.

[91] RATCLIFF J D. I am Joe's body (A Berkley/Reader's Digest Book)[M]. New York: Penguin Group,1986.

[92] REISFIELD G M,WILSON G R. Use of metaphor in the discourse of cancer[J]. Journal of Clinical Oncology,2004,22(19):4024-4027.

[93] RICHARD I A. The philosophy of rhetoric[M]. Oxford:Oxford University Press,1936.

[94] ROCH E,CLARE J,O'KEEFFE D P,et,al. Selections from the buffet of food signs in radiology[J]. Radio Graphics,2002,22(6):1369-1384.

[95] ROSSMAN G B,WILSON B L. Numbers and words:combining quantitative and qualitative methods in a single large-scale evaluation study[J]. Evaluation Review,1985,9(5): 627-643.

[96] SOLOMON A. The noonday demon:an atlas of depression[J]. Scribner,2001,27-29.

[97] SOMMER E, DORRIE W. Metaphor dictionary[M]. London:Independent Pub Group, 1996.

[98] SHOKOUHI H,ISAZADEH M. The effect of teaching conceptual and image metaphors to EFL learners[J]. The Open Applied Linguistics Journal,2009,2:22-31.

[99] SONTAG S. Illness as metaphor[M]. New York:Farrar,Strauss & Giroux,1978.

[100] TASHAKKORI A,TEDDLIE C. Mixed methodology:combining qualitative and quantitativeapproaches[M]. London:SAGE Publications,1998.

[101] TASHAKKORI A,TEDDLIE C. SAGE handbook of mixed methods in social and behavioral research[M]. London:SAGE Publications,2003.

[102] TASHAKKORIA,TEDDLIE C. SAGE handbook of mixed methods in social and behavioral research[M]. 2nd ed. London:SAGE Publications,2010.

[103] UNGERER S,FRIEDRICH,SCHMID H J. An introduction to cognitive linguistics[M]. 2nd ed. London:Routledge,2006.

[104] VYJEYANTHI S P. Using metaphors in medicine[J]. Journal of Palliative Medicine, 2008,11(6):842-844.

[105] WICKMAN S A, CAMPBELL C. The co-construction of congruency: investigating the conceptual metaphors of Carl Rogers and Gloria[J]. Counsellor Education & Supervision,2003,43:15-24.

[106] WILLIAMS W D,MIO J S,WHITNEY P. Metaphor production in creative writing[J]. J Psycholinguist Res 21,1992,497-509.

[107] ZHAO H, COOMB S, ZHOU X. Developing professional knowledge about teachers through metaphor research:facilitating a process of change[J]. Teacher Development, 2010,14(3):381.

[108] 蔡基刚. 制约我国大学英语教学方向转移的因素分析[J]. 外语研究, 2010, 120(2): 40-45+112.

[109] 陈家旭. 英汉隐喻认知对比研究[M]. 上海: 学林出版社, 2007.

[110] 董宏乐, 杨晓英. 概念语法隐喻理论对阅读教学的指导意义[J]. 国外外语教学, 2003(4): 37-41.

[111] 杜惠玲. 认知视角下的隐喻理论探索与英语教学应用研究[M]. 南京: 东南大学出版社, 2019.

[112] 胡壮麟. 认知隐喻学[M]. 北京: 北京大学出版社, 2020.

[113] 焦伟达. 概念隐喻与中国大学生英语水平的关联度[D]. 长春: 吉林大学, 2009.

[114] 林书武. 国外隐喻研究综述[J]. 外语教学与研究, 1997, 109(1): 11-19.

[115] 刘畅. 概念隐喻与中国英语教学: 实证研究[D]. 长春: 吉林大学, 2007.

[116] 刘振前, 时小英. 隐喻的文化认知本质与外语教学[J]. 外语与外语教学, 2002, 55(2): 48-53.

[117] 陆国强. 英汉概念结构对比[M]. 上海: 上海外语教育出版社, 2008.

[118] 束定芳. 隐喻研究[M]. 上海: 上海外语教育出版社, 2020.

[119] 苏立昌. 英汉概念隐喻用法比较词典[M]. 天津: 南开大学出版社, 2009.

[120] 王守元, 刘振前. 隐喻与文化教学[J]. 外语教学, 2003, 24(1), 48-57.

[121] 王文秀, 王颖, 贾轶群. 英汉对照医务英语会话[M]. 北京: 人民卫生出版社, 2010.

[122] 王寅, 李弘. 语言能力、交际能力、隐喻能力"三合一"教学观——当代隐喻认知理论在外语教学中的应用[J]. 四川外语学院学报, 2004, 20(6): 140-143.

[123] 王寅. 认知语言学[M]. 上海: 上海外语教育出版社, 2007.

[124] 魏耀章. 认知能力和语言水平对中国英语学习者隐喻理解和生成的影响[D]. 上海: 上海交通大学, 2007.

[125] 严世清. 隐喻能力与外语教学[J]. 山东外语教学, 2001, 83(2): 60-64+88.

[126] 赵振华. 概念隐喻和隐喻教学——基于英语专业学生隐喻学习的调查[D]. 桂林: 广西师范大学, 2007.

[127] 周红辉. 从认知角度看隐喻观对英语学习的启示[J]. 齐齐哈尔大学学报(哲学社会科学版), 2006, (1): 134-136.

[128] 朱炜. 原型范畴理论对英语词汇教学的启示[J]. 江苏教育学院学报(社会科学版), 2005, (1): 98-101.

List of Abbreviations

CM	Conceptual Metaphor
CMT	Conceptual Metaphor Theory
EFL	English as a Foreign Language
EGP	English for General Purposes
EMP	English for Medical Purposes
ESP	English for Specific Purposes
GE	General English
LM	Linguistic Metaphor
MC	Metaphoric Competence
MCT	Metaphoric Competence Test
ME	Medical English
MEELI	Metaphor Enriched English Language Instruction
MIP	Metaphor Identification Procedure
NECC	The National College Entrance Examination
NVivo	N(Nudist)+Vivo
SLA	Second Language Acquisition
SPSS	Statistics Package for Social Science

Appendices

Appendix A Semi-structured Interview Protocol

Interview Protocol Project: Teachers' Understanding of Metaphor and Metaphor Enriched Instruction.

Basic Information About the Interview

Time if interview:

Date:

Place:

Interviewer:

Interviewee:

Position of interviewee:

Recording information about interview:

1. What are the main challenges in your EGP teaching?

Possible probes:

(1) Do you think vocabulary is a big problem of English teaching for first-year students? Why? Please explain.

(2) Do you think speaking is a big problem of English teaching for first-year students? Why? Please explain.

(3) Do you think reading is a big problem of English teaching for first-year students? Why? Please explain.

(4) Do you think writing is a big problem of English teaching for first-year students? Why? Please explain.

2. What are the main challenges in the students' EGP learning?

(1) Do you think vocabulary is a big problem of English learning for first-year students? Why? Please explain.

(2) Do you think speaking is a big problem of English learning for first-year students? Why? Please explain.

(3) Do you think reading is a big problem of English learning for first-year students?

Why? Please explain.

(4) Do you think writing is a big problem of English learning for first-year students? Why? Please explain.

3. To what extend do you know about metaphor?

Possible probes:

(1) Have you studied metaphors systematically?

(2) Do your know the cognition mechanism of different kinds of metaphor?

(3) Will you learn the contemporary metaphor theories?

(4) Is it necessary to study metaphor when you prepare for your lecture? Why? Please explain.

4. Have you implemented metaphor in your instruction? Which issues need to be considered?

Possible probes:

(1) Will you compare the literal meaning with metaphorical meaning?

(2) Do you think it is important to understand the mechanism of metaphor for students? Why? Please explain.

(3) How long will you spend time on metaphor instruction?

(4) What are the issues needed to be considered in the process of implementation?

5. Do you think metaphor enriched approach will help the students' learning and teacher's instruction?

Possible probes:

(1) Do you think metaphor enriched approach will enhance students' English language competence? Why? Please explain.

(2) Do you think metaphor enriched approach will enhance students' Medical English learning? Why? Please explain.

(3) Do you think metaphor enriched approach will enhance students' interest of English learning? Why? Please explain.

(4) Do you think metaphor enriched approach will enhance students' metaphoric competence? Why? Please explain.

(5) Is it a good method to help the students' transition from General English to Medical English?

6. What will be faced when adopting the metaphor enriched approach?

Possible probes:

(1) Do you think what is the biggest problem when applying metaphor enriched approach

for teachers? Why? Please explain.

(2) In your opinion, what is the biggest problem when applying metaphor enriched approach for students? Why? Please explain.

(3) Will you want to solve the problem with your colleagues?

(4) Will you spend more time and energy on this approach if it is effect?

Appendix B　Metaphor Cognition Questionnaire

Dear Students,

　　The purpose of this study is to obtain your opinion about your metaphoric competence. To measure and determine your level of metaphor, your responses to this questionnaire is vital. Please read the instructions and record your answers in the spaces provided. Please answer all the questions completely and honestly. If you have any questions about this questionnaire, please feel free to contact me immediately.

　　Confidentiality will be maintained and no information obtained from this study shall be disclosed in any manner that will identify you. Therefore, in order to ensure that all information remain confidential, please DO NOT include your NAME. Participation is strictly voluntary and you may refuse to participate at any time.

　　Thanking you for your cooperation.

隐喻认知调查问卷

亲爱的同学们：

　　此份调查问卷旨在获得您关于隐喻学习的态度和目前状况。您的答案对准确获得测量结果至关重要。请阅读说明并在空白处写下答案。衷心希望您能坦率、诚实、全面地回答所有问题。如果您对问卷上的问题有疑问，请随时与我联系。

　　为了确保信息的保密性，请您以匿名的方式填写，我们会严格保密，绝不公开您的个人信息。受访者完全自愿参与此项调查并可随时退出。

　　感谢您的支持！

1. This questionnaire asks for information about metaphor cognition and Medical English.
本问卷询问关于隐喻认知和医学英语方面的信息
2. This questionnaire should take approximately 20 minutes to complete.
填写本问卷大概需要20分钟。
3. Most questions can be answered by marking the one most appropriate answer.
大部分问题应该选择最合适的选项

| 1 = strongly disagree | 2 = disagree | 3 = agree | 4 = strongly agree |
| 1 = 非常不同意 | 2 = 不同意 | 3 = 同意 | 4 = 非常同意 |

Part 1 Metaphor Cognition

1. I know that there are many metaphors in General English 我知道语言中到处都存在隐喻	1	2	3	4
2. I know that metaphor in English articles can make language more vivid 我知道英语文章中使用隐喻可以使语言表达更生动形象	1	2	3	4
3. I find teachers always use metaphors in their instruction 我发现教师在教学中经常使用隐喻	1	2	3	4
4. I know that some conceptual metaphors in English are different from those in Chinese 我现在很清楚,英语中有些隐喻概念和汉语不同	1	2	3	4
5. I know that some metaphorical expressionsin English are different from those in Chinese 我现在很清楚地知道,英语中有些隐喻语言表达式和汉语不同	1	2	3	4
6. The image of compared object will immediately flash in my mind when using metaphors 在使用隐喻时,我的大脑里会马上闪现对比对象的形象	1	2	3	4
7. I will understand metaphor from the context in the process of reading 阅读过程中,我会结合上下文来理解隐喻	1	2	3	4
8. I will consciously apply metaphors which I have learned in the classroom in my writing 我会将课堂上学到的隐喻使用到我的写作中	1	2	3	4
9. When communicating with English native speakers in English, I often discuss metaphors with them 当于英语母语者交流时,我经常使用隐喻	1	2	3	4
10. I often try to express my ideas through new metaphors 我经常使用新的隐喻表达我的想法	1	2	3	4

Part 2 Metaphor and Medical English

11. I know that there are many metaphors in Medical English 我知道医学英语中存在很多隐喻	1	2	3	4
12. I am sensitive to metaphor in articles in the process of reading medical journals 阅读过程中我对文章中出现的隐喻很敏感	1	2	3	4
13. Metaphors help me to memorize medical words 隐喻有助于我理解医学单词	1	2	3	4
14. Metaphors help me to understand the medical terms 隐喻有助于我理解医学术语	1	2	3	4
15. Metaphorical expressions help me to understand the illness 隐喻性表达有助于我理解疾病	1	2	3	4
16. I think it is interesting to understand medical articles from the perspective of metaphors 我认为从隐喻角度来理解医学文章使学习过程更有趣	1	2	3	4
17. I realized that metaphor can express meanings which cannot be explained by non-metaphor language 我意识到使用隐喻可以表达一些非隐喻语言无法表达的含义	1	2	3	4
18. I will use metaphors to explain conditions of illness to my patients in future 未来我会用隐喻去和病人解释病情	1	2	3	4

Thank you for your cooperation!
谢谢合作!

Appendix C Metaphoric Competence Test

(The statistics of the test is for academic use only and any personal information in questions will not be disclosed.)

(本测试统计数据仅供学术研究使用,所涉及答题者个人的任何信息均不公开。)

A. Metaphor Recognition (40%, 15 minutes)

Metaphor is a set of expressions or stories to explain or introduce one concept by using human or speakers' experience. Although the content of the expression does not seem to be true literally, it has actually established a deep link between the two concepts. For example, "Time is a bird", although "time" cannot really become a "bird", the "bird" flying reminds people of "time" flies. The sentence "The piano is a spoon" is not a metaphor, because it is difficult to see the internal relationship between "spoon" and "piano". Another example, "Treating disease is fighting a war" is a metaphorical expression (conceptual metaphor). This metaphorical expression gives us a better understanding of the processes and result of treating diseases. The mapping process is as follows.

Source domain	Mapping	Target domain
War	⟶	Disease
Field	⟶	Body
Enemy	⟶	HIV/bacteria
Arm	⟶	Medicine
Defense system	⟶	Immune system
Win	⟶	Recover
Lose	⟶	Die

隐喻指人们常用一个熟悉的概念去表达一个抽象的概念或作者特意要描述的一个含义。虽然表达的内容从字面上看似乎并不成立,但实际上却在两个概念之间建立了一种深层次上的联系。例如,"Time is a bird",虽然"时间"不可能真正成为"鸟",但是"鸟"的飞翔让人想到了"时间"的飞逝。而句子"The piano is a spoon"则不是一个隐喻,因为很难看出"勺子"与"钢琴"有什么内在联系。再如,"Treating illness is fighting a war"是一句隐喻性表达(也称概念隐喻)。这一隐喻性表达使我们更好地理解治疗疾病的过程和结果。从始源域到目标域的映射如下。

始源域	映射	目标域
战争	⟶	疾病
战场	⟶	身体
敌人	⟶	艾滋病病毒
细菌	⟶	武器药品
防御系统	⟶	免疫系统
胜利	⟶	康复
失败	⟶	死亡

Please tell which expression is metaphorically expressed with your choice of the grade. Please fill in the brackets before the selected grade.

(1) This sentence is obviously not a metaphor.

(2) This sentence may contain some kind of metaphorical expression, but I can not find it.

(3) This sentence is metaphor, but not very convincing.

(4) This sentence is obviously a metaphor.

请按所给的四个等级标准,判断下列各句是否是隐喻性表达、在多大程度上是隐喻性表达。请将所选等级填入每个等级标准前的括号里。

(1)此句明显不是隐喻。

(2)此句可能有某种隐喻性表达,但看不出来。

(3)此句是隐喻,但不十分令人信服。

(4)此句明显是个隐喻。

(　) 1. I'm feeling down.

(　) 2. My job is a jail.

(　) 3. He led a dog's life when he was young.

(　) 4. Speech is silver, silence is gold.

(　) 5. From the plane we had a bird's eye view of London.

(　) 6. Is her husband a man or a mouse?

(　) 7. He has learned that happiness is gold.

(　) 8. Unfortunately their relationship turned sour after one was promoted.

(　) 9. That event was the spark that started the war.

(　) 10. He was in a dark mood after the examination.

(　) 11. I couldn't see my own flesh and blood insulted in this way.

(　) 12. It might make him embarrassed if you pull his leg in the meeting.

(　) 13. The death penalty for murder works on the principle of an eye for an eye.

(　) 14. You must be green to believe that!

(　) 15. Music is death.

(   ) 16. Their marriage was on the rocks.

(   ) 17. He dived right into the problem.

(   ) 18. The two contestants are neck and neck.

(   ) 19. The gold medal has become a white elephant for him.

(   ) 20. She is the apple of her father's eye.

B. Metaphor Interpretation (30%, 20 minutes)

Please list the interpretations of the following metaphor as much as possible which means why these two concepts can constitute a metaphor, and what is the relationship between them. The more explanations, the better. You can use Chinese if it is necessary.

For example: Time is money.

It can be explained like this:

1) Both are valuable commodity.

2) Both are limited resource.

请为下列隐喻写出尽可能多的解释,即说明为什么两者可以构成隐喻。两者间有何种联系,解释越多越好,但必须合理。

例如:Time is money.

可以解释为:"both are valuable commodity" "both are limited resource"……

或者解释为:"都是珍贵的物品" "都是有限的资源"……

1. Love is a journey

_____

_____

_____

2. Ideas are food

_____

_____

_____

3. Depression is falling into an abyss(深渊)

_____

_____

_____

4. Human body is a battleground

_____

_____

_____

5. Brain is a machine
_____
_____

C. Metaphor Production (30%, 15 minutes)

Please complete the following description of "Learning English is…" and "Treating illness is …" in English using your imagination.

请发挥想象力用英语完成下列句子。

1. Learning English is…
(1)
(2)
(3)
(4)
(5)

2. Treating illness is…
(1)
(2)
(3)
(4)
(5)

Appendix D Classroom Observation Checklist

Researcher: Teacher:
Class Observed: Unit:

Metaphor enriched class structure	Outstanding	Good	Fair	Poor	Not observed
1. Clearly states goals or objectives for the metaphor-related content	5	4	3	2	1
2. Clearly explains metaphor theories	5	4	3	2	1
3. Interprets metaphors in general English or Medical English	5	4	3	2	1
4. Links General English with Medical English in terms of metaphor	5	4	3	2	1
5. Assigns and analyzes the metaphor enriched homework	5	4	3	2	1

Comments: _____
_____
_____

Teaching strategies	Outstanding	Good	Fair	Poor	Not observed
6. Employs non-lecture learning activities (small group discussion, student-led activities)	5	4	3	2	1
7. Employs other tools/instructional aids (technology, video)	5	4	3	2	1
8. Provides students opportunities to use metaphors	5	4	3	2	1
9. Times activities appropriately	5	4	3	2	1
10. Supports high-level thinking	5	4	3	2	1

Comments: _____
_____
_____

Teacher's use of materials	Outstanding	Good	Fair	Poor	Not observed
11. Provides well-designed metaphor-related materials in an organized manner to meet the objectives	5	4	3	2	1
12. Uses high reliable metaphor-related materials	5	4	3	2	1
13. Uses moderately difficult metaphor-related materials	5	4	3	2	1
14. Adopts various metaphor-related resources (pictures, video) as supplement	5	4	3	2	1
15. Relates metaphor concepts to teachers' or students' experience	5	4	3	2	1

Comments: _____

_____

_____

Teacher's use of language	Outstanding	Good	Fair	Poor	Not observed
16. Uses metaphorical expressions in the process of instruction	5	4	3	2	1
17. Uses clear questioning or coaching	5	4	3	2	1
18. Engages students actively	5	4	3	2	1
19. Explains important ideas simply and clearly	5	4	3	2	1
20. Makes evaluation and gives feedback according to students' performance	5	4	3	2	1

Comments: _____

_____

_____

Other Comments:

1. What were the instructor's major strengths as demonstrated in the observation?

_____

_____

_____

2. Based on your observations, what specific suggestions would you offer your peer that can be addressed in the near future?

_____
_____
_____

Teacher's signature_____   Date_____

Researcher's signature_____   Date_____

Appendix E   Student Feedback Questionnaire

Teacher _____   Date _____
Course _____   Class period _____

Instruction: For the closed-response questions on this form, please choose the appropriate one to indicate your attitude to each statement.

> Your feedback is an important component towards the improvement in Metaphor Enriched English Language Instruction. The results will be used in reviewing and improving aspects of teaching content and teaching approach. Your constructive comments are always welcome.

Note. Metaphor Enriched English Language Instruction (MEELI). SA = strongly agree, A = agree, N = no strong view, D = disagree, SD = strongly disagree.

Part I   Feedback on Subject

Please give feedback about your learning experience of the subject, not about the staff member(s). Answer all questions.

A. Your learning experience of the MEELI

Items	SA	A	N	D	SD
1. I fully understand the metaphor theories	5	4	3	2	1
2. I can identify and understand the metaphors of this unit	5	4	3	2	1
3. I have a basic understanding of the nervous system via MEELI	5	4	3	2	1
4. The learning activities (e. g., lectures, discussions, presentations) have helped me to understand the supplementary nervous system knowledge	5	4	3	2	1
5. I better understand medical metaphor concepts and will try to understand new knowledge via it	5	4	3	2	1
6. I think MEELI is a good way to combine General English with Medical English	5	4	3	2	1

B. Open-ended comments

1. What aspects of MEELI are most useful to your learning?

_____
_____

2. How could the MEELI be improved to help you learn better?

_____
_____

Part II Feedback on the Teacher

This section asks for your feedback on the teacher's performance in MEELI. Please indicate your view by answering all the questions below.

A. Teacher's instruction of the MEELI

Items	SA	A	N	D	SD
1. Provides well-designed metaphor-related materials in an organized manner to meetthe objectives	5	4	3	2	1
2. Adopts various metaphor-related resources (pictures, video) as supplement	5	4	3	2	1
3. Explains important ideas or concepts simple and clearly	5	4	3	2	1
4. Encourages students to ask questions and discuss ideas in class	5	4	3	2	1
5. Teacher's instruction stimulates my interestin metaphor and Medical English	5	4	3	2	1
6. Provides students with a valuable learning experience	5	4	3	2	1

B. Open-ended comments

1. What aspects of teacher's instruction are most useful to your learning?

_____

_____

2. How would you like the teaching be changed (if at all), to help you learn better?

_____

_____

Thank you for completing the questionnaire.

Appendix F The Transcript of Students' Role Play on Heart Problem (Ms Liu's Class)

Nurse(S1): Hello, what can I do for you?

Patient's friend(S2): She is not feeling well. Where is the doctor?

Nurse(S1): Yes, but you have to waiting for a moment. you number is 0020. Have a seat, please.

Patient's friend(S2): Okay.

Doctor(S3): Oh, what's wrong with you?

Patient(S4): I felt sick about my heart. Like the ignition system of a car. It seems that it won't be fired as before.

Doctor(S3): How about your examination report?

Patient's friend(S2): Here it is. We got it just now.

Doctor(S3): Let me see. Frankly speaking, it is necessary for you to do a heart bypass operation.

Patient's friend(S2): What's that? Please explain it in details.

Doctor(S3): Let me make a metaphor. There is a traffic jam in your heart blood vessels. All workers have to build a bridge to make the blood vessels unobstructed. The materials from your other blood vessels all substitute.

Patient(S4): Okay. Is there any other pathway?

Doctor(S3): No, you should do an operation. Please make a decision quickly and do not worry.

Patient(S4): Thank you.

Appendix G The Transcript of Students' Role Play on Heart Problem (Ms Wang's Class)

Patient: I don't feel very well. I have a chest pain and sometimes shortness of breath. I also felt dizzy.

Doctor: How long did your symptoms last?

Patient: Maybe one month.

Doctor: Have you ever been to see the doctor?

Patient: Yes, the doctor thought I had suffered a disease called angina cordis. But I doubt that I have got a severe heart attack.

Doctor: Well, can you describe your symptoms in details? For example, when did the pain occur? How long did the pain last? How did you deal with the pain?

Patient: I found that the pain occurred when I was doing the housework or climbing the upstairs. At that time, I felt tightness, pressure and squeezing like a stone on my heart. Sometimes, the pain radiated to the jaw or arms like being shocked by electricity. Usually, the situation lasted about five minutes and I applied the nitroglycerin as self-treatment.

Doctor: Excerpt for the pain, do you have any other symptoms?

Patient: Yes, when the pain occurred, I also felt anxiety, palpitation, indigestion and fatigue. Sometimes I felt sweating.

Doctor: Okay. Let me give you a brief physical examination. Please lie on the bed.

Patient: What am I suffering from? Is that angina cordis or heart attack?

Doctor: According to your case history, it may be a typical angina cordis. I should give you some diagnostic tests, such as ECG, a chest X-ray and blood test to detect the severity.

Patient: Is the disease serious, doctor?

Doctor: Not too bad. Angina cordis is not as serious as heart attack. A massive heart attack is like the permanent closure of a large road which is going to cause traffic chaos. If there is a long-term blockage of a large artery supplying the heart muscle, it's going to cause damage and death to a large section of the heart muscle. Take it easy. With proper treatment, you will get better gradually.

Patient: That is a relief. Thank you very much, doctor.